SEASONAL GUIDE TO THE NATURAL YEAR

A Month by Month Guide to Natural Events

Florida
with Georgia and Alabama Coasts

M. Timothy O'Keefe

Fulcrum Publishing
Golden, Colorado

To my parents, especially my mother, who encouraged my interests in writing, photography and the outdoors. And to Karl Wickstrom, Bill Hallstrom, Lefty Kreh and Vic Dunaway, who published so many of those first efforts.

Maps included in this book are for general reference only. For more detailed maps and additional information, contact the agencies or specific sites listed in the appendices.

Library of Congress Cataloging-in-Publication Data

O'Keefe, M. Timothy.
    Seasonal guide to the natural year : a month by month guide to natural events. Florida with Georgia and Alabama coasts / M. Timothy O'Keefe.
        p.   cm.
    Includes bibliographical references and index.
    ISBN 1-55591-269-9 (pbk.)
    1. Natural history—Florida—Guidebooks. 2. Natural history—Alabama—Guidebooks. 3. Natural history—Georgia—Guidebooks.
    4. Seasons—Florida—Guidebooks. 5. Seasons—Alabama—Guidebooks.
    6. Seasons—Georgia—Guidebooks. 7. Florida—Guidebooks.
    8. Alabama—Guidebooks. 9. Georgia—Guidebooks. I. Title.
    QH104.5.S59038   1996
    508.75—dc20   96-28334
                                                        CIP

Printed in the United States of America
0 9 8 7 6 5 4 3 2 1

Fulcrum Publishing
350 Indiana Street, Suite 350
Golden, Colorado 80401-5093
(800) 992-2908 • (303) 277-1623

The Seasonal Guide to the Natural Year Series

*Pennsylvania, New Jersey, Maryland, Delaware, Virginia,
West Virginia and Washington, D. C.*, Scott Weidensaul
New England and New York, Scott Weidensaul
Illinois, Missouri and Arkansas, Barbara Perry Lawton
Colorado, New Mexico, Arizona and Utah, Ben Guterson
Northern California, Bill McMillon
Oregon, Washington and British Columbia, James Luther Davis
Texas, Steve Price
North Carolina, South Carolina and Tennessee, John Rucker
Florida with Georgia and Alabama Coasts, M. Timothy O'Keefe

Forthcoming Titles

Minnesota, Michigan and Wisconsin, John Bates
Southern California, Judy Wade

GEORGIA AND ALABAMA HOTSPOTS

Seasonal Guide to
the Natural Year

SITE LOCATOR MAP

N

LIST OF SITES
Alabama

1. Gulf State Park
2. Mobile-Tenshaw Delta
3. Dauphin Island
4. Weeks Bay National Estuarine Reserve
5. Mobile Bay
6. Gulf Shores
7. Bon Secour NWR

LIST OF SITES
Georgia

1. Okefenokee NWR
2. Suwannee Canal Recreational Area
3. Harris Neck NWR
4. Cumberland Island National Seashore
5. Blackbeard Island NWR
6. Savannah Coastal Refuges
7. Okefenokee Swamp Park

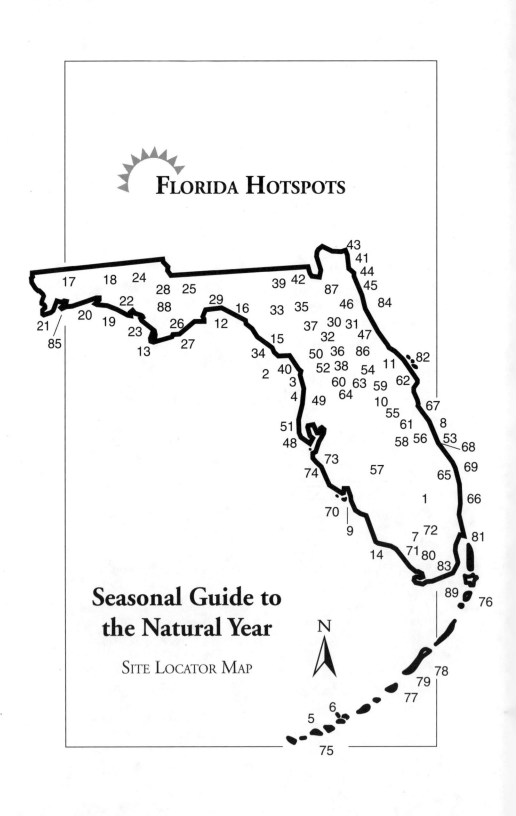

LIST OF SITES
Florida

1. Loxahatchee NWR
2. Cedar Keys NWR
3. Chassahowitzka NWR
4. Crystal River NWR
5. Great White Heron NWR
6. National Key Deer Refuge
7. Florida Panther NWR
8. Hobe Sound NWR
9. J. N. "Ding" Darling NWR
10. Lake Woodruff NWR
11. Merritt Island NWR
12. St. Marks NWR
13. St. Vincent NWR
14. Ten Thousand Islands NWR
15. Andrews Wildlife Management Area
16. Big Bend Wildlife Management Area
17. Blackwater River State Forest
18. Falling Waters State Recreation Area
19. Grayton Beach State Recreation Area
20. Henderson Beach State Recreation Area
21. Perdido Key State Recreation Area
22. St. Andrews State Recreation Area
23. St. Joseph Peninsula State Park
24. Florida Caverns State Park
25. Lake Jackson Mounds State Archaeological Site
26. Ochlockonee River State Park
27. St. George Island State Park
28. Torreya State Park
29. Wakulla Springs State Park
30. Devil's Millhopper State Geological Site
31. Gold Head Branch State Park
32. Gainesville-Hawthorne State Rail-to-Trail
33. Ichetucknee Springs State Park
34. Manatee Springs State Park
35. O'Leno State Park
36. Paynes Prairie State Preserve
37. San Felasco Hammock State Preserve
38. Silver River State Park
39. Suwannee River State Park
40. Waccasassa Bay State Reserve/ Cedar Key Scrub State Reserve
41. Big Talbot Island State Park
42. Cary State Forest
43. Fort Clinch State Park
44. Guana River State Park/Wildlife Management Area

45. Little Talbot Island State Park
46. Ravine State Gardens
47. Washington Oaks State Gardens
48. Caladesi Island State Park
49. Crystal River State Archaeological Site
50. Homosassa Springs State Wildlife Park
51. Honeymoon Island State Recreation Area
52. Rainbow Springs State Park
53. Blue Cypress Water Management Area
54. Blue Spring State Park
55. Bull Creek Wildlife Management Area
56. DuPuis Reserve State Forest
57. Highlands Hammock State Park
58. Lake Kissimmee State Park
59. Lower Wekiva River State Preserve
60. Rock Springs Run State Preserve
61. Three Lakes Wildlife Management Area
62. Tosohatchee State Reserve
63. Wekiwa Springs State Park
64. Withlacoochee State Forest
65. MacArthur Beach State Park
66. John U. Lloyd Beach State Recreation Area
67. Sebastian Inlet State Recreation Area
68. St. Lucie Inlet State Preserve
69. Jonathan Dickinson State Park
70. Cayo Costa State Park
71. Collier-Seminole State Park
72. Fakahatchee Strand State Preserve
73. Myakka River State Park
74. Oscar Scherer State Park
75. Bahia Honda State Park
76. Key Largo Hammocks State Botanical Site
77. Long Key State Recreation Area
78. John Pennekamp Coral Reef State Park
79. San Pedro Underwater Archaeological Preserve
80. Big Cypress National Preserve, Ochopee
81. Biscayne National Park, Homestead
82. Canaveral National Seashore, Titusville
83. Everglades National Park
84. Fort Matanzas National Monument, Summer Haven
85. Gulf Islands National Seashore, Pensacola
86. Ocala National Forest
87. Osceola National Forest
88. Apalachicola National Forest
89. Florida Bay

Contents

CONTENTS

Acknowledgments

Information for a book of this scope comes from many places over an extended period of time, and any attempt to credit all those who assisted in this endeavor is bound to be incomplete. Nevertheless, I would like to thank the following for their significant help: William W. Schroeder, oceanographer, Dauphin Island Sea Lab; Mark Van Hoose, biologist, Dauphin Island; Ralph Havard, biological technician, Marine Resources department, Dauphin Island; Mark Smith, education and training specialist, Florida park system; Peter C.H. Pritchard, Florida Audubon Society; Laura Lowery, wildlife biologist, Ocala National Forest; Vernon Compton, forestry resource administrator, Blackwater River State Forest; and Michael Keys, wildlife biologist, Osceola National Forest.

Introduction

Something is out of kilter in a world where children's petting zoos have become popular mini–theme parks. For many children, a petting zoo is their first exposure to animals other than pets. These youngsters have never touched a cow, seen a pig or fed a chicken. What an illustration of just how divorced we have become from the natural world around us.

Indeed, all of us tend to be dominated by man-made artificial time, a world in which clocks and calendars determine our schedules even as they obscure the deeper rhythms of days and seasons. It is a wonderful thing to rediscover these more fundamental cycles, to enter and observe a world not dictated by wristwatches but by such things as temperature and the length of the day.

In the Southeast, nature reveals herself throughout the year in an astonishing variety of guises, all delicately in time with the seasons. At Crystal River National Wildlife Refuge, hundreds of endangered manatees congregate in the clear spring waters every winter to escape the potentially deadly cold ocean temperatures. At Canaveral National Seashore and all along the Florida East Coast, the world's largest nesting population of loggerhead turtles crawls ashore from May to August to dig their nests and lay their eggs in the sand above the high-water line. At Okefenokee National Wildlife Refuge, hundreds of alligators may fast for as many as six months out of the year, their cold-blooded metabolism virtually dormant during the coldest months. At St. Marks National Wildlife Refuge, thousands of monarch butterflies gather every October as they pause on their marathon journey to winter over in the high forests outside of Mexico City. And every spring in Everglades National Park, thousands of herons, ibis and egrets cluster on the mangrove trees to create one of the most spectacular nesting sights anywhere: trees covered by the white feathers of so many birds it seems the trees are draped in down.

The real world unfolds in its own time. To appreciate nature, one must understand—and respect—its pace. The guidebooks in the *Seasonal Guide to the Natural Year* series are designed to help the wildlife observer do just that. Instead of merely listing intriguing places to visit, *Seasonal Guide to the Natural Year: Florida with Georgia and Alabama Coasts* stresses the element of time: When to go is emphasized just as strongly as where to go. This book directs those who want to see some of the Southeast's most spectacular wildlife attractions to the likeliest spots in the likeliest months.

Four unique viewing opportunities are offered for every month of the year; the natural history of the event or species is described and several hotspots, or outstanding viewing sites, are suggested. The "Shorttakes" chapters within each season briefly list one, two or more additional wildlife events and likely viewing areas. And finally, "A Closer Look" chapters focus on an especially interesting feature for that month.

The three states included in this volume have some of the most unusual animals and habitats of any place in North America, even the world. The elevations are flat and low, so strenuous climbing is never a problem. And although the area is one of the country's warmest, the terrain is more like thick jungle than open empty desert: scrub cypress, forest swamp, palm hammocks, tropical hammocks, salt marshes, freshwater marshes, dry prairies, pine flatwoods, sandhill areas and North America's only coral reef system. With so much diversity, there is always something new to discover on land or under the sea. This region also contains some of the world's most unique—and endangered—plants and animals, ones you are not likely to see anywhere else.

General Tips, Cautions and Suggestions

Virtually every spot recommended in this book is on public land. This is especially true for Florida, which has the nation's most aggressive program for buying and protecting land in what is also one of the country's fastest growing states. Common sense and generous doses of courtesy will always work on your behalf when pulling onto the sides of roads or venturing into areas on or adjacent to private land to view wildlife. Be extremely careful in deciding where to pull off the road: Always make sure that your vehicle will not impede traffic and that the roadside is actually good, hard soil, not soft sand or mud, which would necessitate the assistance of a tow truck in order to extricate your vehicle. Be especially careful about driving on beaches where it's permitted. Every year visitors lose their cars to the sea because they park near the water's edge, go for a walk and never think about the consequences of an incoming tide.

Many of the places suggested here require visitor fees. The best way to hold down this expense is through the purchase of a $25 annual Golden Eagle Pass, which allows the holder's vehicle and all passengers into almost all federal lands, including national parks, national monuments and national wildlife refuges. It pays for itself after just half a dozen visits, and it can usually be purchased at most of the places at which it can be used.

Given the varied temperatures one can encounter in the Southeast both in winter (freezes but little snow) and summer (where every day is in the 90s), it's best to be prepared for every extreme. Sun lotion, brimmed hats, polarized sunglasses, mosquito repellent and extra liquids are essential everyday items. Binoculars are always important, and so is a full tank of gas, because some of the suggested viewing areas are in fairly remote spots where gas stations are not always common. Good maps are also a must. All of the state welcome stations have free road maps and guidebooks. Free to members are the American Automobile Association (AAA) maps and guidebooks for each state; they are a wealth of information. The maps available in the national forest ranger stations are crucial for finding one's way. Most of the state parks supply free pamphlets with a map showing both roads and nature trails. Distances covered in many areas tend to be quite short, so additional maps are not really needed.

January

Notes

1

Viewing Manatees

The manatee is one of Florida's most endangered animals and also one of its most popular. Florida has the nation's only remaining resident population of manatees, whose population estimate ranges between 2,200 and 2,600 animals. The mammals are sometimes called "sea cows" because they eat only plants.

Manatees are regarded as the basis for the mermaid legend, which is one of history's great jokes. Indeed, when Columbus encountered a manatee in the New World in 1493 (he was the first European to record such a sighting), he mistook it for a mermaid, commenting that the creature was not as handsome as myths and artists had depicted it.

A manatee's face, adorned with spiked-hair on heavy jowls, is more akin to that of a walrus than to some sexy seductress. Its head is tacked onto a fat, sausagelike torso that ends in a broad tail. Taken as a whole, the creature appears the result of some bizarre genetic experiment.

Yet, from a distance a manatee might on occasion be mistaken for a creature that is half-human, half-fish. Sometimes when a manatee feeds, it floats vertically in the water and uses both its flippers to sweep food toward its mouth. With its head and arms bobbing above the waterline, a manatee could resemble a person. When a manatee is startled or frightened, it may slip under water with a flip of its tail. Hence a creature with a human head and the tail of a fish.

Actually, manatees can trace their origins back an estimated 55 to 60 million years to an animal in Africa and Eurasia that abandoned the land for the sea. Closely related to the elephant, this creature remained an air-breathing mammal but adapted so well to its new marine environment that it became too specialized ever to return to land. Its front legs, for instance, became a pair of flippers, and its back legs evolved into a broad, beaverlike tail. A fully grown manatee may weigh over 2,000 pounds and become almost

12 feet long. The average manatee weighs only about 1,000 pounds, though.

Despite the manatee's weird appearance, there is still something majestic, almost regal, in the way the animal moves and acts. It moves slowly, never appearing to be in any hurry. But with just a couple of flips of its tail a manatee can outdistance the fastest human swimmer.

Although they appear dumpy and slow, manatees are fast swimmers. They were also the basis for the mermaid legend.

In summer, Florida's manatees may range as far north as the Carolinas and as far west as Louisiana and Texas. But as the weather turns cooler, manatees—like a lot of other travelers—seek out the warm waters of Florida. Fossil evidence indicates this has been the limit of the manatee's range for the last 10,000 years, the period since the last Ice Age.

Adult manatees, which have no natural enemies in the wild, also have no means of defending themselves. They lack both claws and teeth. Confronted by danger, their only defense is to swim away.

Cold weather is one of the greatest threats to manatees. In spite of their blubbery appearance, manatees do not have a thick fat layer to insulate them from the cold. They have to seek out warm water when the water temperature drops below 68 degrees, which typically occurs around mid-November. Manatees that suffer prolonged exposure to water temperatures of less than 60 degrees often die.

Historically, manatees wintered at the southern tip of Florida or in selected natural spring runs. Construction of warmth-generating power plants has allowed manatees to winter farther north. Unfortunately, some plants are in the middle of the state's most developed regions and therefore totally devoid of forage areas. This predicament requires resident manatees to go for long periods of time without food during severe cold spells.

However, it is the dredging and filling of the coastal grazing and breeding grounds that makes manatee survival so precarious. As much as 80 percent of the sea-grass beds that manatees once depended on have been destroyed since 1960, not only by dredge-and-fill projects but by the runoff from pesticides, oil from roadways and other toxic substances. Loss of its shallow-water habitat has pushed the manatee into deeper areas and more traveled waterways that it must share with boats and boat propellers.

As a mammal, a manatee must rise to the surface periodically to breathe. This may occur every four to five minutes or every ten to fifteen minutes. Often it is only the tip of the manatee's nose that is exposed above the surface. Or the manatee may float just a few feet below the waterline—too low to be seen but not low enough to escape a boat's propeller blades. The manatee's gray color can make it almost impossible to see from the surface.

For most of their history manatees have enjoyed an ideal existence. They are able to move freely into all types of water—salt, fresh, muddy or clear—and live there without competition from any other animal. They are the only marine mammals who eat plants. So, for millions of years, all manatees did was eat and sleep, consuming as much as 10 percent of their body weight every day, grazing for between six and eight hours, then resting the remainder of the time. With so many advantages, it's no wonder manatees became the "lazies" of the marine mammal world. Survival was so effortless and uncomplicated that manatees never needed to create a complex social structure as other species did.

The most complex interaction in the manatee world occurs between a calf and its mother. Manatee calves remain almost constantly at their mothers' sides for about two years. It is up to the mother to teach the young animal the simple but all-important survival lessons: migratory patterns, location of the feeding grounds and winter refuge sites. This is why orphaned manatees raised in captivity rarely survive when released in the wild as adults. They don't know the necessary survival skills.

Manatees communicate by squeals and squeaks, and mothers up to 200 feet away have been known to respond at top speed (10–15 mph in short bursts) to their calves' squeals.

Because of the two-year training period needed for each calf, females produce offspring only every three to five years. Their gestation period is about 13 months. This slow reproductive rate is another reason why manatees are endangered today. A good resource guide about these fascinating animals is *Manatees: Our Vanishing Mermaids.*

Hot Spots

From December to mid-February, Florida's **Crystal River National Wildlife Refuge (NWR)** is the only place in the world snorkelers can swim with the West Indian manatee in relatively clear water. As many as 300 adult manatees and their calves overwinter in the constant-72-degree Crystal River. As an endangered species, manatees may not be harassed by swimmers, which means chasing or touching them is not allowed. The best time to view them is early in the morning on a cold weekday (a wetsuit is mandatory). Avoid the weekend crowds of divers and fishermen. Manatees don't mind a few snorkelers at a time, but when a horde of flippered folk show up, the animals move away from the most accessible viewing areas. The town of Crystal River is located about 80 miles north of Tampa at the junction of U.S. 44 and U.S. 19. For complete information on facilities at Crystal River, write the Crystal River Chamber of Commerce, 1801 Northwest Highway 19, Suite 541, Crystal River, FL 34429; or call (904) 795-3149.

Homosassa Springs State Wildlife Park has no special manatee season. Instead, manatees are present every day, making it the only place where the animals can be seen in their natural surroundings year-round. An underwater observatory makes it possible to come nose-to-nose with the creatures in the 45-foot-deep natural spring, which pumps millions of gallons of water per hour. The spring is the headwaters of the Homosassa River, which meanders for nine miles to enter the Gulf of Mexico.

Raising manatees in captivity is expensive. The average adult eats 100 to 200 pounds of romaine lettuce daily, which adds up to more than $30,000 worth of salad per animal per year. Park rangers offer educational programs on the manatees several times daily. Bleachers for these programs are next to the main spring. In addition to the manatee viewing available 365 days a year, visitors have miles of nature trails to walk and can also cruise the Pepper Creek by tour boat. The park opens daily (including holidays) at 9 A.M. and closes at 5:30 P.M. The last ticket is sold at 4 P.M.

The park is located 75 miles north of Tampa and 90 miles northwest of Orlando near the Gulf of Mexico and the town of Homosassa. The park entrance is a quarter-mile west of U.S. 19 in Homosassa Springs. For complete information, call (904) 628-2311.

Located at 7530 North Boulevard in Tampa, the small, 24-acre **Lowry Park Zoo** is ranked one of the top three zoos for its size by the American Association of Zoological Parks and Aquariums. With 1,600 animals representing 272 species (including 31 threatened or endangered species), the zoo features manatees as a main attraction. Lowry Park's Florida Manatee Hospital and Aquatic Center is a special rescue, care and recovery facility for injured or ill manatees. Animals that regain their full health there are released back into the wild. Although the aquatic center is available for viewing as part of the general admission fee, behind-the-scenes tours of the hospital are conducted Wednesday through Sunday only. Call (813) 935-8552 to verify this schedule.

The **South Florida Museum and Bishop Planetarium** is home to Snooty, the internationally famous manatee living in captivity longer than any other manatee in the world. Snooty was born in 1948 at an aquarium in Miami, making him the first manatee ever recorded born in captivity. In 1949 Snooty was moved to the town of Bradenton, where he eventually became Manatee County's mascot. Today the 8-foot-long, 800-pound Snooty is enjoying life as the Bishop Museum's star attraction. Over a million visitors have seen him, and his annual birthday party has become a major area tradition. His birthday, with free cupcakes, punch and a birthday card contest, is held on the Saturday closest to July 21, his actual birthday. The museum hours are 10 A.M. to 5 P.M. Tuesday through Saturday; noon to 6 P.M. Sunday; closed Monday. Snooty is fed several times daily. The museum is located at 201 10th Street West, Bradenton; (813) 746-4132.

Blue Spring State Park is another of the state's most important natural manatee wintering refuges. A half-mile boardwalk skirts the length of the spring run, allowing easy viewing of the 30 to 40 manatees that spend each winter here from mid-November to mid-March. The boardwalk, which is wheelchair-accessible, has several platforms extended over the constant 72-degree water that provide excellent views of the manatees. The spring flows into the St. Johns River. Once the St. Johns warms up, the manatee herd disperses until the following season. Since there is no vegetation growing in the spring run, manatees sometimes make short forays into the river for food.

The best time for manatee viewing is early in the morning, shortly after the park opens. Blue Spring is very popular on weekends, and it's best to be in line when the park opens at 8

A.M. Those who arrive late may find the park is full and have to wait outside until there is an empty parking space inside. Park rangers offer special audiovisual programs when the manatees are in residence. For complete information, contact Blue Spring State Park, 2100 West French Avenue, Orange City, FL 32763; (904) 775-3663. Campsites and vacation cabins are available.

The **Big Bend Station** owned by Tampa Electric is a warmwater discharge area that attracts a sizable herd of manatees in cold weather. Tampa Electric provides access to this remarkable sight through an observation platform that is open only from December through March. Closed on Monday and Tuesday, it opens at 10 A.M. every other day except Sunday, when it opens at noon. From I-75 in Tampa, take the Apollo Beach Exit onto Big Bend Road. Go west toward the Gulf until you reach a sharp turn to the left. The viewing center is located here; (813) 228-4289.

Port Everglades at Fort Lauderdale is a busy shipping center, but manatees come in winter to take advantage of the warmwater discharge plant. The **Port Everglades Ocean Life Viewing Center** is found by taking I-95 and exiting at the State Road 84/Southwest 24th Street Exit. Go east, which will take you right to Port Everglades itself. Turn right when the road approaches the water and look for the designated parking area.

Sea World of Florida launched its Manatee Rescue and Rehabilitation program in 1976. Today, one of several Sea World main attractions is Manatees: The Last Generation?, a 300,000-gallon habitat made to resemble a lush tropical lagoon. Visitors can observe manatees either from the surface or enjoy a spectacular diver's-eye view of the small manatee herd through a 126-foot-long acrylic panel that spans one side of the exhibit. **Walt Disney World's Living Seas** at **Epcot** also houses a manatee exhibit that is separate from the main aquarium.

Since the early 1970s the **Miami Seaquarium** has participated in the recovery and rehabilitation of more than 65 manatees. It also houses one of the most prolific manatee breeding colonies anywhere in the United States. The Miami Seaquarium is located at 4400 Rickenbacker Causeway, Virginia Key, Miami; (305) 361-5705.

2

Wintering Sandhill Cranes

One of the largest birds that migrates to the Southeast in winter is the northern sandhill crane. An estimated 10,000 sandhill cranes migrate every fall from their breeding grounds in Michigan and Wisconsin, arriving in the Southland between mid-October and late November.

Sandhill cranes are as distinctive as their name. A fully mature bird may be as tall as 4 feet and have a wing span of 7 feet. They are mostly gray in color (sometimes with reddish brown stains) with long black spindly legs, a bustle of tail feathers and a long neck. Mature adults also have whitish cheeks and a red patch atop their heads, and immature birds have brown heads and necks. Florida also has its own subspecies of sandhill cranes that is nonmigratory and classified as a threatened species due to its small population.

Sandhills stand out not only because of their size but also their song. The cranes have a windpipe that is several feet long, which some have likened to a French horn. Actually, the loud trumpeting sound—which can be heard for up to two miles—sounds more like a rusty nail being pulled out of a piece of wood. For this reason, some refer to them as the "rusty nail birds."

Considering the bird's raucous call, often made in flight, it's not surprising to learn that sandhill cranes are a close cousin of the whooping crane. The sandhills, in fact, were once referred to as the "whooper." The two species look nothing alike: The whooping crane's feathers are all white.

Both the northern and Florida sandhill cranes have a remarkable mating dance. A male and female face each other, then leap into the air. With wings extended and their feet thrown forward, they bow to each other while making loud croaking calls. They repeat the performance more than once.

Although their name implies otherwise, sandhill cranes make their large saucer-shaped nests in wet prairies, the margins of marshy lakes, low-lying pastures and isolated ponds. Pickerel ponds seem to be the preferred habitat because the vegetation hides the nests from bobcats and other predators.

Both parents build the nest, which may be as much as 4 feet across and constructed in water about one to one and a half feet deep. Aquatic plants and dead sticks are the main nesting material. Like the birds, the eggs are sizable, about 4 inches across. They are deposited anywhere from late February to April and take about a month to incubate, a process in which both parents are involved.

Sandhill cranes are unusually tall and stand between 3 and 4 feet high. They nest in Florida from January through June.

A typical egg clutch has a pair of eggs, though the number can vary between one and three eggs. The eggs are buff colored and have olive markings.

Newborn chicks are covered in a golden down. It takes them about two months to develop the strength and the primary feathers needed for their long flight home. Juveniles stay with their parents for about a year.

The bird's diet is quite varied and includes aquatic plants, berries, grass shoots, seeds and many different kinds of animals such as insects, worms, birds' eggs and small mammals.

Hot Spots

Sandhill cranes nest in wet prairies. There are many such places, but public access to them is often limited to those with four-wheel-drive or a boat. The following are places where you can realistically see sandhills without turning the search into a major expedition.

Georgia's **Okefenokee Swamp NWR** sometimes has as many as 1,000 sandhill cranes wintering over. It may be necessary to reach the prime viewing spot by small boat; these are readily available for rental at the eastern, main, entrance to the refuge near Folkston. From I-95, take the Kingston Exit and go west on Highway 40 to Folkston. From Folkston, go 11 miles southwest to the main entrance to the **Suwannee Canal Recreation Area.** The refuge is open daily but hours vary. Everything needed for exploring the swamp, including overnight trips into the wilderness, can be found here. Call (912) 496-3331.

Florida's main wintering ground is the 20,000-acre **Paynes Prairie State Preserve** just south of Gainesville in North-Central Florida. Between 1,500 and 2,500 birds migrate here annually, compared to the resident 25 to 30 breeding pairs. One of the best viewing locations on this huge land tract is on the north rim along the La Chua Trail, a popular hiking trail. An observation platform, which sits in the middle of the prairie basin, is considered the best spot. The La Chua name is a holdover from when much of this great preserve was the largest and best-known Spanish cattle ranch of the 1600s.

Probably the second-best place in Florida for sandhills is the 5,000-acre **Lake Kissimmee State Park,** named for Florida's

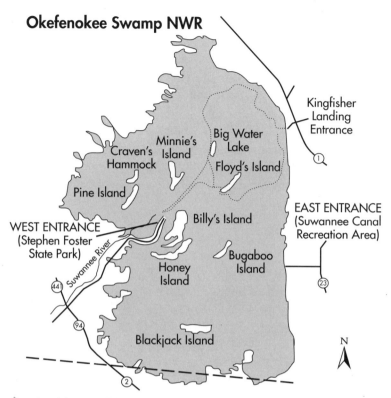

third-largest lake, which the park borders. You can hike the wilderness on two trails, the North Loop and the Buster Island Loop, both just under 6 miles. The trailhead for each starts from the parking area. Contact Lake Kissimmee State Park, 14248 Camp Mack Road, Lake Wales, FL 33853; (813) 696-1112. Take State Road 60 and go east for 14 miles from the town of Lake Wales. Signs mark the turnoff to the park.

Sandhills, both residents and winter visitors, are found in the **Ocala National Forest** and its dozens of small lakes and ponds. One option is to obtain a map from the ranger station and take the forest roads west off State Road 19 north of the city of Umatilla. There's a good chance of seeing (if not hearing) the cranes on any of the numerous shallow-water lakes. Hopkins Prairie, north of State Road 40, is a particularly good spot. Perhaps the easiest way to see the birds is to drive State Road 42 along the south end of the forest, where they are quite common on private land in the cattle pastures.

The **Sunnyhill Restoration Area** in the Oklawaha River Basin is another excellent place to see wintering and resident sandhills. The restoration area includes 9 miles of the Oklawaha River, which is being returned to its original state. Access to the land is only through group tours, and advance arrangements must be made. Contact the St. Johns Water Management District, (904) 821-1489. The entrance is 5.9 miles east of the town of Weirsdale on County Road 42.

A resident population of sandhills can usually be seen in the wet prairies along State Road 70 both east and west of U.S. 27 in the Lake Placid area.

3

Nesting Bald Eagles

As the United States expanded, wilderness areas were developed and pesticides like DDT were introduced into the environment, which caused bald eagle populations to decline dramatically. As a result, most Americans have observed their national symbol only on TV nature programs or on postal delivery trucks.

Considering the human population explosion in Florida since 1900, this may come as a surprise—but the chances of seeing bald eagles on the nest are better in Florida than anywhere else in the lower 48 states. Florida's bald eagle population in the mid-1990s numbered about 667 nesting pairs. Outside of Alaska, Florida has more nesting bald eagles than any other state in the nation.

As witnessed in real life, the bald eagle is more than an impressive symbol. Capable of growing 3 feet in height and with a wing span of almost 8 feet, it is a giant among birds. The bald eagle, *Haliaeetus leucocephalus,* is unique to North America. It belongs to a group of avians known as fish or sea eagles. Of the eight fish eagles that exist worldwide, only one, the bald eagle, is found in the Western Hemisphere.

Young bald eagles are a mottled chocolate brown and white. The distinctive white head and dark body aren't attained until the bird matures, in about its fifth year. With all that white plumage the eagle certainly isn't bald, and it was never considered to be. The confusing name is based on an old usage of the word *bald* that also meant *white.*

Florida's bald eagles are considered part of the southern subspecies that nests in Mexico, the southern Atlantic states, Louisiana, Texas, Oklahoma, Arizona and southern California. Southern bald eagles tend to be smaller than the northern subspecies, and they nest in winter instead of spring.

Eagles normally nest in the same area, and sometimes the same tall tree, year after year, yet they often travel thousands of miles between seasons. As primarily fish and carrion eaters, most of

Florida's nesting eagles are found within a mile of a coastline or some permanent year-round body of water. Unlike ospreys, which are often confused for bald eagles, eagles usually avoid nesting in man-made structures such as channel markers, utility poles and the like. They prefer live trees. Outside of Florida, bald eagles nest in the spring and summer, when food is at its most abundant. Florida eagles, on the other hand, nest in winter, when prey is plentiful throughout the peninsula. For instance, in the dry winter season fish are more concentrated when ponds shrink or dry up.

Immature bald eagles like this one do not gain their distinctive white head and dark coloring until their fifth year.

Bald eagles, which pair for life, usually begin returning to their nests in late September or early October. This is the time to begin looking for the dramatic aerial displays of courtship, when the birds catch each other's feet in midflight and, with their wings and legs outstretched, tumble close to the ground, parting only just before striking the earth.

Early nesters may begin laying eggs in November, whereas late nesters may wait until mid-January. A tall pine tree is the favored habitat for Central and North Florida eagles. The nests are commonly as much as 80 to 100 feet up in and just below the top of a tree. Eagles in South Florida often use mangrove trees for their nests; situated only 20 feet off the ground, these nests are often the easiest to see.

A bald eagle nest, like the birds themselves, is an impressive size. It is the largest nest of any bird in North America, and the same nest is constantly added to, year after year. It may eventually weigh as much as 2 tons. The largest ever recorded in Florida was 10 feet wide and 20 feet deep.

Eagles will use sticks as long as 6 feet to weave into the frame of a nest. Smaller sticks are added and intermixed with the large ones. Weeds and grass, sometimes with dirt still attached, are placed at the bottom.

Nests are shaped according to the tree. Cylindrical nests are formed when a tree's branches grow upright. Broader cup-shaped nests are made where the branches are more spread out. From scratch, a nest takes only about four days to build. Eagles sometimes have more than one nest in an area, though they will use only one during a breeding season.

Females lay two or three eggs, several days apart. The eggs are twice the size of the average chicken egg. Both parents take turns during the incubation period, which lasts about 32 days. The eggs are turned about once an hour so they will warm evenly. To transfer body heat, both parents develop a brood patch in their lower breasts where feathers are absent and the blood vessels are close to the surface.

The chicks emerge several days apart. It takes a chick about 24 hours to break out of its shell using an "egg tooth," a sharp point at the top of its bill that wears off after about a month. This is survival of the fittest from the start: The parents never help a chick break out of its egg.

When food is scarce, the parents do not prevent the older and larger chick from taking most of the food, even if this results in the death of its siblings. The parents never regurgitate food for their young. Instead, the chicks devour bites of food torn off for them by their parents.

A newly hatched chick weighs about 3 ounces and bears a thick coat of gray down. It is able to fly at about eight weeks. It will leave the nest at about ten to twelve weeks but may remain in a tree near the nest for another four to six weeks so that it can still be fed by its parents. Then, beginning around April, the eaglets will fly north, going perhaps as far as Canada, a distance of over 2,000 miles. An estimated one-half of Florida's eaglets do not survive beyond their third year. A mature eagle in the wild may live 25 to 35 years, and in captivity as long as 50 years.

It's believed that bald eagles are able to spot items two or three times more distant than humans can see. Their vision, among the best of all animals, is what the eagles rely on to hunt their prey. They typically use their feet to grasp and kill their prey.

When capturing another bird in flight, the eagle will fly below its quarry, turn upside down and snatch the victim by its breast. When fishing, the bald eagle is a stunning, majestic sight as it swoops down and grabs a fish with its talons, often not even getting its legs wet. However, as Ben Franklin (who favored the turkey as our national symbol) noted, bald eagles are of definite "bad moral character" because they steal food from other birds. The neighborhood bully, the bald eagle may swipe food from ospreys, which share the same kind of habitat, and will also steal from other eagles as well.

Hot Spots In distinguishing bald eagles from other large birds that might inhabit the same area, remember that a bald eagle always soars with its wings held flat. Turkey vultures, which are of similar size, fly with a distinctive V-shape to their wings. From a distance, a bald eagle's head seems almost as prominent as its tail. Black vultures, on the other hand, have a much smaller head. Ospreys, which are fish hawks, are smaller and nest in man-made objects as well as dead trees; bald eagles normally prefer live trees.

The heaviest concentration of bald eagle nests anywhere in the Southeast—as many as 150—are located in the Prairie Lakes Unit of the **Three Lakes Wildlife Management Area** southeast of Orlando. This former ranchland is situated between several lakes; the lakes are now ringed with eagle nests. Prairie Lakes is considered the best place to see eagles in Florida year-round. To find the Prairie Lakes Unit, take State Road 523 (Canoe Creek Road) for 9 miles northwest of the town of Kenansville. The entrance is on the left. However, management hunts are also conducted here; check with the Game and Fresh Water Fish Commission, (904) 732-1225.

Paynes Prairie State Preserve just south of Gainesville has several unusually accessible nests at Lake Wauburg on the Micanopy side of Paynes Prairie. The place to stop is a small picnic area right off the major highway, Highway 441. The nests should be visible from this spot. In addition, nearby Orange Lake and Lake Lochloosa have plenty of bald eagle activity during the nesting season.

Ocala National Forest offers rich bald eagle habitat. It borders the St. Johns River and contains hundreds of lakes and several freshwater springs within its 383,000 acres. Bald eagles may be seen almost anywhere but are most numerous around Lake George. It takes a little bushwhacking to get close to some of the nests in remote swampy areas. Eagles don't put their nests openly on the lake edge, where they would be easy to see. The easiest way to spot eagles is to take the ferry across Lake George from the community of Salt Springs. It's quite common to see eagles from the ferry. There is also a nest at Lake Delancy. For more information, call (904) 625-2520.

Withlacoochee State Forest near Brooksville has an easily accessible nest site on the Richloam tract near the fish hatchery. It's possible to get fairly close by car, then hike to the nest. Look for bald eagles around the ponds near Mud Lake Road at **Lake Woodruff NWR** near DeLand. All of the ponds have walkable dikes surrounding them. Another good spot is **Lake Kissimmee State Park** near Lake Wales. It's not unusual to see as many as a dozen eagles in the same day. Several birds nest in the park, but the most reliable and easily accessible nest is near the replica of an 1876 cow camp.

The **Merritt Island NWR** near Titusville is another reliable area. Check at the visitor center on State Road 406 for the location of currently occupied nests. Just north of Fort Myers is **Pine Island,** reached by taking State Road 78 from U.S. 41. Pine Island's main road is County Road C-767 (Stringfield Road). Drive the 15-mile road in any direction and start looking for nests, which are usually quite plentiful.

The **Charlotte Harbor Environmental Center** has a couple of hiking trails that should put you in view of the bald eagles that nest here from December to April. On U.S. 41 southeast of the city of Punta Gorda, turn south on Highway 765 (Burnt Store Road). Go for 1 mile to the entrance. The center phone number is (813) 575-4800.

In **Everglades National Park,** look for bald eagles at Paurotis Pond and at the very end of the park road at Flamingo.

In the Panhandle, the clear, rich waters of **Wakulla Springs State Park** are lined with several nests, and the birds can frequently be seen flying overhead. **St. Marks NWR** just south of Tallahassee usually has bald eagles nesting by November or December. Remote **St. Vincent Island NWR,** with 8 miles of Gulf shoreline, is another good site, but a private boat is necessary to reach it.

4

It's a Shad, Shad Story

January winds in Florida can be cold and bitter, and the water temperature is normally low enough that largemouth bass and bream are essentially dormant. Although most people are at home watching the football play-offs at this time, dedicated anglers near Orlando will be bundled up and taking advantage of the annual shad run in the St. Johns River.

The American shad is the southern version of the Pacific salmon. Like the salmon, a shad begins life in fresh water but spends most of its adulthood in the ocean. And when it is time for the fish to spawn, it returns to fresh water, presumably to the very same river where it was born.

Spawning shad, which average from 3 to 5 pounds, enter the St. Johns River near Jacksonville in early winter, when the water temperature ranges between 56 and 66 degrees, which occurs typically in late November or December. If the river water goes above 66 degrees, the shad stop "running" until the temperature plunges again.

The spawning season starts in January and continues through late March and into early April, though in some years the fish have been caught as late as mid-May. The first three months of the year typically offer the best angling, subject to the vagaries of the weather.

After spawning, the shad die, and their bodies are consumed by alligators, turtles, vultures and other animals. Nature's sanitation corps is a very effective one on the St. Johns. Unlike the aftermath of a salmon run, it is rare here to see many shad floating on the surface or washed up on the shoreline.

Newly spawned shad remain in the St. Johns until late September or early October, by which time they range between 4 to 6 inches in length. The young shad leave the river and remain in the open ocean for three to five years, then return to spawn and die.

If shad are similar to salmon in their life cycle, they are more like hundred-pound tarpon when it comes to fighting on hook and line. Like tarpon, the shad is a dazzlingly bright creature with large silver scales. A shad jumps like a tarpon too, often catapulting itself in the air as soon as it is hooked. And also like the tarpon, the shad is generally considered inedible. The shad is a fish to be hooked, fought with and released.

With the proper lure, hooking a shad should not be difficult, but boating the tissue-mouthed fighters can be tricky. Because of their tender mouths, the best way to land a shad is to net it. Releases, however, are easy. Give the fish a little line and they will usually free themselves right at the boat.

Shad are usually caught by trolling slowly against the current. In the St. Johns that means motoring south, for this river is one of the few in the world that flows north. Normally, anglers troll as slowly as possible. Troll too fast and the lure may start catching herring, which stay closer to the surface than shad do. Go too slowly and the hooks may snag clamshells off the bottom. The level at which the lures run can be adjusted by letting out more line or reeling some in. A good rule of thumb: If the shad aren't biting, let out more line.

Since the whole purpose of fishing for shad is to fight the fish, the lighter the tackle, the better. An 8- or 10-pound test spinning rig is more than sufficient. Once a fish is on, it's wise to put the motor in neutral in order not to drag the shad through the water needlessly.

A typical shad rig is a three-part combination: a 5-foot piece of 20-pound test monofilament leader with a small spoon at the end, a jig tied on about midway and a keel sinker that is tied to the fishing line. The keel sinker is essential for trolling because it keeps the lures down with the fish and minimizes line twist.

The jigs and spoons come in different colors, and the fish do seem to have definite preferences at various times. Rather than guess in advance, check at one of the fish camps for the hot color of the moment. The camps will have rigs made up and ready to sell.

At times a shad will strike suddenly and viciously, and an angler may find himself concerned with the safety of his light tackle. On other occasions the hookup feels like a snagged log or some other debris. Then the rod will suddenly jump to life, and there will be no more doubt about what has been hooked.

Fly fishing for shad is sometimes more effective than trolling. The first shad ever caught in Florida, in fact, was caught on a fly rod. The year was 1942, and the fisherman was a New York angler after largemouth bass. He used a plastic worm on a fly rod to catch a 6 $\frac{1}{2}$-pound shad. Previously it had been thought that shad would ignore a hook and could be captured only by commercial fishing nets.

Fly fishing for shad requires a 5- or 6-ounce fly rod with weighted line and a reel containing at least 40 to 50 yards of 4-pound test monofilament as backing. Essential to success is getting the lure down where the shad are, which is often close to the bottom. This means wet flies weighted with $\frac{1}{8}$- or $\frac{1}{4}$-inch diameter glass beads on the leader just above the fly. Not only will this make the fly sink faster, but it will add more flash to the lure. Red is a favorite color for beads, although orange, pink and yellow also have their followers.

Hot Spots Although the first St. Johns shad was caught on hook and line near the city of DeLand, all of the shad fishing today takes place south of the city of **Sanford**, below **Lake Monroe.** This is a beautiful stretch of river with almost no development. Palm trees line the banks in many places, and the wind rustling through the palm fronds sounds like falling rain.

Open pastures adjoin the waterway throughout much of the region. It's common to see mixed herds of Brahman cattle moving slowly along the banks, grazing in the fields or standing knee-deep in the river, munching on water hyacinth. Small white cattle egrets often accompany the cattle, sometimes perching on the bovines' backs.

It may seem hard to conceive that there could be so much beauty and such magnificent fishing within sight of a major highway, the stretch of State Road 46 between the towns of **Sanford** and **Geneva.** There are several fish camps here with rental boats and shad rigs. **Marina Isle Fish Camp** is where the river and State Road 46 meet just east of Lake Jessup. The next major access to the St. Johns is on State Road 50 where it crosses the St. Johns between **Orlando** and **Titusville.** There's another fish camp here too, but most of the angling efforts are off State Road 46, where the fish seem much more dependable. A saltwater-fishing license is required of all anglers unless they are fishing from the riverbank.

5

January Shorttakes

Rare Snail Kites

The snail kite, also called the Everglades kite, is doing well enough recently that it's possible to make some predictions about where to see these wintering birds. As their name implies, snail kites live off snails, the same apple snails that limpkins dine on (see chapter 44). The kites gather their snails deftly by hovering above the water and snatching them. This requires lots of open space. Probably the most reliable viewing spot is along the **Tamiami Trail** (U.S. 41) just west of Miami. One usually good place is the Miccosukee Restaurant, just across from the Everglades National Park Shark Valley visitor center. It's impossible at most places along the heavily traveled trail to pull over. However, the first fishing access area after leaving Miami does offer a turnoff, and it's possible to wander along the road for several miles here. The stretch of **State Road 78** bordering the northwest shore of Lake Okeechobee between Moore Haven and the town of Okeechobee is another usually reliable region. In addition, **Loxahatchee NWR** near West Palm Beach has an active snail kite restoration program. Here at least you can call and check ahead to discover your odds of seeing the birds; (407) 734-8303.

Exploring Biscayne National Park

Biscayne National Park is the nation's only national park that is 95 percent covered in water. Its 181,500 acres extend from the mainland to the edge of the Gulf Stream in the Atlantic Ocean. All of the park is open and accessible to anyone, but the offshore islands are bearable only during the coolest months, from December through April. The mosquitoes are so thick the rest of the time that boat trips aren't even scheduled.

However, the 32 barrier islands on the park's easternmost border are a unique and interesting world unto themselves. They are ancient coral reefs that emerged thousands of years ago, following the last Ice Age. Imprints of fossilized corals are present in many of the rocks on the islands today. Like the mainland, most of the islands are fringed with mangroves. Their interiors, however, are more characteristic of the West Indies than Florida. Jamaican dogwood, strangler fig and small stands of mahogany populate many of these jungle islands, the plant seeds carried here by wind, wave and in the digestive tracts of birds. Two of the most visited landfalls are **Elliott Key**, with its offshore camping facilities and hiking trails, and **Boca Chica Key**, with its stone lighthouse.

Biscayne National Park is located near Homestead. From U.S. 1 in Homestead, take North Canal Drive east until it ends at the only developed area, the visitor center at Convoy Point. Boat trips to the nearby islands can be arranged here. The small stone jetty near the visitor center is often a good place to see shorebirds, black skimmers and double-crested cormorants. A canoe trip through the nearby offshore cays (rentals at the visitor center) should find brown pelicans, ospreys and double-crested cormorants. Call (305) 247-2044.

Nature Walks Where the Buffalo Roam

Come to **Paynes Prairie State Preserve** near Gainesville in the middle of summer and you'll seriously wonder why the state is protecting such desolate wilderness. However, the abundant wildlife present here in the winter months makes it very clear and very understandable why this is an important state preserve. Paynes Prairie is an unusually diverse landscape that includes plenty of wet prairie, marsh, open water, swamps, pine flatwoods and hammocks, and each one is heavily populated with the appropriate species of plants and animals. The history of the area is also quite unusual: This was once the largest Spanish cattle ranch in the nation, and it was once even attacked by pirates (who had to travel many miles overland to get here). To make this 18,000 acres more accessible and more understandable, the staff has an aggressive field-trip program in the cooler months. The activities cover everything from a morning nature walk to overnight camping trips. Who knows, you might even get to see the bison roaming freely here. Bison? They were once native to the region, and the state has reintroduced a herd of the animals. That's just one of the surprises you're apt to encounter at Paynes Prairie, located just south of Gainesville on U.S. 441. For a current schedule of activities, call (904) 466-3397.

Paynes Prairie State Preserve

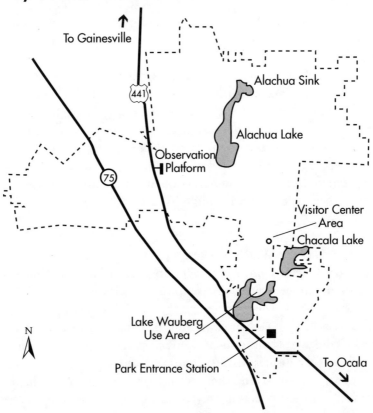

6

A Closer Look: Florida Brings Back the Bald Eagle

Florida's effort to restore its own bald eagle population has worked so well that the state's eagles have been used to help the eagles start a comeback in many Southeastern states and Oklahoma. In fact, all the bald eagles nesting in Oklahoma today are from Florida.

The restoration process was simple: Steal eggs from Florida bald eagle nests and transfer them to eagles in other states to raise. An estimated 80 percent of the time the Florida eagles "double clutched," or laid a second clutch of eggs to replace the stolen ones. Eggs from Alaska's more abundant bald eagle population weren't considered for two reasons: That species is larger, and the population's eagles might not be able to tolerate warmer temperatures.

Until recently, bald eagles were extinct in most of the Southeast except for Florida. The birds disappeared for several reasons. The millions of acres of pine forest that once covered the Southeastern states were either cleared, parceled up or transformed completely through fire-control efforts. In addition, bald eagles were trapped, hunted and poisoned by many ranchers and farmers who considered the birds a threat to their livelihoods.

Perhaps the greatest death toll resulted from the popularity of pesticides like DDT following World War II. For almost three decades, until DDT was banned in 1972, it poisoned bald eagles and many other bird species, such as the brown pelican. A persistent chemical, DDT does not break down easily but is stored in the fatty tissues of the creature ingesting it (including humans). Further, the effects of DDT compound over time. The chemical is subject to the nasty phenomenon known as biological magnification, where the concentration actually increases significantly on each level of the food chain. Thus, even after DDT was banned in 1972, the poison stayed in the tissues of adult eagles for the rest of their lives.

DDT severely interfered with the reproductive process by destroying hormones such as estrogen. That in turn caused eagles and other birds to lay eggs with abnormally thin shells that often broke. Even if a shell didn't break, frequently the egg didn't hatch because the thin shells couldn't supply enough calcium for the bones of the growing embryo. The impact was horrendous. By 1963, the entire bald eagle population of the lower 48 states consisted of only 417 nesting pairs.

Florida's bald eagle count declined dramatically during this same period, but the Sunshine State was fortunate because not as much DDT had been sprayed, and the coastlines continued to provide the kind of rich habitat that bald eagles have always needed.

In the 1990s, Florida alone can count 667 nesting pairs, a truly secure bald eagle population—but Florida is unique. The only other southeastern state to attain triple digits is Louisiana, with just 103 nesting pairs. In all of Texas, only 37 nesting pairs can be found, with 20 in Arkansas, 8 in Mississippi, 10 in Alabama, 17 in Georgia, 22 in Tennessee, 88 in South Carolina, 8 in North Carolina and 10 in Kentucky.

Outside Florida and Louisiana the bald eagle still has a tenuous hold on existence. Yet that may not stop it being upgraded from endangered to threatened on the Endangered Species List. Although the protection afforded would not change, the obvious message would be that the bald eagle is no longer in any imminent danger of extinction. That could foster the dangerous impression that the bald eagle isn't a species of concern any longer, a conclusion that is clearly erroneous. The numbers simply aren't there yet.

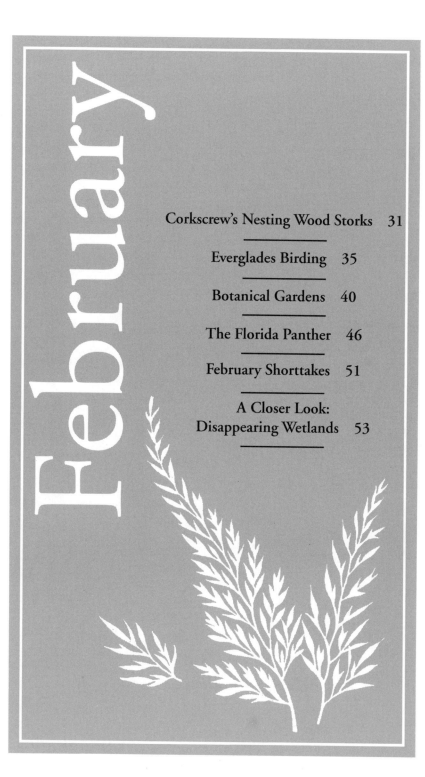

February

Notes

7

Corkscrew's Nesting Wood Storks

One of Florida's finest birding areas is the 11,000-acre Corkscrew Swamp Sanctuary in Southwest Florida just north of Naples. February is one of the best times of year to visit, when the world's largest population of wood storks nests here.

In addition to the wood stork colony, the sanctuary also contains the nation's largest remaining subtropical old-growth bald cypress forest. Bald cypress here tower 130 feet high and are as many as 700 years old. These are the oldest trees in all of eastern North America.

Corkscrew Swamp Sanctuary is owned and operated by the National Audubon Society. Access to the swamp is provided by a 2-mile-long boardwalk that goes into the heart of the sanctuary. During the winter dry season wading birds and other animals concentrate in the pools near the boardwalk. Among them is the endangered wood stork, which nests here in greater numbers than anywhere else.

Wood storks are impressive birds. They have white bodies and a 7-foot wingspan. The tail, wing tips, trailing edges and legs are black, but the feet are pink. The wood stork's distinctive head, which lacks feathers, is dark and capped with a light horny plate. The wood stork goes by many names, including wood ibis, Spanish buzzard, gannet, preacher, ironhead and flinthead.

In the 1930s wood storks numbered an estimated 75,000 birds. Unfortunately, like most of today's other endangered species, the population declined dramatically due to habitat loss. Wood storks need wetlands that undergo seasonal flooding followed by drying. Unfortunately, the continued practice of draining and eliminating wetlands has imperiled the birds. Wood storks require shallow water for finding fish. They feed with their bills slightly open in the water until they make contact with a fish.

Today, only an estimated 4,000 to 5,000 nesting wood stork pairs remain, and the vast majority of wood stork nesting occurs in Florida. The nests are big and bulky and built at the tops of high trees. The birds are not bashful about being around other wood storks and often nest by the hundreds or thousands in the same vicinity. An average clutch is two to four white eggs.

The National Audubon Society began protecting both wood storks and great egrets from plumage hunters in this area as far back as 1912, well before this became an established sanctuary. It wasn't until 1954 that the society began assembling land to create the preserve.

The area here was roadless until the 1950s. Canoes, horses or swamp buggies were all that could travel this extremely wet terrain. Any high-elevation areas with pines and cabbage palms were usually turned into camps. Today the sanctuary boardwalk meanders close to the Bird Rookery Camp, which was first used by plumage hunters, then by Audubon wardens.

Although this was a very isolated region until the 1960s, development now encircles it. Yet the Corkscrew Swamp still feels, as someone once said, "a million years from Miami." Or any other urban area.

The sanctuary boardwalk goes over a tremendous variety of terrain. Initially it passes through sections of wet prairie, areas that are not wet enough for cypress or dry enough for pines. In this region, grasses and sedges are the dominant vegetation until spring and summer, when the prairie turns into a brilliant showcase of wildflowers.

Despite all the standing water, mosquitoes are not nearly as bothersome here as one would expect. That's due to the numerous mosquito fish that feed on great quantities of mosquito larvae.

In February, the huge forest of bald cypress appears remarkably bare. Bald cypress are so named because of their winter leaf-shedding, which renders them very dead-looking. The tree's skin is a dingy gray and covers a highly prized dark-colored wood. Making homes, furniture and paneling from cypress trees accounts for why there are so few virgin stands of cypress remaining. How scarce the wood has become is well illustrated by the sanctuary boardwalk. The first sections were made of cypress, but the wood became so scarce that the walkway had to be finished with a rotproof pine called lighterwood.

At Corkscrew Swamp there are many more animals to see than just wood storks: There are another 200 bird species, including the largest of Florida's common woodpeckers, the pileated, with its red crest and black-and-white feather pattern. Cardinals, too, are common, and look for white ibis, green herons, anhinga, great blue herons and limpkins. Other winter visitors include catbirds, phoebes and ruby-crowned kinglets.

The wood stork's distinctive featherless head has prompted many other names, including flinthead and ironhead.

To locate the Corkscrew Swamp Sanctuary, take Exit 17 from I-75 and go east on State Road 846 for about 16 miles. A sign leading to the swamp will be on the left. The facility opens at 7 A.M. December through April, and at 8 A.M. May through November. The boardwalk closes at 5 P.M. year-round. For more information, contact Corkscrew Swamp Sanctuary, National Audubon Society, Route 6, Box 1875-A, Naples, FL 33964; (813) 657-3771.

Hot Spots Although the majority of wood storks nest in the **Corkscrew Swamp Sanctuary,** there are several other good sites as well. Wood storks are also common along the **Tamiami Trail** (U.S. 41), which extends between Miami and Naples. In late afternoon, wood storks, along with other birds, feed on the catfish in the canals. In the **La Belle area,** wood storks inhabit may of the same areas as do the sandhill cranes. They can often be seen in the fields on County Road 832 off State Road 29. Continue south on State Road 29 and look for wood storks around the bridges.

In Central Florida, wood storks nest in several areas, including the cypress trees around the **Cypress Gardens** attraction near Lake Wales. In the field on the other side of the St. Johns River at **Mullet Lake Park** wood storks frequently feed in winter. To find the small park, which has limited camping and a boat ramp, take State Road 46 east from Sanford and turn left at Mullet Lake Park Road, located on the left after the Marina Isle Fish Camp.

Orlando Wetlands Park, which is closed for hunting from October 1 through January 20, also hosts wood storks during winter. Take State Road 50 from Orlando to the town of Christmas. Go north on County Road 420 (Fort Christmas Road) for 2.3 miles and turn right onto unpaved Wheeler Road. The parking lot is on the left, another 1.5 miles east.

It's possible that you might see nesting wood storks in Georgia's **Okefenokee Swamp NWR,** but Florida's Corkscrew Swamp is a certainty.

8

Everglades Birding

Traditionally, the best place to view wading birds in all of North America has been the Everglades, the largest remaining subtropical wilderness in the continental United States.

The terrain of the Everglades, mostly a shallow plain of saw grass that grows in water only about 6 inches deep, is ideal wading-bird habitat. This blanket of water, which has been likened to a tropical primordial soup of algae and bacteria, nourishes snakes, turtles, fish and insects, which in turn feed the incredibly rich population of birds.

Unfortunately, the bird population has suffered severely in recent years, but it is still worth visiting the Everglades to take part in Florida's classic version of the African big game safari. The Everglades is still the best there is, simply because there is nowhere else like it. The counts may be lower, but you might see as many as 300 bird species here.

To maintain the shallow water level so essential to birds and other wildlife, the Glades has always relied on the summer overflow from Lake Okeechobee, located 60 miles north of the park. Lake Okeechobee, the second largest freshwater lake in the continental United States, could always be relied upon to send down a sheet of water 50 miles wide that thoroughly watered and flushed the saw grass all the way to the Gulf of Mexico. This annual flood was followed by a six-month dry season. Birds and animals adapted and patterned their lives based on this seemingly eternal, alternating cycle.

But beginning in the twentieth century, attempts were made to regulate the water flow so that farmers and cattlemen could take advantage of the rich soil. A hurricane in 1938 caused considerable destruction and killed 1,800 people, which prompted the federal government to dam and dike Lake Okeechobee so it wouldn't happen again. Another disaster occurred as a result, but this time it was the Everglades wildlife that was devastated. Lake Okeechobee's floodwaters are essential for maintaining proper water level because almost four-fifths of the area's annual rainfall is lost to evaporation and runoff. When Lake Okeechobee's annual overflow was disrupted, so was life in the Everglades.

The loss of bird life is sickening. Since the 1930s, waterbird numbers have declined 93 percent. Today, about 18,500 waterbirds inhabit the park, compared to the estimated 265,000 that lived here in the 1930s.

One virtually decimated species is the snail kite, whose entire North American population by the 1960s declined to only about two dozen birds. Snail kites feed predominantly on apple snails, which lay their eggs above the high-water line. If there is too much water, the snail eggs die. Wood storks, considered one of the key barometers of the Everglades's health, are still in considerable trouble. Since the 1960s, they have dwindled from 6,000 individuals to just 500.

If that isn't bad enough, the water quality has become downright toxic in various places due to high levels of mercury. Add the mercury to tremendous runoff of farm nutrients from the sugar and farming industries (one dairy cow produces as much raw waste as 20 people) and the future looks bleak. The excess nutrients kill beneficial algae and promote the growth of harmful marsh vegetation. Even so, the fields of saw grass are still hanging in there.

Hot Spots Over a million people a year visit **Everglades National Park,** the second largest national park in the contiguous United States (after Yellowstone). The main park entrance is about an hour south of Miami near Homestead. Take the Florida Turnpike (toll road) from Miami to Homestead. The Everglades is about another 20 minutes away. The park's richness is mind-boggling: 2,000 species of plants, 51 types of reptiles, 17 assorted amphibians, 40 different mammals and an assortment of 347 avians. In the winter dry season the bird life concentrates mostly around the permanent bodies of water, which makes it quite easy to observe. This is by far the best time of year for birding. Mosquitoes are at their least bothersome then, too.

Royal Palm Hammock is on the left, just 2 miles from the entrance. The half-mile-long **Anhinga Trail** is located here. The park's single most popular trail is named for one of Florida's most distinctive birds. The anhinga is also called the water turkey and snake bird because it swims almost totally submerged, with only its snaky-looking long neck and head above water. It captures food by diving underwater and spearing fish with its beak. The anhinga is frequently spotted perched on a branch with its wings spread as if in a state of alarm. The bird is actually drying its feathers. The anhinga lacks the oil glands needed to keep its plumage dry, and if it didn't drip-dry regularly, it would become so waterlogged it would sink.

Follow the paved trail to a boardwalk that penetrates a sawgrass prairie. Along the way look for sora, smooth-billed ani, least bittern and great white heron. The **Gumbo Limbo Trail,** named for the tree with the distinctive red bark, is also located here. The foliage is higher and thicker, which makes birding more difficult. Try scanning the hammock at the end and beginning of the trail, where the growth is more open. Look for a variety of warblers as well as the short-tailed hawk.

At the **Long Pine Key Campground and Picnic Area,** the slash pine are particular favorites of warblers, including the pine and yellow-rumped. This is a good place for owling: barn, barred and screech. The whippoorwill is frequently heard here. Similar birds are along the **Pinelands Trail.**

Try calling barred owls at **Mahogany Hammock,** even during the day. The results may be pleasantly surprising. Bald eagles are frequently seen in the area. And look for white-crowned pigeons feeding on the ground.

By February the birds should be concentrating around places like **Paurotis Pond** (named for the paurotis palms in the area) and **Nine-Mile Pond.** Both are good sites for short-tailed hawks, ospreys, herons, bald eagles and what many consider to be the emblematic bird of the Everglades—the roseate spoonbill. Unfortunately, like many other wading birds, roseate spoonbills are not as common anymore. (If you miss spotting one here, look again at **Mrazek Pond** near Flamingo.)

Around the ponds, both migratory and the smaller resident cormorants, Caspian terns, mottled ducks and swallow-tailed kites may also be present during the day; look for limpkins and white-crowned pigeons early and late.

Waterfowl have always been particularly fond of **West Lake:** American widgeon, ruddy duck, pintail, shoveler, scaup (lesser and ring-necked) and teal (green- and blue-winged). The white-crowned pigeon is often sighted over the lake late in the day. Take the boardwalk along **Mangrove Trail** for an incredible concentration of American coots. (This lake is also a rare opportunity to sight the almost extinct American crocodile.)

To this point it hasn't been necessary to walk very far, but the outstanding opportunities make it worth the 2-mile walk on **Snake Bight Trail.** But go well protected against mosquitoes, which are only slightly less numerous than the leaves on the red and black mangroves here. Although the bugs may repel *you,* they are easy fast food for the many small land birds. The mangroves here also serve as important bird rookeries. Isolated from most land predators, mangrove islands provide secure nesting. At the end of the trail, the boardwalks over the mudflats have produced significant spottings, especially rare sightings of the greater flamingo and even the Key West quail dove. But don't build up any hopes about the flamingos. They are still as rare as hen's teeth.

When water levels are low, **Mrazek Pond** is one of the best places in the park for bird photography; the place is crowded with many different species. Because of this site's easy access, flocks of birders can make it difficult to see the birds.

Stretch your legs again at the 2-mile-long **Bear Lake Trail.** It passes through tropical woodland where you may find white-crowned pigeons and numerous land birds. Unfortunately, the flamingos are long gone from the small fishing town of **Flamingo,** the gateway to Florida Bay and its mudflats. But keep an eye out for shorebirds, sandpipers, ospreys, egrets, pelicans and bald eagles in this area.

In the late 1880s Flamingo was an important trading center for the plumage of the snowy egret, which once thrived here in huge numbers. Not only egrets but roseate spoonbills were killed to supply plumage for women's clothing. Adult birds were attacked on the nest, when their plumage is at its finest, and they are easiest to kill. The young were left to die. The National Audubon Society is responsible for ending this horrendous slaughter.

Eco Pond Trail at Flamingo is just a short 0.5-mile loop, but it can be loaded with birds and other animals, including wading birds, songbirds and alligators. The best bird-watching is early and late from the ramped viewing platform.

Shark Valley is located in the northernmost sector of **Everglades National Park.** The entrance is nowhere near Homestead but is located 30 miles west of Miami on U.S. 41; a 15-mile-long hard-surfaced trail bores directly into the Shark Valley wilderness. It's a great place, but be prepared to share it with lots of other people. It's wise to arrive the first thing in the morning when the Shark Valley gates open, at 8 A.M. Beginning on the hour at 9 A.M. and continuing almost until closing, the park operates a two-hour tram ride along the road to view birds, gators, deer, turtles and other animals. At the end of the road is a 50-foot-high observation tower that provides a wonderfully panoramic look deep into the Glades. The tram returns by a different road that parallels the first, so the scenery is totally different. Rental bikes also are available so that people can explore individually. The best tram trips for birding are usually the first and last ones of the day. Reservations are highly recommended for the tram ride from December through March; (305) 221-8455. The tram is handicap-accessible.

9

Botanical Gardens

Florida's climate ranges from a transition zone between temperate and subtropical conditions in the northern section to a true tropical climate in the Keys. And although Charles Darwin was referring to South America when he penned these words on the voyage of the *Beagle,* they seem equally appropriate for characterizing the subtropical and tropical regions of Florida: "Epithet after epithet was found too weak to convey to those who have not visited the intertropical regions, the sensation of delight which the mind experiences ... . The land is one great wild, untidy hothouse, made by nature for herself."

Florida typically receives a large amount of rain: 50 to 65 inches annually, which works out to 148 billion gallons per day. As a result of these warm, wet conditions, the Florida landscape is a lot more jungly than anywhere else in the country. In fact, many of the plants and trees here are more closely associated with the Caribbean than with North America. Ironically, the state is on the same latitude as some of the world's largest deserts (including the Sahara and Arabian). However, no part of the Florida peninsula is more than 60 miles from the ocean, which accounts for the frequent high humidity.

Although some temperate palm trees, like the cabbage palm, may now range as far as North Carolina, the original home of many Florida trees and plants is outside this hemisphere. The common date palm, for example, is native to Egypt and the African continent, while the origins of the Canary Island and India date palms are obvious. Florida's grandest palm of them all, the royal palm, is a transplant from Cuba.

Citrus fruit, Florida's most famous crop, is also foreign to this hemisphere. Oranges and grapefruit, once native to the Orient, were transplanted to India, the Mediterranean and finally to this side of the Atlantic. Columbus himself is credited with planting the first citrus plant seeds in the Western Hemisphere on the island of Haiti. By 1579, citrus was recorded growing in great abundance around the Spanish city of St. Augustine.

Growers using hothouses and other devices have turned ornamental plants into a big business for Central and South Florida. The small city of Apopka, located just outside Orlando, calls itself the Indoor Foliage Capital of the World, claiming to produce more than 60 percent of the world's indoor ornamental foliage.

In the wild, the tremendous diversity of plants that grow the length of the peninsula is one of the most appealing—and perplexing—aspects of the Florida landscape. Easily the best place to see such profusion and clear up the confusion is at one of the many public gardens scattered the length of the state.

Sunken Gardens in St. Petersburg is among the many gardens that will be dazzling in color this month.

Hot Spots Gardens have always interested Florida visitors. The state's very first tourist attraction was a garden display: Cypress Gardens, which opened in 1936 near Winter Haven. The following gardens are listed alphabetically rather than geographically.

Audubon House and Gardens. Wildlife artist John James Audubon never owned this Key West house but supposedly stayed here in 1832 during a bird painting visit. The house, displaying antique furniture and original engravings by Audubon, has a small, lush tropical garden featuring exotic native plants. An admission fee is charged. Open daily 9 A.M. to 5 P.M. on the corner of White-head and Greene Streets, Key West; (305) 294-2116.

Bok Tower Gardens. One hundred fifty-three acres of beautifully landscaped gardens that feature thousands of exotic and native plants. A marble and coquina stone carillon performs recitals at 3 P.M. Guided nature tours are offered at noon and 2 P.M. from January 15 to April 15. Picnic facilities are available. An admission fee is charged. Open daily 8 A.M. to 5 P.M. Near Lake Wales on County Road 17A, 1 mile east of the junction with U.S. 27; (813) 676-1408.

Cypress Gardens. More than 8,000 varieties of plants gathered from 75 different countries, sharing 208 acres with electric-boat rides, a glass-enclosed butterfly conservatory and water-ski shows. Several minigardens have special themes, such as the Oriental Gardens and All-American Rose Garden. The Plantation Gardens contain both herb and scent plants as well as plants that attract butterflies. Special flower festivals, such as the Spring Flower Festival from mid-March to mid-May, are held throughout the year. An admission fee is charged. Five miles southeast of Winter Haven on State Road 540; (800) 282-2123 in Florida, (800) 237-4826 elsewhere.

Eden State Gardens and Mansion. The Old South is recalled with magnolia trees, live oaks festooned with Spanish moss and azaleas and camellias that envelop an 1898 mansion built in the Greek Revival style. Guided 45-minute tours of the house, filled with Victorian, Empire and Colonial antiques, are available hourly from 9 A.M. to 4 P.M. Thursday to Monday. The gardens are open from 8 A.M. to dusk. An admission fee is charged. At Point Washington, near Panama City in Eden State Park, 1 mile north of U.S. 98 on County Road 396; (904) 231-4214.

Fairchild Tropical Gardens. A striking spot not far from downtown Miami. Eleven lakes dot the 83 acres that grow palms, cycads, orchids, vines, flowering trees and exotic plants from around the world. The admission fee includes a tram tour. Open 9:30 A.M. to 4:30 P.M. daily except Christmas. On Old Cutler Road, 10 miles southeast of Miami; (305) 667-1651.

Flamingo Gardens. Loaded with plants and trees native to subtropical areas, plus several bird exhibits. A tram tours the park's wetlands. Also features a greenhouse growing tropical plants and a 200-year-old live oak hammock. An admission fee is charged. At 3750 Flamingo Road, Davie, near Fort Lauderdale. Take the exit off the Florida Turnpike. Open daily 9 A.M. to 5 P.M.; (305) 473-0010.

Florida Cactus. This is a working nursery growing 500 different cactus species, but visitors are welcome. Free admission. Located on Peterson Road in the town of Plymouth, off U.S. 441 west of Apopka. Open weekdays 7 A.M. to 5 P.M., and on Saturdays from 7 A.M. to noon; (407) 886-1833.

Florida's Sunken Gardens. A small, 5-acre garden with thousands of tropical trees and plants along with rare birds and animals. Several bird and animal shows are offered throughout the day. An admission fee is charged. At 1825 4th Street North, St. Petersburg. Open daily 9 A.M. to 5 P.M.; (813) 896-3187.

Four Arts Gardens. Small but varied, with a jungle garden, a Chinese garden, a tropical fruit garden and a moonlight garden. Free admission. In the Four Arts Plaza, Palm Beach. Open daily 10 A.M. to 5 P.M.; (407) 655-7226.

Fruit and Spice Park. Twenty acres containing more than 500 varieties of spice, fruit and nut trees from around the world. Also a banana grove and an herb and vegetable garden. There is a small admission fee. Located 4.75 miles north of Homestead on State Road 997, then 1 mile west at the sign. Open 10 A.M. to 5 P.M. daily except Christmas, January 1 and Thanksgiving; (305) 247-5727.

Jungle Larry's Zoological Park at Caribbean Gardens. As the name implies, this is both a zoo and a garden. Tram rides travel through 52 acres of tropical species that include banyan trees, palms and bamboo. An admission fee is charged. At 1590 Goodlette Road, Naples. Open daily 9:30 A.M. to 5:30 P.M.; (813) 282-5409.

Kanapaha Botanical Gardens. Sixty-two acres and a 1-mile walkway with plants that attract hummingbirds and butterflies, along with wildflowers and carnivorous plant species, also a fern grotto and lily pond. There is a small admission fee. At

4625 Southwest 63rd Street, Gainesville. Open 9 A.M. to 5 P.M. Monday, Tuesday and Friday; from 9 A.M. to dusk on Wednesday, Saturday and Sunday; (904) 372-4981.

Leu Botanical Gardens. A 57-acre park with a formal rose garden, a tropical plant conservatory and floral clock that features a variety of different plants over the seasons. Also a major camellia collection and desert garden. The Leu house is restored to its original late-1800s style. An admission fee is charged. At 1730 Forest Avenue, Orlando; go 0.75 mile north of the junction of U.S. 50 and U.S. 17/92, then 0.5 mile east on Virginia Drive. Open daily 9 A.M. to 5 P.M. except Christmas; (407) 246-2620.

Maclay State Gardens. These gardens (an impressive 307 acres) were begun in 1923 by a businessman and his wife and later acquired by the state. Camellias, azaleas, magnolias, dogwoods and many native plants are featured. A small admission fee is charged. Located off U.S. 319, just north of Tallahassee. Open daily 8 A.M. to sunset; (904) 487-4556.

Morikami Museum and Japanese Gardens. This 140-acre park highlights a charming re-creation of a Japanese garden and house by using rocks, plants and water in a distinctive design. Such may seem out of place in South Florida, but the museum commemorates a Japanese farming colony established nearby in the beginning of the 1900s. Various festivals are held throughout the year. An admission fee is charged. At 4000 Morikami Road, Delray Beach; take I-95 Exit 42 and go west on Lincoln Boulevard for 3.5 miles, then 1 mile south on Carter Road. Open Tuesday through Sunday 10 A.M. to 5 P.M. Closed Christmas, January 1, Easter, Memorial Day, July 4 and Thanksgiving; (407) 495-0233.

Ravine State Gardens. A long-established 85-acre garden begun in 1933. Erosion by the St. Johns River created the ravines, which contain native wild plants. Camellias and azaleas complete the landscaping in other areas. With many winding trails plus picnic facilities. A small admission fee is charged. On Twigg Street off State Road 20 near the town of Palatka (site of a major azalea festival in March). Open 8 A.M. to dusk daily; (904) 329-3721.

Sarasota Jungle Gardens. Bird and reptile shows, plus many exotic and native animal species in 10 acres of tropical gardens that include several walking trails. An admission fee is charged. Two blocks off U.S. 41 at Myrtle, north of Sarasota. Open daily 9 A.M. to 5 P.M.; (813) 355-5305.

Selby Botanical Gardens. The setting on these 14 acres couldn't be finer for this major collection of orchids, other exotic plants, a botany museum and bookstore. Some plants are available for sale. An admission fee is charged. On South Palm Avenue at U.S. 41 in Sarasota. Open daily 10 A.M. to 5 P.M. except Christmas; (813) 366-5730.

Vizcaya. Best known as a lavish estate with 34 elaborately decorated rooms, the 10-acre gardens are equally spectacular. Various gardens, including formal Italian gardens with the requisite marble figures, are formed by hedges and walls. One of the most famous is the Garden for the Blind, where visitors can smell the plants and feel the statuary. The word *Vizcaya* is Basque for "elevated place." There is an admission fee. At 3251 South Miami Avenue, Miami, just south of the Rickenbacker Causeway. Open daily 9:30 A.M. to 4:30 P.M.; (305) 250-9133.

Walt Disney World. This is one of the most elaborately landscaped places in the world. Of special note are the topiary animals and cartoon characters, some of which are located near the hotels. Park there to avoid the admission fee.

World of Orchids. Thousands of orchids in an enclosed rainforest setting, so the occasional Central Florida frost is never a problem. The flowering plants are changed periodically. Also featured are both an indoor and outdoor garden with palms, ferns, bamboo and more. Guided tours available. An admission fee is charged. Near Kissimmee west of I-4; take U.S. 192 west, then turn onto County Road 545. Open daily 10 A.M. to 6 P.M. except Christmas, January 1, July 4 and Thanksgiving; (407) 396-1881.

10

The Florida Panther

The Florida panther is one of the earth's most endangered animals. Only an estimated 30 to 50 individuals remain in the wild. The Florida panther is also one of the Sunshine State's two official state mammals, along with the manatee.

The Florida panther is a subspecies of what is called a mountain lion, cougar or puma in other parts of the country. Although cougar attacks have occurred in western states, there has never been a recorded attack in Florida.

The Florida cat is actually misnamed. Typically, the name *panther* is assigned only to black felines, yet Florida's cat, like other cougars, is tan-colored. Why the discrepancy? One theory suggests that early settlers who sighted it at night thought it was black. Or the name could be derived from the Greek name for leopard, for the cat's young are spotted and the adults lack a mane. Correct or not, "panther" is the accepted name for Florida's feline.

Ironically, only 200 years ago cougars were among of the most broadly distributed animals in the Western Hemisphere. They ranged from the tip of South America to Canada and were found in every region of the United States. Today the Florida panther is the only cougar that survives east of the Mississippi. The rest were hunted to extinction.

The Florida panther is naturally camouflaged. Tawny-colored along the back and lighter on the lower chest, belly and inner legs, its pelt closely mimics that of the white-tailed deer, its primary prey.

The Florida panther has several distinctive characteristics not found on western cougars: a cowlick in the middle of the back and a crook at the end of the tail, features that may be the result of inbreeding in the small population. The Florida panther also is lighter in weight and darker in color, with smaller feet and longer legs than other cougar subspecies.

Males and females look alike, but males tend to be bigger and to have a larger head. Males weigh between 100 and 150 pounds and measure up to 7 feet from the tip of the tail to the nose. Females range from 65 to 100 pounds and measure about 6 feet.

People in every section of Florida claim to have seen wild panthers, but most of the remaining animals are believed to inhabit the remote regions of the Big Cypress–Everglades region of South Florida. However, verified sightings have also come from Central Florida, in Seminole and Indian River Counties.

Several factors account for the tiny surviving panther population. In Florida as well as the rest of the country the panther was

The Florida panther is one of the world's most endangered animals. Only between 30 and 50 remain in the wild. Most live in the remote Everglades.

aggressively hunted for decades because of the belief that cougars attacked livestock. Although it's generally not recognized, Florida has always been one of the nation's top cattle producers. To encourage elimination of the panther, a $5 bounty was placed on the animals in the late 1800s.

Cattle again affected the panther in the 1930s and 1940s, when white-tailed deer were slaughtered by the thousands in an attempt to eliminate the tick that causes Texas cattle fever. Most recently, the large-scale clearing of wilderness areas for human development has further reduced the number of cats.

Panthers mark their territories with *scrapes* that consists of a small pile of soil, pine needles and leaves about 6 inches long. Feces, urine or a discharge from the anal glands may also be deposited on the scrape. Females generally avoid leaving any scent. They will often cover their feces, especially if they have young, because males have been known to kill and eat kittens as large as 50 pounds.

A large carnivore like the panther requires extensive hunting space. Studies have shown that adult males stake out a territory and may range over 400 to 500 square miles within a single month.

A panther's diet includes rabbits, raccoons, wild hogs, birds, armadillos and, when food is scarce, even grasshoppers. Annually, adult panthers require between 35 to 50 animals with the food value of a deer (ten raccoons, for instance, are said to equal the food value of a single deer).

Able to sprint up to 35 mph over short distances, a panther usually ambushes its prey. It brings down a deer with a bite that severs the spinal cord at the spot where the neck and head join. A panther may take several days to consume its kill. Between feedings, the cat covers the carcass with leaves and dirt.

Breeding occurs at any time of year but is most common between November and March. Once the female is no longer in heat (estrus lasts from 8 to 11 days), the male leaves the area. Gestation lasts about three months, and the typical litter numbers one or two kittens. A newborn weighs only about a pound. Its eyes do not open for one or two weeks. Teeth begin appearing at about two weeks. Although a young cat can eat meat after six weeks, the mother continues nursing it for about two months. She needs about two years to train a kitten fully in hunting skills.

Chaotic panther family life makes it difficult for any kitten to survive. Males do not assist in supplying food for the young and, as mentioned, have been known to kill and eat young cats. Consequently, the mother must leave her kittens unprotected when she hunts, and she could be gone for two days or more. Male kittens will also be at risk any time adult male panthers visit the mother for breeding.

When the female is ready to mate again, she leaves her offspring abruptly: She makes a kill and departs while her young are still feeding. From that point, the youngsters are totally dependent on their own skills for survival.

Although panthers are quite stealthy when hunting, they are notorious for making a surprising variety of noises. They have been known to chirp, whistle, moan, peep and growl; kittens, in fact, chirp to communicate with their mother. Some people claim that a panther sometimes makes a cry that will stand a person's hair on end.

Because the Florida population is so low, Florida panthers in captivity may be bred with cougars from other parts of the country and the offspring released into the wild. Although most of the panther population is currently in Central and South Florida, the new releases may be made in North Florida, such as in the Apalachicola National Forest and areas near Georgia's Okefenokee NWR and Florida's Osceola National Forest, which together form a huge wildlife corridor.

Unfortunately, not even the remote Everglades is a safe haven for the big cats. A dead panther was found there with levels of mercury in its remains so high they would have been fatal for a human. Precisely how mercury is entering the South Florida environment is still not known.

Hot Spots

Although the Florida panther once ranged from Texas and the lower Mississippi River Valley as far north as Tennessee and South Carolina, the only place you're apt to see a panther in the wild today is South Florida. The 27,000-acre **Florida Panther NWR** near Naples is closed to the public. Open for visitors are several adjacent areas where panthers are known to roam. They include the **Fakahatchee Strand**, the **Bear Island Unit** of **Big Cypress National Preserve**, the

Raccoon Point area of the Big Cypress National Preserve; and the eastern region of **Everglades National Park.**

The optimal times to see a panther are early or late in the day, the same times when deer tend to feed most actively. Don't look for panthers only in the woods. They are good swimmers, and one cat was sighted swimming a river that is about a mile wide.

With only 30 to 50 animals remaining in the wilderness, your chances of spotting a Florida panther are, quite frankly, dismal. You would do better to track down captive animals, something not suggested for any other species in this book. Some commercial operations keep their panthers confined in small zoolike cages (always a depressing sight), but, fortunately, there are a couple of displays where the cats have plenty of room to roam in natural habitat. One of the best places is in the Everglades, at **Kissimmee Billie's Swamp Safari,** operated by the Seminole tribe on the Big Cypress Reservation southwest of Clewiston and an hour's drive west of Fort Lauderdale; call (800) 949-6101. In the Panhandle, 6.5 miles south of Tallahassee at Lake Bradford, is the 52-acre **Museum of History and Natural Science.** It too keeps its panthers in a large, natural, open area. Otters, bobcats and white-tailed deer are also present at the museum. For its current hours, call (904) 576-1636.

11

February Shorttakes

Tracking Black Bears

Although they are rarely seen, black bears live in many parts of North and Central Florida. In fact, they are not very far outside the huge Orlando metropolitan area. Take I-95 east from Orlando to the State Road 46 Exit near Sanford and turn left onto State Road 46. The last 6 miles before the city of Plymouth are loaded with bear-crossing warnings. Bears have frequently been killed here at night. The best places locally to see bear signs are in the **Lower Wekiva Preserve,** off State Road 46, and **Wekiwa Springs State Park** near Apopka.

In the **Osceola National Forest,** the **Big Gum Swamp Wilderness** in the north-central part of the forest almost guarantees black bear tracks. Simply follow any of the fire lines that go off through the woods into the swamp or any of the old tram roads left by past logging. Walk on any one of these, and you should be able to find bear tracks in the mud, small bay trees that have been clawed down or palmettos that have been ripped up. This is a tremendous amount of sign, though the chances of seeing the actual animal itself is remote. Call (904) 752-2577 for more information.

Go Take a Long Walk!

Florida is not usually thought of as a good place to hike, probably because for about half the year it's too hot and too humid to hike comfortably. Yet Florida has more than 3,000 miles of designated hiking trails, an expanding rails-to-trails program, plus the **Florida Trail,** the 1,000-mile-long hiking corridor that runs from the western tip of the state to the Everglades. These walks in the wilderness are truly the best way to see the natural, unspoiled Florida and the plants and animals that populate it. Although the Everglades this time of year is like a crowded theme park, the trails are like a forest church, quiet and undisturbed. There are many Florida Trail links that are interrupted by private land holdings, yet the single longest stretch is over 450 miles, from the western edge of the Apalachicola National Forest to the southern tip of the Ocala National Forest. Membership in the Florida Trail Association makes it possible to hike even the privately held corridors. For information, contact the Florida Trail Association in Gainesville at (904) 378-8823. Many state and local parks also have excellent hikes that are not part of the Florida Trail. These walks, along with the Florida Trail, are detailed in *The Hiker's Guide to Florida.*

Osceola National Forest

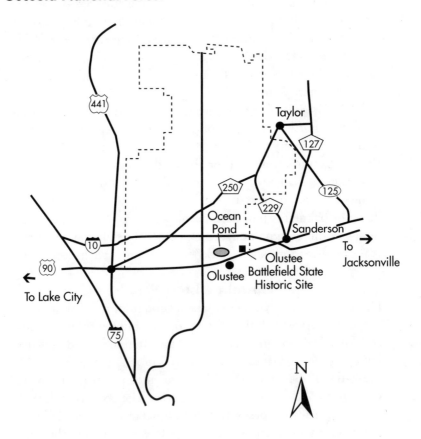

12

A Closer Look:
Disappearing Wetlands

Fresh and saltwater marshes provide some of the earth's richest habitat. Unfortunately, wetlands have been under serious assault in this country since 1763, when George Washington decided to drain Virginia's Great Dismal Swamp in order to increase available farmland.

Until recently, the notion has persisted that marshes and wetlands could be put to "better" use by draining them to grow crops, build shopping centers or create more pastureland. The idea that wet, marshy places might have some value all by themselves was never considered, no doubt because of the dense mosquito populations usually found in these locations. Today, more than 50 percent of the nation's wetlands have been drained, channelized, filled or dammed. It's estimated that about 1,000 acres of wetland are lost in the United States every day.

Wetlands are defined as areas inundated by surface water or groundwater often enough to support vegetation typically found in saturated soil. That includes marshes, bogs and swamps. Unfortunately, wetlands are sometimes very easy to convert into highly desirable property. When situated on the coast or adjoining a scenic lake or river, each wetlands parcel is a potential "waterfront" tract once it's been drained dry and built up high.

In the twentieth century, Florida's 20 million acres of wetlands existing at the beginning of the century have been reduced to just 8 million acres. The realization that wetlands are important for all the state's residents—human as well as wildlife—happened almost too late. Now, even the most ardent developers would agree (if only in private) that wetlands provide many vital benefits to the state's overall welfare. Consider the following: Saltwater wetlands and marshes serve as buffers that absorb potentially damaging wave energy generated by storms, particularly hurricanes. They provide shelter, breeding and nursery grounds for just about every type of animal: birds, shellfish and fish, reptiles, amphibians, mammals and invertebrates.

Coastal wetlands and nearby waters are the habitat of some of the nation's most endangered wildlife: manatees, whooping cranes, wood storks, brown pelicans and even the American crocodile. Both improve water quality by filtering nutrients, waste and pollutants before they reach other nearby surface water. They supply habitat for many unique plants.

Freshwater wetlands are crucial for collecting water and recharging underground water supplies, in particular the Floridan aquifer. And marshes and wetlands in their natural state provide indispensable recreational opportunities to bird-watchers, photographers, hunters and anglers. Wetlands and marshes may also act as climate stabilizers.

The importance of wetlands in secondary sewage treatment cannot be overemphasized in Florida because, in some ways, the sandy peninsula is nothing but one big septic tank. The state's limestone base is like a sponge that absorbs oil, gasoline, soft drinks, sewage—whatever is poured on it. Wetlands function like a kidney to filter out these pollutants before they reach the underground aquifer, one of the most important sources of Florida's drinking water.

The economic value of the coastal wetlands along the entire Gulf Coast from Florida to Texas is staggering: Traditionally, as much as a third of the entire U.S. marine sport-fishing catch has come from this area. Wetland-dependent species include the most popular sport species: sea trout, redfish and flounder.

Today, wetlands enjoy far greater protection than they ever have, but the tremendous losses suffered previously will have impact for decades to come: Their destruction created lifeless black holes totally unsuitable for wildlife and wildlife-watching. Yet learning late is better than never learning at all. Future generations will appreciate what has been preserved and understand it was done so that they, too, might share in the natural beauty of today.

Isn't that what saving for the future is really all about?

March

Notes

13

The Wily Armadillo

It seems that almost everyone's introduction to the armadillo occurs on a highway. Most people see their first armadillo either while it's foraging in the grass beside the thoroughfare, or they encounter it as roadkill, a messy spot on the roadway.

Although fossil records indicate that armadillos have been around in one form or another for 65 million years, it's obvious they have yet to realize that the automobile is their greatest threat. Perhaps it's because some of their ancestors weighed several tons and they never had to worry about being in the road. They should avoid highways since their brain is quite small, and they aren't very bright.

Yet they *are* cute. And spring is the time of year to see armadillos traveling in family groups as the female looks after her four sexually identical newborns. This close relationship will last over the next few months, until just before the next breeding season.

Armadillos mate anytime between July and December. A single fertilized egg is implanted in the uterus, and four sexually identical embryos develop from this one egg. After a gestation period of at least 150 days, the female bears four identical-appearing offspring that are born with their eyes open. The newborns' shells, initially pliable, begin to harden after a few days. The hardening process isn't completed until the animal reaches its full size.

Newborn armadillos stay with their mother through spring and summer, then are left to forage on their own when the female must attend to the next breeding season. The youngsters do not become sexually mature until their second year. The life span of an armadillo in the wild is between four and seven years.

Armadillos are so unique among mammals that they have been incorrectly named both popularly and scientifically. The name *armadillo* comes from the Spanish for "little armored one," referring to the armadillo's *carapace,* or tough shell, something no other mammal wears. However, this outer covering is not at all like the exoskeleton of a tortoise. Instead, the carapace is made of modified skin tissue and, despite its imposing appearance, accounts for less than 20 percent of the animal's weight. The average adult is about 2 $\frac{1}{2}$-feet long, weighs about 14 pounds and males are larger than females.

Armadillos are also incorrectly placed in the animal order Edentata, meaning "toothless," yet armadillos do have primitive peglike teeth. The scientific name, *Dasypus novemcinctus,* translates as "nine-banded rabbit-turtle," which is what the Aztecs called the animal. Anyone who tastes cooked armadillo can partly understand the comparison to rabbit.

An armadillo shell actually consists of three major sections. Both the shoulder and pelvic shield are joined together by the bands, which may number from eight to eleven, though nine is most common. In turn, bands are connected by folds in the skin, which allow the animal to bend like an accordion. The shell is not flexible enough for the animal to roll up into a protective ball, but it will curl up to protect its vulnerable underbelly. The leathery covering that protects the head, ears and tail is much tougher than the animal's soft, hairy underbelly.

In the open, a person or a dog can normally outrun an armadillo, but few creatures try to charge into thick underbrush after it. Armadillos have always been a challenge to catch because their sense of hearing and smell are quite good. Yet anyone who decides to capture an armadillo should first ask themselves two questions: Why do I want to catch it, and what in the world am I going to do with it once I do?

Armadillos may be small, but they do have curved, sharp claws, four on each front leg, five on each hind leg. These claws can inflict severe damage on humans or dogs and should be respected. The claws are not intended for attacking animals or birds but for burrowing and digging out insects. However, armadillos are not strictly insectivorous, for they have been recorded eating dead birds, frogs and even earthworms. Plants are not a significant part of their diet.

As insect eaters, armadillos do not need large tracts of territory to locate food. Studies in Florida show that armadillos range over areas as small as 2.5 acres to as large as 35 acres. Armadillo territories sometimes overlap, but the animals are not aggressive toward one another because they don't have to compete for food as carnivores do.

Armadillos, like rabbits, are ground dwellers. Their cool, damp burrows, which may extend for as far as 10 feet, also function as apartments that spiders, mosquitoes and other insects hide in. Armadillos seem to ignore these easy pickings until prolonged bad weather keeps them confined or hunting is poor; then, it's snack time! In pursuit of an armadillo, never put a hand in its burrow. Armadillos share their burrows with rattlesnakes, rabbits, cotton rats, opossums and skunks.

Of the estimated 27 different species of armadillo, only the nine-banded is found outside Central and South America. The most widespread of all the armadillos, the nine-banded has been expanding into the United States since about 1850. It came in through Texas, then introduced into Florida. How armadillos first entered Texas, whether on their own or transported by humans, is still uncertain. The armadillos could possibly have been introduced by humans who were increasingly recognizing the animal's potential as food.

The nine-banded armadillo was introduced into Florida by a serviceman from Texas during World War I.

Florida's armadillo population was established by a soldier from Texas who released a pair of armadillos during World War I in the Hialeah area of South Florida. In 1922, a youngster near Miami captured Florida's first recorded wild armadillo, much to the surprise of local zoo officials, who had no idea what in the world the animal was. Later, armadillos escaped from zoos in Cocoa and other parts of Florida, all of which helped establish the animal's residency. The armadillo now thrives in every part of the state except the Everglades, where its burrows flood too easily.

What is the role of the armadillo in the Southeast: Just a curious oddity or a highly destructive pest?

For many years armadillos were blamed for destroying the eggs of ground-nesting birds, particularly quail eggs. However, studies revealed that most armadillos would not eat a quail or chicken egg even when the egg was placed in front of it.

Understandably, armadillos are not popular with urban gardeners, for armadillos like to root around in the soil at night, destroying the flower beds. Armadillos also make a mess of golf courses and football and baseball fields.

Armadillos do have a unique role in a very specific type of medical research. The armadillo is one of the few animals (in addition to humans) that can contract Hansen's disease, or leprosy. An estimated 12 to 14 million people worldwide still suffer from this dreaded condition. Although leprosy can often be controlled by sulfone drugs, an antileprosy vaccine is considered the best means of preventing its occurrence in the first place.

Consequently, armadillos have been used as laboratory animals to provide the leprosy microbes needed to develop such a vaccine. Not only can armadillos be infected with the disease, it turns out the disease naturally occurs among armadillos in the wild. There are several somewhat unsettling documented cases of humans being infected with leprosy after capturing (and getting scratched by) an armadillo. Fortunately, leprosy is still considered the least infectious of all the contagious diseases affecting humans. So, no, there is no need to go out and eradicate the armadillo.

Better simply to observe it, photograph it and if you still feel an overwhelming desire to chase and capture one—wear leather gloves.

When the female is out feeding with her identical brood in late spring and summer, she tends to be fairly cautious. She is most often seen early and late. Otherwise, the appearance of an armadillo cannot be predicted in specific places during specific seasons. Armadillos, like their food, are present year-round, and the creatures don't have to roam a good deal. And like alligators, armadillos may pop up at any time, anywhere.

It's not uncommon to see armadillos feeding on the side of heavily traveled highways in rural areas after dark. Some of the best places to spot armadillos are wildlife management areas, national wildlife refuges and state parks. They can sometimes be found on barrier islands grubbing in the sand dunes. They are also plentiful in the sandhills of the **Apalachicola, Osceola** and **Ocala National Forests.** In the **Withlacoochee State Forest** near Brooksville, try both the **Colonel Robbins Nature Trail** and the **McKethan Lake Nature Trail.** If the animals aren't present, their triangular-shaped holes should be quite apparent.

Consider the armadillo an animal of opportunity that could present itself at several points during any seasonal visit.

14

Roseate Spoonbills

The colorful pink roseate spoonbill is unquestionably the emblematic bird of Florida. Therefore, by all rights it ought to be the official state bird, but it's not. The 1927 legislature chose instead the mockingbird, a year-round resident whose Latin name means "a bird of many tongues," something old-time politicians themselves were familiar with.

The roseate spoonbill was almost extinct by the middle of the twentieth century, but the bird is returning quite strongly. Its broad, flattened beak, whose tip is not too different from the shape of a manatee's tail, is characteristic of the bird, young and old. The bill is important in feeding, during which the bird moves its bill from side to side underwater in search of shrimp and small fish. The flat bill also comes in handy for searching soft, shallow, muddy areas for insects and crustaceans.

More than anything else, the preservation of the bird's shallow feeding areas in Florida Bay and elsewhere is paramount to the roseate spoonbill's survival.

In Florida Bay and other parts of South Florida, roseates nest during November and December. In Central Florida, breeding occurs several months later, around April. In all areas the nests are built in low, dense mangroves or trees, often in the same territory as the nests of herons and ibis. Roseate spoonbills, which normally lay three eggs, build sturdy, deep nests made of sticks.

Immature birds display a soft pink on their wings and back that darkens with age. They attain their bright pink mature colors at about three years of age. The pink is accented by a distinctive orange tail and shoulders, rump and chest patches that are all bright red. The skin on the sides and back of the neck is a dark black.

A little gaudy overall, perhaps, but it's no wonder plume hunters wanted these birds so badly that they almost completely exterminated them.

Hot
Spots

Roseate spoonbills nest not only in South Florida's shallow **Florida Bay** but as far north as **Tampa Bay** and the **Merritt Island NWR**. Expansion to eastern Central Florida is so recent that many birding guides have yet to note it. The spring and summer of 1995 were banner seasons for the number of roseate spoonbills seen around Tampa Bay, possibly a consequence of the bay's own healing. After the nesting season, some birds will disperse farther north, ranging to St. Augustine on the Atlantic Coast and the Panhandle along the Gulf Coast.

In the early 1900s, roseate spoonbills were almost hunted to extinction for their colorful feathers, which were used to decorate women's hats.

In summer, look for roseate spoonbills at **Fort Matanzas National Monument,** off A1A 15 miles south of St. Augustine. A free ferry takes visitors to the monument daily from 9 A.M. until 4:30 P.M. At the mouth of the **Alafia River** are two spoil islands/ bird sanctuaries. Spoil islands are man-made landfalls created by dredging or maintaining river channels. Usually located just to the side of a channel, the barren dirt mounds quickly become populated with native vegetation thanks to the seeds that are blown or washed ashore. Direct access to them is not permitted, but they can be viewed from a boat. Roseate spoonbills nest here frequently.

Fort DeSoto County Park on Mullet Key near St. Petersburg is fairly reliable for spoonbill sightings. Located on Mullet Key, it's reached by traveling west on the Pinellas Bayway, then turning south onto State Road 679; follow signs to the park.

In the **J. N. "Ding" Darling NWR** on Sanibel Island, spoonbills usually appear year after year. Spoonbills also appear in summer on the offshore islands at nearby **Carl Johnson State Park,** located on State Road 865 south of Fort Myers. **Fakahatchee Strand State Preserve** near Everglades City could have roseate spoonbills at any time.

In **Everglades National Park,** look for roseates at **Paurotis Pond** in winter and at **Eco Pond** in summer. In the **Keys,** look in the flooded area behind the church at Mile Marker 93 during the winter months. At Mile Marker 22, only a short distance from Key West, look for roseate spoonbills on the mangroves surrounding **Twenty-Two Mile Pond** on Cudjoe Key. The pond is right across from the mile marker. Also look for them in the ponds near the **Key West airport.**

On the east coast, look for spoonbills in the estuary at **John D. MacArthur State Park.** In North Palm Beach, take U.S. 1 to Ocean Boulevard (A1A) and turn east. The entrance is less than 2 miles away.

15

Spring Wildflowers

The perennial shower of wildflowers begins early, in March, and the display is always an exceptionally fine one. After all, it was in the spring of 1513 that their number, variety and splendor so inspired world explorer Ponce de Leon that he named a newly discovered territory the "land of flowers," or *Florida*.

Already landscaped with thousands of indigenous trees, plants and shrubs, Florida's growing conditions proved so agreeable that European settlers added hundreds of new varieties to the native flora. Today there are an estimated 3,500 different species growing around the state.

Two of the easiest and most obvious places to see wildflowers in Florida are along two heavily traveled interstate highways. The state has planted 200 miles of crimson wildflowers along I-10 between Tallahassee and Jacksonville, and 215 miles of annual phlox along I-75 from Tampa north to the Georgia state line. In all, over 1,000 miles of highway have been planted with wildflowers statewide. Some roadside flowers will be familiar, but others will be new discoveries because they are endemic or imported perennials from Mexico, Asia and the Caribbean that thrive in the Southeast's moderate temperatures.

It surprises many first-time visitors that the wildflower season in Florida is year-round. Like a florist's display, they bloom in the accompaniment of several roadside plants. The most notable are the bright green ferns. Scores of different fern species grow continually in swamps and ditches and some, such as the cinnamon fern, mimic the main wildflower season and flower exclusively in spring.

As enduring and delightful as they are, ferns are not what sets the fields, plains and roadsides afire. Much of the color comes from several varieties of phlox, particularly the purple needlelike flowers of the creeping phlox, which grows low to the ground in compact tufts in open fields and pinelands as far south as Orlando. Common throughout the entire region is the annual phlox, actually native to Texas, which exhibits the showy purple flowers found along roadsides and in open places.

Adding to spring's mantle of purple is the Florida violet, which, despite its name, is found in adjoining states as well. These low-to-the-ground flowers are abundant in open woods and clearings everywhere.

Spring also ushers in the red poppy mallow to Northwest Florida and Alabama, plus the even more striking Turk's-cap, or wax mallow, a bushy shrub whose scarlet pendant flowers never open fully. The yellow Jessamine adds a splash of contrast to the hammocks, thickets and clearings. Its climbing woody vines often collect and merge to form a striking sight.

A few of the most colorful flowers, such as the columbine, are rare in Florida but quite common farther north. The brilliant flowers of the columbine, found only in three Panhandle counties, are pollinated by hummingbirds seeking the nectar at the end of the plant's spurs (spurs that happen to be just as long as a hummingbird's bill).

The roadsides and fields offer the most obvious arrays of wildflowers, yet don't ignore some of the greatest color shows of both wildflowers and shrubs that occur in more out-of-the-way places, the swamps and long stream banks. Characteristic wetlands shrubs include the ti-ti (also called leatherwood) and the black ti-ti, both of which produce long, showy racemes of fragrant flowers.

There are many more spring wildflowers, hundreds more, and the only way to appreciate what you're viewing is with a good guidebook. *Florida Wild Flowers and Roadside Plants* by Bell and Taylor and *The Guide to Florida Wildflowers* by Taylor are the definitive works. With more than 500 plants identified through text and color photographs, the books are good companions throughout the year.

The vibrant colors that begin in March are not like the momentary color flashes of autumn, a brief moment of glory that too quickly fades and disappears. Many spring wildflowers remain in bloom through the summer and sometimes as late as fall. And the early arrivals will be joined later by others that don't reveal their full brilliance until the hot days of summer. Spring is only the beginning of the wildflower season.

Hot Spots In the timber-managed state and national forests, areas that undergo prescribed burns often have some of the best wildflower habitat, because the fires remove much of the shady forest canopy.

Along the Alabama coast, the predominant wildflower habitat is the pitcher-plant bog (see chapter 37). The spring wildflower season here tends to be spread out, and there is no big burst of color. Fall is better, though the main color tends to be yellow, and black-eyed Susans are most common from late September to the first frost. **Gulf State Park** offers one of the better floral displays, with swamp rose mallow, seashore mallow, sundews, golden asters, bay and ti-ti all in one convenient place.

Georgia's **Okefenokee NWR** comes alive in March as golden club and bladderworts begin to bloom on the prairies. At Florida's **Blackwater River State Forest,** the best wildflower viewing is along the hiking trails. These include the **Bear Lake Recreation Area Loop Trail,** which goes through a number of systems. The **Wire Grass Trail** also offers good wildflowers most of the year. Another good Panhandle hotspot is **Florida Caverns State Park** near Marianna. The forest and swamp border the scenic Chipola River.

In the **Apalachicola National Forest,** it's the Post Office Bay savannahs area on the **Apalachee Savannahs Scenic Byway** in the southwestern section of the forest. The wildflowers share the same savannahs as the carnivorous plants do.

In **Osceola National Forest,** the trails leading from the Olustee Battlefield and the Mt. Carrie Wayside Park (on U.S. 90 across from the Columbia Correctional Institution) pass through good wildflower displays. The palmetto cover is far less dense in this southern part of the forest, providing better wildflower habitat for blazing stars, goldenrod, aster, milkweed and orchids, all of which grow in profusion following a summer burn. Wild azaleas grow along the **Middle Prong of the St. Marys River** in the northwest section in the vicinity of the East Tower.

San Felasco State Preserve near Gainesville has some colorful displays, as does nearby **Paynes Prairie State Preserve,** which has more than 700 wildflower species—thanks to the great variety of habitat, including wet prairie and sinkholes. Wild-flowers last well beyond spring and into the fall here. **Tosohatchee State Reserve,** which borders the St. Johns River, can also be quite good. It is located on Taylor Creek Road, off State Road 50 near the town of Christmas. In Southwest Florida, **Corkscrew Swamp Sanctuary** can be an excellent spot.

16

Swamp Walks

Cypress swamps are moody, mysterious places. For many animal and plant species, these remote sheltered regions represent the heart and soul of the remaining wilderness. Naturalist and explorer John Muir offered a poetic description of a cypress swamp, the first one he ever encountered, during his thousand-mile walk in 1867 from Indiana to Cedar Key, Florida: "The whole forest seems level at the top, as if each tree had grown up against a ceiling, or had been rolled while growing. This taxodium is the only level-topped tree that I have seen. The branches, though spreading, are careful not to pass each other, and stop suddenly on reaching the general level, as if they had grown up against a ceiling … . The winds are full of strange sounds, making one feel far from the people and plants and fruitful fields at home."

Many creatures live in the swamp, though they are not always easily seen. Gray squirrels, raccoons, otters, black bears, alligators and white-tailed deer all may be sighted. Turtles and snakes are also common residents. As many as 16 different snakes can be seen from the boardwalks, including water snakes and eastern cottonmouths. A swamp's thick canopy of cypress trees also provides essential roosts and secure nesting sites for hundreds of species of waterbirds.

Swamps also grow many distinct and unusual food sources. For instance, from March through September you'll often see small white snail eggs the size of BBs just above the waterline on trees and plants. Most likely these are apple snail eggs, and the egg masses contain anywhere from a handful to as many as 75 eggs. The adult snails are an important food source for both limpkins and the rare Everglades kite.

A dense cypress swamp is truly eerie in its stillness and closeness. Forbidding they may appear, but freshwater swamps are hardly the cesspools they may seem. Swamp water is not normally stagnant or fetid, as is popularly imagined. Instead, swamp water often flows very slowly, as the movement of floating debris reveals. Even when the water level drops low enough to end the flow, the water is still quite pure thanks to the roots of the water plants, which release oxygen into the water. This in turn oxidizes the organic matter so the water remains pure. Only when swamp water is low enough to form isolated pools is the water likely to turn foul, but only until the next rainy period.

Cypress trees, of course, are the main characteristic of these swamps. Protruding above the water near these trees are what appear to be short, bark-covered stumps. They are the cypress knees, which create added stability for a tree and may also "breathe" for it.

Swamps are not only among the best places to view animals, they are one of the best places to see some of the most distinctive plants in the Southeast. Southern swamps are remarkable for the tremendous number and variety of air plants attached to the cypress trees. The plants are often piled one after another on the tree trunks and branches, like Christmas decorations. In the late afternoon or early morning, the plants block the slanting sunlight so that it filters through in random, spooky patterns.

Undoubtedly the best known air plant, or *epiphyte,* is the Spanish moss hanging from cypress tree limbs like spider webs in the

A boardwalk, like this one at Corkscrew Swamp Sanctuary near Naples, is the easiest way to examine the amazing plant and animal diversity found within a cypress forest.

corners of an abandoned house. Spanish moss is one of the most recognized and emblematic symbols of the South. Like many air plants, it is a member of the pineapple family. It is not parasitic, so it will not kill the tree on which it is draped. The moss receives all of its nourishment from the air. However, Spanish moss definitely *can* damage a tree by shading out the leaves. The moss exhibits its own bright green flowers in late spring. Spanish moss spreads from tree to tree by sending out small seeds with a silky parachute that are spread by the wind. At one time Spanish moss was used for filling pillows, mattresses and car seats.

Because swamps undergo an alternating cycle of drought and high humidity, some air plants have developed tough skins in order to reduce moisture loss. Others rely on thick stems in which to store their precious liquid; many air plant stems are vase-shaped in order to collect water at their base. One of these is the yellow catopsis, a light yellowish green plant. The water stored in its leaves also attracts insects and frogs and other animals. In turn, the plant depends on the animals' fecal matter for important nutrients.

Ferns, among the most common plants of the cypress swamp, come in exhaustive varieties. The most common is appropriately called the swamp fern, which grows best in deep shade. Probably the most famous fern is the resurrection fern. During periods of drought, its curled brown leaves make it appear dead, but following a heavy rain the leaves return to their vibrant green. Another interesting fern is the strap fern, with its swordlike leaves. It doesn't even resemble a fern at all. In the United States, the strap fern is limited to South Florida.

A green layer of duckweed, or possibly even water lettuce, may cover some pools of water. Duckweed is one of the smallest of all flowering plants. Each tiny plant contains two or three leaves and a short root. The much larger water lettuce takes its name because of its similarity in both looks and size to iceberg lettuce. Water lettuce appears to die out after frost or drought, but it typically returns in time.

Unappetizing to humans, perhaps, but a cypress swamp is clearly an essential broth of life for hundreds, if not thousands, of plant and animal species.

Hot Spots

Georgia's famed **Okefenokee Swamp** has two very different boardwalks. At the **Suwannee Canal Recreation Area** near Folkston on the swamp's east side is a rambling 4,000-foot boardwalk. Much of this old boardwalk passes through open areas, and it's possible to see for greater distances than in many Florida swamps. The number of swamp residents here is staggering: 42 mammals including black bear, 58 reptiles, 32 amphibians and 233 birds. A good day here from March through June, or October through December can be breathtaking. The **Okefenokee Swamp Park** at the northern end near Waycross is more reliable year-round for watching wildlife because the animals are always more concentrated. The north-end boardwalk, however, is far shorter.

Most of Florida's swamp boardwalks are located in the central and southern part of the state. All of them are wheelchair-accessible. One of the best times for swamp boardwalking is during the winter dry season, when birds and animals congregate in the greatest numbers around the remaining pools of water. One of Florida's most northerly swamp boardwalks is at the **Morningside Nature Center,** which offers a stroll through a cypress dome in the city of Gainesville. Warblers, pileated woodpeckers and great crested flycatchers are present in the cypress forest in spring and summer. Open daily from 9 A.M. to 5 P.M. Take U.S. 441 to Gainesville, then go east for 3.5 miles on East University Drive.

Florida Power and Light operates the 400-acre **Barley Barber Swamp** near Indiantown on Florida's east coast. A 1-mile boardwalk loops through this superb cypress swamp. Reservations are required one week in advance for access. A naturalist will explain the plant and animals that inhabit the region; call (800) 257-9267. Barley Barber Swamp is located at Florida Power and Light's Martin Power Plant, 8 miles north of Indiantown on State Road 710. Just past the railroad tracks is the sign, "Wait Here for Swamp Tours."

Highlands Hammock State Park near Sebring was one of the state's first parks and is where the last sighting of the ivory-billed woodpecker occurred. The boardwalk is one of many excellent short hikes. There's also a ranger-led tram tour throughout the property. From U.S. 27 north of Sebring, turn west onto County Road 634; (813) 385-0011.

Access to the **Reedy Creek Swamp** is offered on an 1,800-foot boardwalk at the **Osceola Schools Environmental Study Center.** Bald eagles and a rookery of great blue herons are present in winter and early spring. White ibis and great egrets are other dry-month residents. Also look for alligators and turtles. From the town of Kissimmee, go west on U.S. 17/92 4 miles to Poinciana Boulevard. At Poinciana, turn left and go 6 miles to the entrance; (407) 846- 4312.

On Florida's southwest coast near Fort Myers, the **Six Mile Cypress Slough Preserve** offers a 1.2-mile boardwalk that passes through a natural wildlife corridor for bobcat, turkey and white-tailed deer, all year-round residents. Alligators, raccoons, warblers, bald eagles and snowy egrets are also present. Two observation platforms and a photo blind offer unusually good picture-taking opportunities. Take I-75 south of Fort Myers to Exit 22 (Colonial Boulevard). Go west 0.5 mile to Six Mile Parkway. Turn south (left) and proceed 3 miles. Turn east (left) on Penzance Crossing. The entrance is a tenth of a mile from the intersection.

The **Corkscrew Swamp Sanctuary** offers one of the state's premier boardwalks (see chapter 7). The trail proceeds for 2 miles through the nation's largest old-growth cypress forest. The largest nesting colony of wood storks in the country takes up residence here in late winter. Owned and operated by the National Audubon Society, the facility opens at 7 A.M. from December to April, at 8 A.M. May through November. The boardwalk closes at 5 P.M. year-round. Go east 21 miles on State Road 846 from U.S. 41 north of Naples. Turn left at the sanctuary sign; (813) 657-3771.

The **Big Cypress Bend Boardwalk** provides the best access to the **Fakahatchee Strand State Preserve,** considered one of Florida's greatest natural resources. Many endangered species inhabit this long, narrow old-growth cypress stand, including the Florida panther, wood storks, Everglades mink and the Florida black bear. Alligators, otters, turtles, ibis and egrets are common. The boardwalk is on the north side of U.S. 41

(Tamiami Trail) just west of the junction with State Road 29; (813) 695-4593.

A combination trail and boardwalk passes for 1.2 miles through pine flatwoods, saw-grass marsh, palm hammock and cypress wetlands at the **J. W. Corbett Wildlife Management Area's Hungryland Boardwalk and Trail.** Bobcats and white-tailed deer are often seen here early and late. Barred and screech owls, river otters and pileated woodpeckers frequent the cypress dome. Unusually good interpretive signs outline both the plant and animal communities. From I-95 north of West Palm Beach take the Northlake Boulevard Exit. Go west for 12.3 miles and turn right onto Seminole Pratt Whitney Road. The entrance to the J. W. Corbett Wildlife Management Area will be on the right. Follow the signs for 0.7 mile to the Hungryland Boardwalk and Trail.

The boardwalk is slightly less than a half-mile long at the **Loxahatchee NWR,** but this section of northern Everglades swamp is incredibly full of air plants and ferns. Listen for woodpeckers. Anoles and basking snakes are the principal animals sighted here. Take Exit 50 off I-95 in West Palm Beach. Go west on U.S. 98 for 7 miles to U.S. 441. Turn south (left) and proceed another 13 miles. The refuge entrance is on the west (right).

Alabama's **Mobile-Tenshaw Delta** does not yet have boardwalks, but it does have one very interesting wildlife tour. Located only a short distance from Mobile, the tour travels for over 25 miles up the Chickasabogue Creek and into the delta. Avoid taking this tour during the sweltering summer heat; early mornings are bearable, but the afternoon is not. Take I-10 from Mobile and turn north on I-65. Travel north for 13 miles and take Exit 13. Go east on Highway 158 for 2 miles, to Highway 43. Turn right and after 0.5-mile look for the Chickasaw Marina on the right. For information, call (334) 460-8206.

17

March Shorttakes

Racehorse Foals

Few animals have as much time, money and research placed in the development of their offspring as do thoroughbred racehorses, whose foals will be on display at a select number of horse farms in North-Central Florida. The world's four main centers for raising thoroughbred racehorses are Lexington, Kentucky; Newmarket, England; Chantilly, France; and **Ocala-Marion County, Florida,** where more than 400 horse farms are devoted to the raising and training of thoroughbred racehorses. The Ocala farms have produced winners of the most important races, including the Kentucky Derby, the Preakness Stakes and the Belmont.

What makes Ocala such a good area for raising horses? The Floridan aquifer, the massive underground river that flows down the central part of the state, also runs directly beneath the Ocala area's limestone base. Together, these two features produce some of the nation's richest pastureland. Only a limited number of farms allow visitors. The current list is available from the Ocala-Marion County Chamber of Commerce at (904) 629-8051; fax (904) 629-7651.

One Million Coots

One million is a lot of coots, but that's the typical number present this month near Clewiston on **Lake Okeechobee,** the second largest freshwater lake in the continental United States. To begin counting coots, go west 2 miles from the town of Moore Haven on U.S. 27. Turn right onto State Road 78. Go almost 15 miles to the Harney Pond Canal Access Area. Turn right and go another mile to the lookout tower. Herons and egrets should also be present. Camping is available at Moore Haven.

Largemouth Bass

March is when the largemouth bass fishing really gets going. Florida has some of the finest largemouth bass waters in the nation, and trophy fish over 10 pounds are not uncommon. Visitors would do best to get themselves a guide, because Florida fishing is quite different from that in most places: The lakes are shallow and sometimes weed-choked. Among the best places are the lakes of the **Ocala National Forest, Lake Kissimmee, Lake Tohopekaliga,** the lakes around the town of **Mount Dora,** and **Lake Okeechobee.** Chambers of commerce in all these areas will have the names of local bass guides.

18

A Closer Look:
The Creepie Crawlies

The Southeast has some unusual creepie crawlies inhabiting its wilderness. Knowing that these critters are present and how best to deal with them will make following the natural year a lot less itchy.

The first concern is how one smells: It should be the exact opposite of what is desired by polite society. In the wild, one's body aroma should be as unattractive as possible. Avoid pungent soaps, perfumes and colognes. A good insect repellent, one with a high concentration of DEET, is good for making anyone downright repulsive. However, repellents with more than 30 percent DEET are considered to be toxic when absorbed through the skin.

Long pants and long-sleeved shirts offer less skin surface area for insects to bite. Keep your shirttail tucked in any time you're seated on the ground. Socks and shoes (as opposed to sandals) help deter ankle-biters. Socks should be sprayed with repellent.

In the Everglades and a few other places, staying outside until sunset demands the addition of a beekeeper's hat to keep mosquitoes at bay. Wool gloves without the fingertips provide additional protection for photographers who want to stay past sunset.

A list follows of the worst of the creepie crawlies and some ways to deal with them:

Mosquitoes. Florida has an estimated 67 species of salt- and freshwater mosquitoes. Freshwater mosquitoes are most active during the summer rainy season, but saltwater mosquitoes will put the bite on you year-round. Twilight is often the worst time.

Chiggers. They can be found in the woods almost anywhere. The favorite body areas for these tiny red mites to attack is around the wrists, ankles and waist. Insect repellent helps keep them at bay; so does sulphur powder. Clear fingernail polish brushed on the bites helps smother the chiggers, which burrow into the skin. Calamine lotion helps stop the itching.

Fire ants. They are a problem only if their mound, which looks like a shovelful of dirt, is disturbed. Otherwise they stay underground, out of sight. Some people are highly allergic to these ant bites.

No-see-ums. These are the bane of beach hikers at sunrise and sunset. These virtually invisible creatures feel like they are all teeth. The best protection is ample clothing. Fortunately, no-see-ums are a problem for only about an hour at each end of the day.

Ticks. They are active year-round. In Florida there are several reports of people contracting Lyme disease. A drop of gasoline will sometimes encourage a tick to loosen its grip. Otherwise, tweezers may be required to remove the tick. Be careful to grab it next to the skin in order to extract the head. A tincture of iodine dropped on the bite helps reduce the chance of infection.

Rabid animals. The animal most likely to be rabid in Florida is the cute-looking raccoon. Avoid close contact on general principle. Any raccoon that seems to have lost its fear of people, is overly friendly, too aggressive, scraggly-looking or wobbly on its feet is suspect. The only way to confirm that an animal is rabid is through a brain autopsy. A series of shots are the only effective treatment for a bite from a rabid animal.

Snakes. Despite their healthy numbers in the Southeast, they are rarely a problem. Keep to the trails and the boardwalks. Snakes are no more anxious to encounter people than we are to encounter them. Statistically, you are more likely to be fatally injured by a pig than a snake (so as long as you stay away from pig farms, you should be quite safe). In the event of a snake bite, the best first-aid is to rush the victim to a hospital.

Scorpions. These are not likely to be a problem except for campers, and then only rarely. Scorpions like to crawl into boots and clothing left outdoors. The sting is painful but not fatal.

Alligators. Most aggressive toward swimmers in the breeding season, they are also a potential problem when people have been feeding them, or if a dog is present. Alligators can outrun people in short bursts, but they supposedly cannot run in a zigzag pattern.

April

Notes

19

Heronries

With long gangly legs like those of the flamingo, the heron is among the most distinctive and popular birds. Indeed, the great blue heron, standing 4 feet tall and with a wingspan of more than 6 feet, is emblematic of the Southeast.

When hunting at the edge of lakes, rivers and roadside culverts, the great blue is a solitary stalker, so it could come as a surprise to discover that scores of herons and other species sometimes nest together in some of the most cramped and crowded breeding conditions imaginable. The name for such a heron nesting colony is *heronry*, and the sights, sounds and smells associated with one are unforgettable—especially the smells. So it's not such a bad thing that most heronries are closed to visitors and must be viewed from afar. Anyone with a normal sense of smell probably wouldn't want to get much closer, anyway.

The great blue heron often shares its nesting territory with the tricolored (formerly Louisiana) heron, little blue heron, green heron, the yellow-crowned and black-crowned night herons, the snowy egret, the great egret, anhinga and sometimes even wood ibis.

There may be a couple of ringers thrown in too. Ward's heron, often mistaken for the great blue, is a couple of inches taller and with a wingspan of almost 7 feet. It lives in marshes, lakes and rivers and is more native to the Gulf Coast than the Atlantic.

In South Florida these species may be joined by what are sometimes called "great white herons." Once considered a separate species, these actually are great blues in a white phase. The body is totally white; the bill, legs and feet are yellow and the eye has a bluish green patch around it. This white phase is peculiar to South Florida.

Heronries are normally located close to estuaries or lakes that produce an ample amount of food for the young. Forage may include insects, shrimp, frogs, snakes, lizards, grasshoppers, killifish and other small animals. Perhaps even more remarkable than the activity and confusion of the rookery itself is watching all the birds in flight. The great blues, which walk with their necks tall and proud, appear almost headless in flight as they fold their necks back and draw their heads into their shoulders.

Heron nests are so similar that it is sometimes difficult to distinguish between the nests of different species. The nest, made of sticks and twigs, is a flattened, shallow bowl that may or may not have a lining of softer material. A nesting colony is typically located on an island or mangrove coastline where predators, particularly raccoons, cannot easily reach them.

The great blue heron, which seems to spend most of its time stalking fish, is one of the Southeast's most distinctive birds.

Although a colony will typically return to the same location each year, this is sometimes impossible because the heronry is actually destroying its habitat during each nesting season. The heronry is easy to spot outside of breeding season because of the whitewashed tree leaves near the nest that are thick with guano. The droppings, which eventually cause the branches to become too brittle, kill the trees. Then the colony must shift to neighboring trees or abandon the area altogether.

Heron nests usually contain three to four eggs that are laid days apart. The female begins incubation as soon as the first egg is laid, which means the chicks hatch at different times, or asynchronously, a good survival procedure. The oldest chick begins feeding immediately, chugging down each load of regurgitated food brought by its parents. As the strongest and largest chick, it will monopolize the food at the expense of its weaker siblings once they hatch. In a lean year, the last born may starve to death. Yet better that one chick should survive than none. And when times are good, the whole brood will live.

Hot Spots

In order not to disrupt the birds, most heronries are closed during the nesting season. However, many colonies can be viewed with a spotting scope either from land or, more frequently, from a boat.

At the **Savannah Coastal Refuges, Harris Neck** usually has good numbers of herons, egrets, ibis and wood storks nesting together from spring to September. The amount of nesting is often determined by water conditions. Check with the refuge office first to make sure the birds are present and that access is possible: (912) 652-4415. Reach Harris Neck by going 43 miles south of Savannah on U.S. 17, then east on Highway 131 to the refuge entrance. **Blackbeard Island** has a good-sized heronry at Flag Pond with as many as 1,000 heron, egret, ibis and anhinga pairs. Access is by boat only. Trips can be arranged at Shellman's Bluff, 51 miles south of Savannah.

Okefenokee NWR wading bird rookeries become active in April, though a boat will probably be required to approach them. Rentals are available at the visitor centers.

Visitors need to arrange their own transport to visit the islands at **Cedar Key NWR,** site of one of the largest heron nesting grounds anywhere in the South. Boat tours are easy to arrange, and a few operators specialize in trips for birders. Contact the Chamber of Commerce at (904) 543-5600.

Merritt Island NWR near Titusville is one of the Southeast's great nesting grounds for herons: tricolored, great blue, little blue and green herons, plus ibis and egrets. This location is considered to have the best assembly of all the different species anywhere on the entire U.S. East Coast. Check at the refuge center for location of the most accessible nests: (407) 867-0667.

Nesting blue herons are easily visible in winter and early spring from the boardwalk at the **Osceola Schools Environmental Study Center** near Kissimmee. (Look for nesting bald eagles during the same period too.) The center is open Saturday 10 A.M. to 5 P.M. and Sunday noon to 5 P.M. In the town of Kissimmee, take U.S. 17/92 west 4 miles to Poinciana Boulevard. Turn south (left) and go 6 miles to the entrance on the right. For more information, call (407) 846- 4312.

Visitors to **Blue Cypress Water Management Area** near Vero Beach will need their own boats to find the several heronries in this area of cypress swamps, lakes and marshes that form the headwaters of the mighty St. Johns River. The only public facilities are a grassy parking area and a boat ramp. Go 14 miles west of Vero Beach on Highway 60, turn north onto County Road 512 and go 2 miles to the entrance, on the left. Administered by the St. Johns River Water Management District: (904) 329-4377.

The number of active heronries in a single season at **Loxahatchee NWR** is staggering: over 250 in good years. Each heronry differs dramatically in the number of birds. Some heronries are small, but others contain thousands of nesting herons, egrets and ibis. Many are difficult to reach, but the one behind the refuge office on **Marsh Trail** seems like it was placed just for the benefit of visitors. You could see as many as a thousand birds present at the peak of the nesting season. Take I-95 to the Boynton Beach Boulevard Exit and go west to U.S. 441. At U.S. 441, go south for 2 miles to the refuge entrance; (407) 732- 3684.

One of the easiest nesting bird colonies to reach is at **J. N. "Ding" Darling NWR** on Sanibel Island in Southwest Florida. It's located at the end of the wildlife drive (closed Fridays) where egrets, great blue herons and several other heron varieties are perched on fragile-looking limbs over the water. Avoid weekends because this is the most visited refuge in the nation. Canoe trips into the backcountry are easy to arrange. For information, call (813) 472-1100.

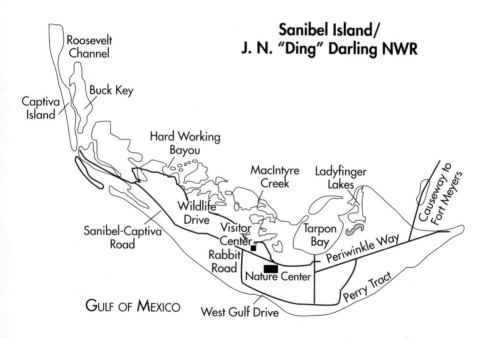

N

The **Great White Heron NWR** covers a number of islands that extend from Marathon to Key West. There is no easy public access to any of the islands. The best bet is to join one of the backcountry canoe or kayak tours that put visitors in good range of the birds. Contact Lost World Adventures, Box 431311, Big Pine Key, FL 33043; (305) 872-1040.

One of the last great stretches of undeveloped shoreline in Southwest Florida is the **Ten Thousand Islands NWR** at the northern end of **Everglades National Park.** The mangroves here attract thousands of herons and egrets. Ten Thousand Island NWR is a new refuge (a satellite administered by the Florida Panther NWR), and facilities are still being developed. For the latest information, call (941) 353-8442.

Heronries are also located in Everglades National Park, particularly near Flamingo, and in **Corkscrew Swamp Sanctuary** near Naples, which are covered in greater detail in chapters 8 and 7, respectively.

In Alabama's Mobile Bay, **Cat Island** is a major rookery for as many as 15,000 pairs of eight different species from May to mid-July when just about every type of heron imaginable is present, including great blues. This is an isolated island that can only be reached by boat from Dauphin Island. It is home to tricolored herons, snowy egrets, reddish egrets, cattle egrets, little blue herons and glossy and white ibis. This is not a place where you will want to spend any time because the mosquitoes will carry you away.

20

Wood Ducks

Generalizations, especially in regard to beauty, seem always open to argument and debate, with one notable exception. For decades now, the male wood duck has been regarded as the loveliest waterbird in all North America, and its iridescent collage of green, purple, yellow, red, buff and blue is one ideal that has never gone out of style. Its Latin name perfectly characterizes the drake's distinctive elegance: *Aix sponsa,* "a water bird in a bridal dress."

As the name implies, the bird is a duck of the woods. In the Southeast, wood ducks generally nest in cypress swamps, the only waterfowl species that does. By nesting in trees, they are able to utilize areas with little ground cover.

The drake's spectacular plumage caused it to be overhunted in the nineteenth century. This, along with the clear-cutting of old-growth forest, severely impacted the wood duck population. Unlike most waterfowl, wood ducks nest in the cavities of old trees made hollow with heart rot. Replanting after timber harvest was of little benefit for wood ducks because the new trees were far too young to furnish the traditional nesting space.

Regulating the hunting of wood ducks was easier than providing new nesting sites until after World War II, when it became common to make boxes that would serve as artificial nests. Wood ducks were agreeable to adapting to the concept, as long as the boxes were placed in the right habitat, and their population rebounded. Wood ducks tend to prefer open swampland. The nests, whether in a tree cavity or box, are padded with down. Nesting boxes, usually placed about 50 feet above the ground, are 24 inches tall and about a foot square. The oval entrance is about 3 inches by 4, with a strip of cloth nailed on the inside so the chicks will have something to grip when it's time to climb out.

Once a box is claimed in spring by a nesting pair, they may return to it year after year. The female, a much drabber gray with a broad white eye ring, lays about fifteen eggs, which hatch after more than a month of incubation. The chicks are born with their eyes open, wide awake and covered in down. Instead of being helpless, they are ready to take on life from the beginning.

The mother induces them from the nest by flying to the ground and calling up to them. The chicks, sometimes as high as 50 feet above her, have no fear of heights and, urged on by their mother's calls, launch themselves from the nest box, their featherless wings spread and feet flailing. Like rubber balls, the chicks bounce when they hit the ground, none the worse for wear.

Once the brood is assembled, the chicks follow their mother in single file to the water. For some, the first day out of the nest will be the last, because snapping turtles are rather fond of wood duck chicks.

The most colorful of all ducks, the handsome male wood duck richly deserves its Latin name, Aix sponsa, *"a water bird in a bridal dress."*

Hot Spots

Blackwater River State Forest has nesting wood ducks right along Highway 191 going north from the town of Milton. After it enters the forest boundaries, **Pitman Creek** is a small creek with a good wetland area around it. The nesting boxes, active in recent years, are visible right from the road. In addition, there is a loop trail that goes completely around the **Bear Lake Recreation Area.** Look for active boxes along here as well.

In the **Apalachicola National Forest,** there are so many natural cavities in trees along the creeks that the ducks often ignore the boxes. It requires a canoe to explore the cypress trees that grow on the creeks along the Apalachicola and Ochlockonee Rivers. However, they do use the boxes at **Franklin Pond** in the forest's western section, making it a good, reliable spot for nesting ducks year after year.

In the **Ocala National Forest, Lake Dorr** has the most nest boxes. The best way to view the nests is to launch a boat at the Lake Dorr campground and simply circle the lake to spot the boxes. Lake Door is on State Road 19 just north of the town of Umatilla.

At the **Paynes Prairie State Preserve** near Gainesville, take the Gainesville-Hawthorne Trail, part of the rails-to-trails system. The pond at Mile 3 is a very active wood duck site.

21

Shorebirds

Professionals who think their work requires too much travel would do well to consider the situation faced by migrating shorebirds, which have to shuttle back and forth between hemispheres to take advantage of the longest days and the greatest food stores. These avians clock enough frequent flier miles in a year for permanent first-class upgrades.

A large percentage of North American shorebirds spend the winter in South America. Once the weather there cools and the days begin to shorten, groups of restless shorebirds will start their trek north. The largest numbers typically return in May, though the earliest birds start appearing on Southeast coasts by April.

The journey is long and arduous. Once the birds leave the South American coast, they may have to wing their way for as much as 80 hours nonstop before reaching North America. And that's flapping the entire time, not drifting with air currents. The fat reserves built up over the previous few months are depleted by the time these migrating colonies reach the North American mainland. The exhausted birds, transformed from healthy to emaciated by their days and nights of continuous flying, are ravenous when they finally land.

But their layover is brief, lasting only about a week or two as they restore themselves for the next leg of their trip to the Arctic and their breeding grounds. Some of the birds will be back this way as soon as August on their return trip to South America. They will have courted, mated and raised their young, who will be accompanying them.

Of course, there will always be stragglers both coming and going, so different varieties of shorebirds will be passing through the region from April to September, plus there are resident populations that nest along the Southeast coast.

Visually speaking, the spring migration is far more enjoyable because the birds will be dressed in their finest plumage in anticipation of the breeding season. Technically known as *full alternate plumage,* the feathers will be freshly molted, dark and crisp, the best the birds will look all season. It's reminiscent of the concurrent high school prom rituals where young men in tuxedos are dressed in an uncharacteristically refined and mature manner.

This is quite different from how the shorebirds will appear after their Arctic visit. Then it will be like the prom's morning after when everyone has a hangover. In fall, with feather edges tattered, the plumage will be faded from constant exposure to the sun and rain, all the once sharp colors quite diminished. Some birds will even be molting into basic winter plumage, which is far more washed out than the courting colors.

The attendant youngsters will tend to look more like one another than their parents. Gray will be their uniform color, and their patterns, though close, will not quite match those of the adults. In fact, everyone tends to be such a look-alike that exact species identification is often difficult at this time of year.

In spring, it's all much less confusing.

Hot Spots The mudflats of Alabama's Mobile Bay's **Cat Island** attract many migrating shorebirds in April on their way to nest in the northern tundra and again in August, when they return to their wintering grounds in South America. There are also a few that nest locally: American oystercatcher, willet, snowy plover, Wilson's plover and spotted sandpiper. Nearby **Bon Secour NWR** has several shorebird nesting areas. Most common are the endangered least tern and the killdeer. The nesting usually occurs in the swale area, behind the beach dunes, in May and June. You'll know when you're close to the terns because they will try to run you off.

Gulf Islands National Seashore near Pensacola is a good hotspot, especially the **Santa Rosa Sound.** All of the Florida Panhandle offshore barrier islands—**St. Joe, St. Vincent** and **St. George**—are good locations.

The oysterbars at **Lower Suwannee NWR** are loaded with migrating shorebirds in March and April, and sandpipers, plovers, turnstones and dowitchers sometimes stand wing to wing by the thousands. Both **Caladesi Island State Park** and **Honeymoon Island State Recreation Area** near Dunedin always have good shorebird populations. Caladesi Island can be reached only by boat; ferry service leaves from Honeymoon Island, which is reached by turning left from U.S. 19 onto Curlew Road, about 3 miles north of Dunedin.

Fort DeSoto County Park near St. Petersburg is located on Mullet Key, which juts out into the Gulf. Shorebirds are always plentiful at **East Beach, the Bayway** and **the Park.** The visitor center makes it easy by supplying a map with all the good birding areas. Travel west on the Pinellas Bayway from St. Pete and turn south on State Road 679. Follow signs to the park; (813) 866-2484.

Continuing down the Gulf, **Cayo Costa State Park** with its 7 miles of beaches has been little developed, so the birding is always good. The ferry to this beautiful barrier island leaves from Bokeelia on Pine Island, some 20 miles north of Fort Myers. **J. N. "Ding" Darling NWR** on Sanibel Island is another shorebird attractor.

On the Atlantic side, don't bypass the 25-mile-long beach at **Canaveral National Seashore. Smyrna Dunes Park** (at Ponce de Leon Inlet south of Daytona) has good views of nesting black skimmers and least terns from April through July. **Little Talbot Island State Park,** between Jacksonville and Fernandina Beach, is excellent for migrating shorebirds as well as a strong resident population. Little Talbot is located on coastal road U.S. A1A. **Fort Clinch State Park** is located on a barrier island, the northern tip of Amelia Island, which faces into Georgia. The beaches and dunes around the old brick fort are another reliable spot for shorebirds. So is Georgia's **Cumberland Island National Seashore,** just a few more miles up the coast.

22

Nesting Brown Pelicans

A squadron of brown pelicans in flight is one of nature's grandest beach scenes. It is remarkable enough that the birds are able to follow one another in a perfect single-file or V-formation. But their ability to flap their wings in perfect synchronization makes them seem telepathically linked. Furthermore, the ability of such a bulky bird to glide effortlessly, for minutes at a time, hundreds of feet above the surf, looks like a violation of the laws of aerodynamics.

Brown pelicans owe much of their aerial grace to their oversized wings, which in design are more akin to those of vultures than to the cormorants and gannets to which brown pelicans are related. The wingspread of a brown pelican ranges between 80 and 85 inches in an adult, compared to an overall body length of 45 to 55 inches.

Typically, a brown pelican's neck is about as long as its body. In flight, the neck is folded to provide a resting place for the large head while the long bill protrudes forward like a pointing rod.

A bird of grace in the air, the brown pelican is like a drunkard when it walks on land. Its big webbed feet, so ideal for paddling in the waves, are set too far back on the body for anything but awkward walking.

Of all the brown pelican's antics, none is more spectacular than its headlong dive into the ocean in search of menhaden, mullet or other fish schooling near the surface. Brown pelicans do not recklessly dive for their catch, depending only on luck. They rely on larger fish that are feeding deeper, out of sight, to spook small fish to the surface. A diving pelican plummets like a hard-flung spear. It is a deadly missile that rarely misses.

A bird usually begins its dive from about 20 or 30 feet in the air. It partly closes its wings and curves its neck to draw its head back toward its shoulders. Just prior to hitting the water, the pelican goes through a number of contortions that are almost too quick for the eye to catch. It folds back its wings and turns its body so it is actually upside down and at about a 70-degree angle as it enters the water. A split second before striking the surface the bird extends its neck so the bill and its pouch are also upside down.

Impact automatically opens the pelican's elastic pouch completely, filling it with water and (the pelican hopes) fish. When a brown pelican pops back to the surface, the first thing it does is sit with its bill lowered so the water can drain out. The pouch is not normally used for storing food, for once the water is eliminated, the bird raises its bill and gulps down the fish. However, the pouch is a excellent scoop when schools of baitfish are plentiful and the pelican can skim them off the surface.

Most of the year, the heads and necks of brown pelicans are white. During the breeding season the heads acquire a distinctive yellow color, and the sides and back of the neck turn dark reddish brown. After courtship is over, the neck and head return to white.

Brown pelicans typically breed in colonies consisting of several hundred, sometimes several thousand, birds. Mangroves are a favorite habitat, but the birds make do with other trees or, if nothing else is available, by nesting on the ground. Whatever the location, the nest must be well above the storm surge and away from the reach of predators, such as raccoons.

A female usually lays between two and three eggs in her large, bulky nest; one clutch a year is normal. The eggs, white and about the size of jumbo chicken eggs, hatch in about a month. Both parents take turns incubating.

The newborn chicks emerge with a thin white fuzz and no feathers. Until feathers appear, the chicks have to rely on their parents' body heat for warmth. Once feathers are present, the chicks actively try to walk on their webbed feet, move their wings and practice holding up their large heads.

Parents take turns collecting and regurgitating food. Feedings may occur up to a half-dozen times a day. The chicks are voracious eaters. They plunge so deeply inside a parent's pouch that at one time it was believed the chicks were actually feeding on blood from the parent's breast. This is why the pelican was used in some Christian religious paintings as a symbol of the atonement, the reconciliation of man and God through Christ's sacrificial death.

Brown pelican chicks spend little time in the nest, only about five weeks. During this period the fledglings learn to fly by standing at the side of the nest and imitating a parent, which typically is standing on a nearby tree branch flapping its own wings. Soon the youngsters will practice their flying by winging and stepping from one tree branch to another.

Parents must also teach fledglings the necessary skill for dive-bombing fish. Parents take this very seriously and have been known to interrupt a youngster's diving practice in midflight if the form is badly off. The watery impact could possibly damage or

The nation's first national wildlife refuge was Florida's Pelican Island. Brown pelicans continue to nest there by the hundreds every spring.

even break a wing while a young bird is learning, but this seems to happen rarely.

Brown pelicans of every age sometimes develop the regrettable habit of frequenting fishing docks for handouts. The birds may become so tame and accustomed to being fed that they will try to intercept fishing lures being cast into the water. Sometimes a bird ends up with a hook impaled in its body or snagged in its pouch, or the pelican may become helplessly entangled in fishing line. If the hooks rip the pouch, the pelican could starve. A good number of brown pelicans brought to rehabilitation centers are there to have their pouches repaired.

Brown pelican populations were severely damaged in many parts of the country by the pesticide DDT. The DDT caused the adults to produce thinner egg shells that could not survive the incubation process. Fortunately, most of Florida's brown pelicans escaped this situation because the pesticide was not widely used throughout the state. Elsewhere in the Southeast, the declining brown pelican populations, along with those of the bald eagle, were important signals that something in the environment was very, very wrong. Florida's current brown pelican population is estimated at about 20,000 birds.

Hot Spots Brown pelicans are saltwater birds apt to be seen anytime, anywhere along the coast. It's uncommon to find a brown pelican in freshwater. The major nesting period is in early spring, although pelicans may nest year-round in the Keys.

Brown pelicans nest on many of the spoil islands in the Indian River in Central Florida, but none is more heavily used than **Pelican Island NWR,** the first national wildlife refuge. Established in 1903, the tiny, 3.5-acre island was protected by executive order of President Theodore Roosevelt to stop the "sport" of randomly shooting and killing birds on the nest. The refuge has since grown to encompass thousands of acres for thousands of nesting brown pelicans as well as egrets, cormorants, ibis and frigatebirds. The original Pelican Island can be viewed with a powerful scope from the town of Sebastian, where a rental boat can also be arranged. The islands are closed to visitors, but the birds can still be viewed from close quarters.

Going south on both coasts, brown pelicans are apt to be seen nesting in the branches of coastal mangroves anywhere the trees are thick and people and predators are scarce. That would include many small islets in the **Keys, Biscayne National Park near Homestead, Ten Thousand Islands NWR** on the northeast fringe of Everglades National Park, **Florida Bay** and the **Flamingo** area in Everglades National Park, **J. N. "Ding" Darling NWR** on Sanibel Island, **Cayo Costa Island** across from Boca Grande, and almost any other concentration of thick mangroves in the area.

Gaillard Island in Alabama's Mobile Bay is considered to have perhaps the largest brown pelican colony in the whole United States. As many as 2,500 different pairs nest there in a single season. It can be visited only by boat.

23

April Shorttakes

Birding the Dry Tortugas

One of the best birding areas—and also one of the least accessible—is the **Dry Tortugas** about 70 miles from Key West. From April to August, an incredible 100,000 sooty terns and brown noddies nest on Bush Key. The best place to view them is from **Fort Jefferson** on nearby **Garden Key**, which will also have plenty of frigatebirds flying over it this time of year. The summer heat can be horrific, so April and May are the best times to visit. However, the seas are also quite rough in these months, too rough even for big charter boats to make the crossing comfortably, so the best bet is to fly over for the day via seaplane.

Trips are available for a half or full day, or—if you truly like to rough it—you can camp out overnight. All supplies must be flown in, including water, since the only facilities available are a toilet. The old fort is now a national monument open to visitors during daylight hours only. Fort Jefferson, one of America's largest fortifications, is where Dr. Samuel Mudd was held prisoner after setting the broken leg of President Lincoln's assassin.

At this time of year birders have been fortunate enough to see rare West Indies species that have been blown off course. These may include the beautiful white-tailed tropic bird, Bahama mockingbird and brown and red-footed boobies.

The Key West Seaplane Service has been visiting the Dry Tortugas for years and is accustomed to dealing with the requests of both birders and campers. They can be reached at (305) 294-6978 or (800) 224-2-FLY; fax (305) 294-4660. They can also advise you on the gear you will need if you decide to stay overnight, which includes a well-screened tent, plenty of bug spray and at least a gallon of water per person. Snorkeling around the fort can be quite good when the winds are calm.

Nesting Roseate Spoonbills

Although roseate spoonbills nest during the winter in South Florida, the nesting season in Central Florida doesn't begin until April. One of the best places to check out is **Merritt Island NWR** near Titusville. Check at the visitor center (closed Mondays) on State Road 402 just east of Titusville: (407) 861-0667.

24

A Closer Look:
Worm Grunting

Walking through North Florida forests, you may hear a particularly strange sound you can't identify. It's a noise that will be repeated regularly, so you might initially mistake it for an animal or bird. But no, no creature alive makes sounds like a bullfrog band accompanied by a chorus of asthmatic pigs.

These are the sounds of worm grunting. Not grunting worms, mind you, but worm *grunting*. People are making that noise as they drive worms from the ground in a somewhat bizarre slithery roundup.

These aren't ordinary worms being grunted. They are native Florida worms and very special—so special that fishermen all over the South are willing to pay a premium to put them on their hooks. They are not only big worms, measuring between 6 and 8 inches, but they're tough, which makes them an ideal bait.

Unlike red wigglers and other worm types, grunt worms cannot be raised on worm farms, though people have tried. They have to be allowed to grow wild in the woods and then lured from the ground. Only a few North Florida counties have grunt worms in quantities large enough to wholesale them: Wakulla, Liberty and Calhoun Counties and the Apalachicola Forest. Selling grunt worms is a sizable enterprise, representing perhaps a million dollars worth of business every year.

Worm grunting has even become a tourist attraction, which just goes to show that if you can offer people something weird enough, they will come. Worm grunting is also known as worm fiddling, and International Worm Fiddling Contests are held every summer in the small community of Caryville. "You must be kidding!" is the usual comment from visitors who accidentally stumble upon the celebration.

Most grunt worms are taken in low, flat, cleared areas of the Apalachicola National Forest. Grunters have their best luck on grassy land or burned areas that have just started to grow back.

How are the worms grunted? You almost have to see it to believe it. A large wooden stake is one of the two key tools. Most grunters prefer to use a stob, or stake, that is 18 to 24 inches long and made of hardwood such as oak. Casual grunters may simply use a flat piece of board. When a grunter reaches his site, he pounds the stob into the ground to a depth of about 12 inches. Then he produces his other worm-calling tool, a piece of cast iron. A chunk of railroad track is a perfect instrument.

The iron is rubbed across the stob. The rubbing produces vibrations that, on a good day, will irritate every worm out of the ground within a 20-foot radius of the stake. In burned areas the stob is often placed next to a palmetto stump or some other large plant root to increase the vibrations.

Proper tuning and pitch are important because the amount of vibration generated is critical. Electric and gas-powered devices are undesirable because they are often too powerful and their vibrations so strong that they kill the worms. On the other hand, if the vibrations are too slight, the worms won't come out of the ground.

Weather is also an important worm grunting variable. When it's too wet, the ground can't be vibrated enough to drive the worms out. After a heavy rain, it usually takes about three days for the ground to regain the proper "conductivity." An overly dry condition also creates problems. In continued hot, dry weather the worms burrow so deep that the worm grunter's vibrations have little effect.

But when conditions are perfect, a single rub can bring up as many as 200 worms. Then the grunter—a lone worker who also gathers his own worms—must work like an octopus. The worms will retreat back into the ground within three to four minutes after the vibrations stop.

There's a knack to producing those good vibrations. The grunter needs to keep his weight center balanced over the stob while applying just the right amount of pressure as he rubs the iron across the wood.

Commercial worm grunters place their harvest in gallon cans that hold about 500 worms each. The worms are then sold to a wholesaler by the gallon. On an exceptional day, a person might gather as many as 14 or 15 gallons before the grunting stops, between 10 A.M. and noon: The worms dig deeper as the day gets hotter.

Wholesalers ship the worms in smaller containers that hold old sawdust, in which the worms can survive for five to eight days. Worms can be grunted throughout the year, but they're collected primarily in spring and summer months when angling activity is at its highest.

Grunt worms may be shipped to Georgia, Alabama, the Carolinas and Tennessee, where they go by several different names. In the Panhandle town of Sopchoppy, they're known simply as earthworms. In other places they are called grunt worms or, in parts of Georgia, Louisiana pinks. Compared to the out-of-state trade, relatively few of the worms are sold in Florida.

Can an area be overfiddled if it's worked too much? Not according to veteran worm grunters. They say the big worms will disappear, leaving only small ones, when an area is scrubbed regularly, but that the situation is usually temporary. The big worms will start reappearing in as little as a week.

May

Notes

25

Nesting Sea Turtles

One of the best places in the nation—indeed anywhere—to view nesting sea turtles is on Florida's Atlantic Coast. A staggering 80 percent of the sea turtle nests laid on the entire East Coast occur between New Smyrna and Boca Raton. Most of these nests belong to loggerhead sea turtles. As many as 15,000 have been counted in a single season (May to September). The only comparable loggerhead nesting beaches are half a world away, in the Gulf of Oman.

Adult sea turtles are sizable animals; even the smallest weighs between 200 and 300 pounds. To closely approach such a large endangered creature on its own territory, without the slightest danger, is remarkable. To do it when the creature is nesting is extraordinary.

All sea turtles are classified as endangered except for the loggerhead, which is listed as a threatened species. Five of the world's eight sea turtle species nest in the United States, and Florida in particular. They are the loggerhead *(Caretta caretta);* the green *(Chelonia mydas);* the leatherback *(Dermochelys coriacea);* the hawksbill *(Eretmochelys imbricata);* and the rarest of all sea turtles, the Kemp's ridley *(Lepidochelys kempi).*

Sea turtle nesting grounds are limited exclusively to the Southeast region. They extend from the Florida Keys to Virginia on the Atlantic Coast, and from Texas through Florida along the Gulf of Mexico. Along the Gulf of Mexico, Florida again claims the greatest nest count (between Pinellas and Monroe Counties), but the nests are far, far fewer than on the Atlantic side. Sea turtles do not nest on the United States's Pacific Coast.

The earliest sea turtle fossils date back about 150,000,000 years, to a time when vast shallow seas covered much of the earth. Sea turtles adapted in several specialized ways because of their watery habitat. Their forelimbs are sleek and paddlelike to propel them swiftly through the ocean. Their shells are more streamlined and less boxy than many land species. Because they spend almost their entire lives in the water, sea turtles developed more than just lungs for breathing. They are able to exchange oxygen and carbon dioxide with the surrounding water thanks to extensive capillary vascularization in their cloacal cavity and their buccal cavity. By circulating water in these cavities and also by reducing their metabolism dramatically, sea turtles can stay submerged from between 40 minutes to 5 hours if they are not active and the water is not too warm.

Sea turtles do not have teeth. Their birdlike beaks and jaws are quite powerful, able to crush, tear or chew food with little problem. Like all reptiles, sea turtles lack external ears. Instead, the sea turtle eardrum is covered by skin.

With a few exceptions, male sea turtles spend 100 percent of their lives in the ocean. Female turtles have only one need of the land: to deposit their eggs. Adult sea turtles are solitary creatures most of the time. Their only true social interaction is said to occur during courtship and mating. Mating may take place on the ocean bottom, the surface or in open water. Mating occurs about 30 days before the females begin nesting. The early-season matings will fertilize an entire season's eggs.

It's a common assumption that sea turtles nest on the same beach where they were hatched. This is not a known certainty because

Scheduled turtle walks to view nesting loggerhead turtles are extremely popular. More loggerheads nest on Florida east coast beaches than anywhere else in the Western Hemisphere.

it's impossible to track a turtle from the time it hatches until it returns to nest. However, once a turtle begins to use a specific beach for nesting, she does appear to return to the same beach season after season.

Since turtles often winter hundreds of miles from their nesting beaches, it is a mystery how they find their way back year after year. Perhaps they follow a special taste or smell that is unique to each region of the ocean or coastline, or they may navigate by the earth's magnetic fields. It's likely that sea turtles employ a combination of senses to construct their natural guidance system.

Another common misconception is that females tend to deposit their eggs around the time of the full moon. The theory is that the full moon creates a higher tide, which in turn will better hide the nesting trails. Excellent logic, but it doesn't appear to be true. Turtles nest during all phases of the moon, with cycles of 10 to about 17 days between nestings.

Turtle eggs incubate for about 60 days. The hatchlings normally break out of the eggs at night. The daytime heat could be fatal to hatchlings, especially if they did not find the sea immediately. The cool of the night is safer, and the cover of darkness foils many predators.

Life is precarious for hatchlings because their small size makes them easy prey for birds and fish. They seem to recognize this, for they totally disappear for their first year of life. Scientists cannot agree where the hatchlings go until they reach 8 to 10 inches in length. Leatherbacks and ridleys are rarely seen until they mature. One popular idea is that the hatchlings go out to sea and live in the drift lines where seaweed and other debris float in long streaks on the surface. Since hatchlings cannot dive more than a few inches, the driftline theory makes a lot of sense.

Wherever they may go as youngsters, sea turtles spend their juvenile and subadult years in bays, estuaries and shallow coastal waters. At maturity they travel to traditional feeding grounds to join other adults. Sea turtles are believed to live for a fairly long time, from 80 to 100 years or more.

Loggerhead turtles nest in Florida from late April to September. An average clutch consists of about 100 eggs. The eggs incubate for about 60 days before producing 2-inch hatchlings that weigh only three-fifths of an ounce.

After nesting, the females travel long distances to their feeding grounds, which may be as far away as Cuba or the Dominican Republic. There are seemingly excellent nesting beaches in those regions and why the loggerheads commute to the United States is anyone's guess. In the past, when turtles were more abundant in the Caribbean, the beaches there may have been fully utilized by greens and hawksbills. Green turtles, incidentally, are not named for their external coloration, which is commonly olive brown with dark streaks, but from the color of their body fat, which was once made into soup.

Adult turtles are of such a size that they have few natural enemies. The need to bury the eggs on land has always been the sea turtle's greatest vulnerability. A sea turtle on shore is a turtle at risk. In the past, there was a natural balance at work as long as the traditional nesting sites were left intact. It was the arrival of Europeans that changed the balance in our part of the world.

Early explorers quickly recognized that sea turtles were an ideal fresh meat source. On sailing voyages, turtles could be kept alive indefinitely aboard ship by keeping them on their backs. Eventually, turtles became popular food in Europe. In England, the clear soup made from the green turtle soon became a status symbol at important banquets. Today, it is not only illegal to kill sea turtles for their meat or to steal their eggs, it is illegal to import turtle products into the United States.

Hot Spots

Alabama's **Dauphin Island** and the nearby beaches along Fort Morgan Peninsula in the **Bon Secour NWR** all attract loggerhead turtles. Compared to Florida the numbers are quite low, with only 40 to 60 crawls a year on Dauphin Island. However, compared to 15 years ago, when a single crawl would have been newsworthy, this is a vast improvement. Considering the amount of territory and the small numbers, however, the chances of actually finding a nesting turtle are remote. Nesting occurs around the beginning of July and the eggs hatch right around Labor Day.

Cumberland Island National Seashore on Georgia's southeasternmost tip is an important nesting ground for loggerheads from May to August, with June and July the best months. Ranger-led activities include turtle walks, but you're allowed to locate your own turtle along the island's 16 miles of white-sand beach. Turtles will almost always be found nesting on the Atlantic side. Never approach a turtle as it crawls from the water; wait until it begins nesting. For the appropriate etiquette, consult *Sea Turtles: The Watchers' Guide*.

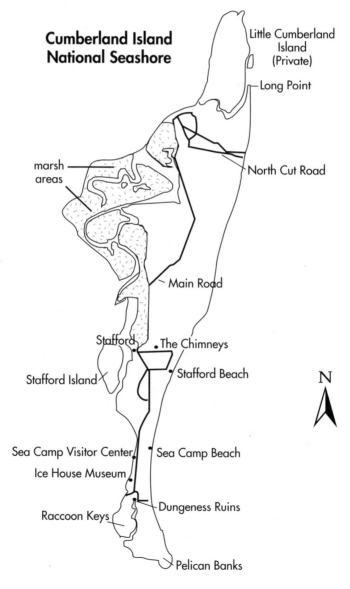

The 45-minute ferry trip to Cumberland Island leaves from the town of St. Mary's; from I-95, take Exit 2 and follow State Road 40 east. Camping is permitted at both primitive and developed sites, but reservations must be made in advance. For turtle, camping and ferry schedule information, call (912) 882-4335 between 10 A.M. and 2 P.M., Monday through Friday.

In Florida, organized turtle walks are incredibly popular. There are far more people who want to view nesting sea turtles than there are spaces for them. Advance reservations are mandatory. All of the programs are held on the east coast, where your chances of viewing sea turtles are best. Only nesting loggerheads, a threatened species, may be viewed on the turtle walks.

In order not to interrupt or disturb the turtles, spectators are not allowed to use a flashlight or take flash photography. Only those scouting for turtles or the group leaders may use flashlights. For pictures of the egg laying—which you generally are permitted to photograph, but verify this ahead of time—you will need fast film and a tripod. Expect mosquitoes to be fierce. Wear long pants, long-sleeve shirts, shoes and socks. Be sure to bring insect repellent.

Canaveral National Seashore/Merritt Island NWR jointly conduct walks. The programs start at 8 P.M. and last until midnight. If a turtle is not sighted by 11 P.M., the watch is canceled. Walks are held at both the northern and southern ends of Canaveral National Seashore. In the northern section, participants assemble at the Canaveral National Seashore Information Center, 7611 South Atlantic Avenue, New Smyrna Beach. Southern walks depart from the Merritt Island NWR Visitor Information Center, 5 miles east of Titusville on State Road 406. Traditionally, more walks are held at the southern end. Reservations for the northern section are made by calling the Canaveral Information Center at (904) 428-3384. Calls are taken May 15 for the June walks, June 15 for the July turtle watches. Reservations for the southern district are taken May 15 for both the June and July programs. Both the northern and southern districts have a road 5 miles long with boardwalks at various intervals. Turtles are observed within one-quarter mile of a boardwalk. Groups are limited to 25 per watch. The age limit is eight years old. In addition, the first Saturday in May is designated as Turtle Day, and the U.S. Fish and Wildlife Service takes reservations for its turtle walks on Canaveral National Seashore; call (407) 861-0667.

The **Orlando Science Center** (743 West Winter Park Street, Orlando), as part of its Summer Adventure Series, offers turtle walks on Friday and Saturday evenings in June and July. Classes are limited to 20 and begin in mid-June. For information/enrollment, call (407) 896-7151. Class members meet at the Science Center at 6 P.M. for an orientation and lecture that lasts between one and two hours. Following the educational presentation, class members carpool to **Melbourne Beach,** where the actual turtle walk is held beginning around 10 P.M. It ends according to when a turtle is found. Since the Melbourne area is the largest nesting area of loggerhead turtles in the Western Hemisphere, the chances of seeing a turtle are unusually good. Also offering turtle walks in the Melbourne area during June and July is the **Sea Turtle Preservation Society of Melbourne Beach.** Their contact number is (407) 676-1701.

The **Sebastian Inlet State Recreation Area** at 9700 South A1A, Melbourne Beach, conducts walks on Friday, Saturday, Sunday and Monday nights in June and July. Reservations are taken two weeks ahead of a scheduled walk. The first call of the day is taken at 9 A.M. Groups are limited to 20 people. Call (407) 589-2147. You can make reservations for up to six persons. Assemble at the McLarty Treasure Museum at 9 P.M. for orientation and a sea turtle presentation. The McLarty Museum is 2 miles south of the Sebastian Inlet Bridge on A1A. The walks are conducted in almost all conditions (including rain) unless lightning is present. The recommended lower age limit is eight years old. The beach walk could be up to 3 miles in length. The program ends at midnight.

Florida Power and Light is a nationally recognized leader in helping protect plants and wildlife, particularly manatees and sea turtles. Turtle walks are conducted Wednesday, Friday and Saturday evenings at the **St. Lucie Nuclear Power Plant** on **Hutchinson Island.** Reservations may be made by calling (800) 334-5483 (Florida only) after May 15. Walks begin at 9 P.M.

with an orientation and education program. Activities usually end by midnight but may last longer if the turtle under observation hasn't completed her nesting. Walks are limited to 50 people, who wait in the auditorium until scouts find a nesting loggerhead. Then everyone is taken by truck to the nearest access gate, so walks are brief. A limited number of spaces are reserved on each walk for guests staying at the three hotels on South Hutchinson Island.

The **Marinelife Center of Juno Beach**, 1200 U.S. 1, Loggerhead Park, Juno Beach, conducts turtle walks on Sunday, Tuesday, Wednesday and Thursday evenings in June and July. Reservations may be made beginning May 1 on a first-come basis: (407) 627-8280. There is a limit of 50 persons per watch, with no restrictions on age. The walks cover about 300 yards of beach. A donation of $2.50 per person is requested. People assemble at 9 P.M. at the Loggerhead Park tennis court pavilion, 1200 U.S. 1, Juno Beach. If no turtle is sighted by 11:30 P.M., the watch is ended. The Marinelife Center is the only turtle hospital between Orlando and Fort Lauderdale that cares for sick or injured turtles. Once the turtles are rehabilitated, they are returned to the sea.

The **John D. MacArthur Beach State Park**, 10900 State Road 703, North Palm Beach, conducts walks on Mondays and Thursdays in June and July that last from one to two hours. Reservations are taken no sooner than the first working day following Memorial Day: (407) 624-6952. Groups are limited to 25. Participants first assemble about 8:30 P.M. at the park's nature center for an educational program on sea turtles. Participants reassemble on the main dune crossover, about midway on the 1.8-mile beach, while scouts are sent to the north and south to locate turtles. Hope for a breeze to keep the mosquitoes down. Sand gnats are sometimes more of a problem. The maximum amount of territory covered by walking is under 2 miles. There are no age restrictions. Normal state park admission fees apply.

John U. Lloyd State Recreation Area, 6503 North Ocean Drive, Dania, holds walks on Wednesday and Friday evenings in June and July. They last between one and three hours, depending on when a nesting turtle is sighted. Reservations are taken beginning May 1; call the park at (305) 923-2833. Each group is limited to a maximum of 25 people with a minimum age limit of six years. The program begins at 9 P.M. with an orientation and presentation at the park's educational facility. You are encouraged to arrive earlier to view the turtle shells and skulls collected over the years. Information brochures are also available. The walk covers about a half-mile of beachfront. Normal state park admission fees apply.

Hobe Sound Nature Center at Hobe Sound holds walks Tuesday and Thursday evenings in June and July. Walks are usually over by midnight but have been known to last until 1 A.M. Make reservations by calling the Nature Center at (407) 546-2067 starting in April. Thirty people are allowed to sign up for each walk, with no minimum age restrictions. Waiting lists are also taken in case of last-minute cancellations. Participants assemble in the center's classroom at the Hobe Sound NWR beginning at 9 P.M. for a 40-minute presentation. The refuge is located on U.S. 1 in southern Martin County. After the presentation, participants drive the five minutes from the Refuge to Hobe Sound Public Beach. Scouts will have arrived ahead of the group to locate a turtle along a stretch of beach that is approximately 1 mile in length. The actual walk to the turtle is normally less than a half-mile. Participants wait in the relative luxury of a covered pavilion with restrooms and drinking fountain until the scouts locate a turtle. Donations are requested.

Museum of Discovery and Science, 401 Southwest Second Street, Fort Lauderdale, during the summer months exhibits a visible nest of live incubating eggs. In addition, you have the opportunity to actually touch two of the live display turtles. The display turtles are not captured specimens but are always animals born at the museum. Organized beach walks take place in the heart of Fort Lauderdale itself on a stretch of beach where the condo lights are not overpowering. Walks are held once or twice a week during the peak nesting season—during the last two weeks of June and the first two weeks of July. Reservations are taken beginning around April 15: (305) 467-6637, ext. 315. Ask for the group-tour administrator. Groups are limited to 50.

Participants assemble at 9 P.M. at the museum for an educational presentation and inspection of the museum's sea turtle exhibits, then caravan to the South Beach parking lot across from the Bahia Mar resort and marina. Depending on the turtle's location, a walk could cover a maximum of 3 miles. There is no minimum age limit. Walks normally end by 1 A.M. at the latest.

26

Pristine Tropical Hammock

This is one place where location was and is everything. Always inconvenient to reach, and with plenty of mosquitoes waiting for those who visit, undeveloped Lignumvitae Key contains the largest virgin West Indian hardwood forest left in the United States. As such, these 280 acres provide what is perhaps the best preserved glimpse anywhere of the tropical foliage that formerly covered many of the Florida Keys. Ignoring the few human additions, Lignumvitae is one of the few places in the Keys where it is possible to imagine that only a handful of people have preceded you.

An estimated 133 species of trees, including poisonwood, strangler fig and gumbo-limbo, all of West Indian origin, constitute the tall forest. It's believed the various species established themselves as seeds that had been carried from other tropical islands by wind, waves and in the digestive tracts of migratory birds.

That this is the only virgin tropical hammock remaining screams volumes about the senseless destruction that's often taken place in the Keys. Many similar hammocks were destroyed to take advantage of the profitable trade in, of all things, snail shells. The different islets of the Keys vary not only in vegetation, but at one time each landfall claimed its own distinctive species of snail. In order to increase the value of particular snails, it was common practice to burn a hammock after enough snails had been collected from it.

Lignumvitae Key never suffered this fate. It had very little human interference, although pirates and the Spanish probably visited. What may have kept more early Europeans away was what still makes a summer visit in the rainy season something of a nightmare: mosquitoes.

The Matheson family, who purchased the island in 1919 for $1, was responsible for keeping the island in its preserved state. Matheson was a chemist and, like Thomas Edison in Fort Myers, very interested in the chemical properties of trees. He cleared 14 acres on which to grow different kinds of non-native trees, but none survived, another reason the island remained pristine.

Today, the four-bedroom house that Matheson built serves as the ranger headquarters. The house was originally used by the caretakers who were in charge of clearing a number of trails and maintaining the island. Although the building was certainly spacious, living in it was a challenge for even true pioneers. All supplies had to be brought in by boat. A windmill generated the only power. Water was always a critical problem. The 12,000-gallon cistern was filled only by the 40–45 inches of annual rainfall (among the sparsest in all of Florida). When guests visited the island overnight, they were expected to bring their own water.

Mosquito spraying did not begin until the 1960s, and screens in the 1930s and 1940s were still a luxury. So the window shutters were often closed, and smudge pots had to be burned inside and outside to discourage the bugs. According to some sources, Floridians who for years lived in this kind of smoke sometimes contracted black lung disease, just as coal miners do, but the Keys fatalities apparently were never associated with the smudge pots.

When the elder Matheson died in the 1930s, the son who inherited the island allowed the 14 acres to regrow naturally. When the last Matheson died in 1953, the new owners decided to modernize the property with a golf course, condos and apartments. To do that, a causeway to the island had to be built, but taxpayers vetoed the bridge. No new development ever took place, and the island was maintained as it was.

Fortunately, a visiting scientist recognized the unique value of the island and began a campaign for its protection. The state purchased the key in 1970 for $2 million, but with certain restrictions: that the carrying capacity be limited to 25 people in the forest or the house at any one time.

The endangered lignum vitae tree, for which the island is named, is one of the rarest as well as one of the world's most fabled trees. In the fifteenth century the tree was catalogued as one of the original species in the Garden of Eden, and some believed that the Holy Grail was carved from it. What helped give rise to such legends is the tree's longevity: It is said to live for a thousand years or more.

Lignum vitae wood, still called holywood in the Bahamas, also was considered to have important medicinal properties capable of curing many serious conditions such as syphilis and impotence. For treatment, scraps of the wood were put into tea bags and boiled. Only the wealthy could afford to buy fresh tea bags; poorer people would buy the used tea bags, and the truly penniless could only pray beneath the wood at church.

Remove all the legends and fairy tales and you still uncover one very impressive wood. Lignum vitae is the second heaviest wood in the three Americas. Only the black ironwood, which weighs 95 pounds per cubic foot, compared to lignum vitae's 80 to 85 pounds, is heavier. Oak, by comparison, is only 55 to 60 pounds per cubic foot.

The lignum vitae natural resins, which help provide its strength, also make the heart of the wood appear as if it has been polished. This oiliness made the wood very popular in shipbuilding wherever lines and ropes were used, because its unusual natural properties reduced friction. Lignum vitae wood in the form of ball bearings is used today in some turbine engines, although less-expensive nylon bearings are replacing the wooden ones.

Lignumvitae Key is in the northernmost range for the tree, which means the specimens here are not necessarily the best or even very impressive. Instead, these trees are under constant stress because the conditions (rainfall, sun, soil pH) are at their extreme limits. The lignum vitae trees on Lignumvitae Key manifest this stress through their small size. A tree that is perhaps 1,000 years old is not some towering giant like a redwood but might be only 35 feet high. The best time of the year to see the tree's delicate blossoms is in May.

Of course there are 132 other types of trees here as well, though they hardly receive the same kind of attention. Just as the snail shells differed throughout the Keys, so do the dominant canopy trees vary from island to island. On Lignumvitae Key, the gumbo-limbo and poisonwood are dominant.

The gumbo-limbo is sometimes locally referred to as the "tourist tree" because of its distinctive red bark, a bright hue similar to that of newly arrived visitors after their first day in the Florida sun—hotter than on any other coast in the continental United States. Gumbo-limbo is important to many bird species because it grows a fruit that is all nut, without any meat. The birds seek out the nuts because the Keys, like most of South Florida, lack the gravel and stones required for some avian digestion.

Gumbo-limbo, long a favorite wood for carousel horses, is in the same family as frankincense, so the cut wood has a very pleasing aroma. And despite the lignum vitae tree's reputation for effecting medical cures, the gumbo-limbo's curative qualities are better documented. Peel back the reddish dead bark and you'll find a living green bark underneath that contains an acid that helps not only headaches but gout and fevers. Locals also use the bark mixed with aloe as a cure for poisonwood, which coincidentally happens to be the other major tree on the island. Poisonwood, in the same family as poison ivy and poison sumac but much more potent, is toxic in every part of the tree except the flowers. It has a compound leaf with five leaflets.

The trails on Lignumvitae Key are pristine in appearance. Thanks to the policy of carefully managing and monitoring visitors, there is no graffiti carved on the trees and no litter on the trail (smoking is prohibited). The park service is also diligent about removing any exotic plant species that might try to settle on the island.

In the 1930s Lignumvitae Key was near the eye of the hurricane that destroyed the Overseas Railroad, which was the first link ever to connect the Keys. Lignumvitae Key and its hardwood forest survived that handily. So, barring some unseen natural or political disaster, this island should appear virtually the same in 3001 as it does in 2001. In a thousand years, some of today's young lignum vitae trees will be just reaching old age. They will be reaching adolescence when our generation passes.

Hot Spots

Even today, **Lignumvitae Key** can be reached only by boat. Located a mile offshore and northwest of Upper Matecumbe Key, access is strictly limited. Boats that meet a ranger for a one-hour organized tour of the forest depart several times daily from **Robbie's Marina** at Mile Marker 77.5, south of Islamorada. The fee is $20 per person; call ahead for reservations at (305) 294-1124.

The snails remain on Lignumvitae Key. They are most easily seen after the onset of the rainy season, when they break out of a protective cocoon that allows them to preserve water. Once on the move they eat lichen growing on the trees and travel as much as 25 feet a day, which can make it challenging for rangers to keep accurate track of individuals to show visitors.

The ranger guide will tell about many other interesting trees, such as the inkwood, a threatened species because so much of it has been cut down. The sap in the tree's cambium layer is a permanent black, which is how the tree gained its name. The inside wood is a very different shade, the color of butter, and this part of the tree was popular for tool handles. The ranger will have many, many more stories. One short visit here is not enough.

Although Lignumvitae Key is one of the state's best-known botanical sites, two other places in the Keys are also noteworthy for their vegetation.

The **Key Largo Hammock State Botanical Site** contains the largest tract of West Indian hardwood hammock remaining in the United States. It is also home to 84 protected species of plants and animals, including the rare American crocodile and the Key Largo wood rat. This is a self-guided walk with brochures sometimes available at the unmanned entrance. Open 8 A.M. to 5 P.M. daily. Located in Key Largo just 0.5 mile north of U.S. 1 on County Road 905, the alternate route into the Keys via Card Sound. For more information, call (305) 451-7008 or 1202.

In Marathon in the Middle Keys, the 63.5 **Crane Point Hammock** holds the last virgin palm hammock in North America. Especially plentiful is the thatch palm, which has been cut down almost everywhere else to build roofs for houses and waterfront bars. The site, which also contains the remnants of an old Bahamian village, is located in the middle of Marathon on the grounds of the **Museum of Natural History of the Florida Keys**, 5550 Overseas Highway, Marathon, FL 33050; (305) 743-9100. Open 9 A.M. to 5 P.M. daily except Sundays when hours vary according to the season.

27

Eastern Scrub Jays

The scrub jay is one of Florida's friendliest songbirds as well as one of its most threatened. Although scrub jays thrive in the western United States and Mexico, east of the Mississippi they exist only in Florida. At one time the range of the Florida scrub jay extended over 7,000 square miles. But now so much of its habitat has been transformed for agricultural and urban use that the scrub jay population has dwindled dramatically. For example, the healthy population of birds that once ranged all along the Atlantic Coast has been fragmented into isolated communities. In 1987 the situation was serious enough that the Florida scrub jay was classified as a threatened species.

As their name implies, scrub jays live in a highly specialized territory, one where tall trees provide canopy cover over no more than 20 percent of an area. In ideal scrub jay habitat, oaks between 3 and 8 feet tall blanket between 50 to 90 percent of an area, while sparse vegetation no higher than 6 inches (or perhaps only bare ground) covers the remaining region.

The Florida scrub jay looks similar to the far more common blue jay. Both are the same size, about 12 inches in length, but the scrub jay is paler in color and lacks a crest. The scrub jay also lacks the white wing spots and white tail-feather tips typical of the blue jay. Instead, the scrub jay wears a collar of blue feathers that separates its white throat from its gray underparts, and it has a white line over the eye that blends into a whitish forehead. The white forehead and eyebrows distinguish the Florida jay from those of western states.

Highly intelligent birds, scrub jays sometimes become very tame, and some like to be hand-fed peanuts. At the golf courses where families of the birds reside, scrub jays will sometimes boldly perch on a person's shoulder or head in hopes of a handout. It's not uncommon for entire neighborhoods to adopt families of friendly scrub jays, a concern for some conservationists who feel the birds should not be fed by humans. A feeding ban of any sort is not likely to work, for both scrub jays and people like interacting with each other.

Although scrub jays will happily take peanuts from people, their normal diet is quite varied. It includes both plants and animals. Acorns, the main staple during fall and winter, are consumed year-round. In spring and summer, insects become the main food source, supplemented by frogs, mice, toads, lizards, snakes and birds' eggs. Corn, sunflower seeds, saw palmetto drupes and greenbrier berries are also eaten when available.

The family life of scrub jays is unusually complex. A family, which consists of a breeding pair and some of their offspring, establishes its own territory and vigorously protects it from other scrub jays. A family's territory may average between 5 and 50 acres, though 25 acres is most common.

The breeding pair, which mate for life, are usually around three or four years of age. Their mating season is short, from early March to late May and sometimes into June. A nest is built between 3 and 10 feet above ground in one of the scrub oaks. Nests, made of twigs and lined with finer material, are used only once. The average clutch is three greenish brown-spotted eggs that hatch after about 17 days. Seventeen is also the average number of days that it takes for the nestlings to fledge from the time they hatch. The juveniles are distinctive, with a dusky brown head and neck that lasts until their first molt, following the first summer.

Unlike any of Florida's other songbirds, both non-nesting females but particularly males remain part of the family for several years. These hangers-on serve as valuable helpers by defending the family territory and feeding the nestlings and fledglings. However, helpers do not assist in nest building or incubating. Not surprisingly, studies have shown that breeding pairs with helpers raise their young more successfully than do birds without helpers.

Fire is essential for maintaining scrub jay habitat. An area needs to be burned every 5 to 20 years in order to keep scrub vegetation at the proper height. As scrub jay habitat becomes more scarce, the birds are seemingly able to adapt and live indefinitely in recreational and residential regions as long as some scrub, or open or green areas, exist nearby.

Hot Spots It's possible to attract scrub jays to you with owl calls and squeaks. Scrub jay vocalizations are not as raucous as those of blue jays.

You'll find scrub jays in numerous places, some quite easy to reach. For instance, around the parking lot at **Fort Matanzas National Monument** south of St. Augustine on Highway A1A. The **Ocala National Forest** has some of the state's best remaining oak scrub territory, and it's easily reached by driving the forest roads; you'll need to get a map from one of the ranger stations. Driving south on U.S. 27 from Ocala south to Lake Placid is sometimes good for spotting scrub jays. In Lake Placid, the **Archbold Biological Station** has more than 5,000 preserved acres of land, and its resident scrub jays are one of the station's ongoing study projects.

On the east coast, the **Merritt Island NWR** has excellent scrub habitat between the visitor center and Playalinda Beach at the Canaveral National Seashore.

Oscar Scherer State Park is one of the best places on the west coast to find scrub jays, particularly in the scrub northwest of Lake Osprey. From the town of Osprey, go 2 miles south on U.S. 41. For more information, call (813) 483-5956.

In Southwest Florida, scrub jays are common and quite tame along the entrance road at the **Franklin Lock Recreation Area** near Naples. The area around **La Belle** in the Lake Okeechobee area offers good spotting possibilities on County Road 731 (Thigpen Road), State Road 74 and State Road 29 at the first culvert.

But perhaps the most reliable place to see scrub jays up close and in big numbers is at **Jonathan Dickinson State Park** on the lower east coast near Jupiter. It would be rare indeed if you did not find plenty of tame scrub jays, particularly where the road crosses over the railroad tracks. If the birds prove elusive, start "pishing" and see what happens, especially if you have peanuts.

28

Ospreys: Bald Eagle
Look-Alikes

If Leonardo da Vinci hadn't thought of the helicopter first, then the American osprey surely would have inspired someone else to invent the machine. This distinctive bird with the brown-and-white head performs a remarkable imitation of a hovering helicopter as it seemingly hangs in the air, its beating wings holding it in one spot. It's almost as if the bird is pausing to plot its speed and trajectory before swooping down on its prey.

Overall, the flight of the osprey is rather relaxed; it glides because it does not have to take other birds in flight or animals on the ground. When it spots a fish near the surface, the osprey drops vertically, feet-first, to snare the fish in its talons. The osprey's feet are well adapted for taking such slippery prey: They have sharp spinelike projections that make it easier to grip the fish.

Often mistaken for the bald eagle, the American osprey is frequently found in that bird's company since the two often share the same territory, yet an osprey is only a small shadow of America's national symbol. A more compact bird, it is only 22 to 25 inches in height compared to the bald eagle's more lofty 35 inches. However, its wings are unusually long for its size, extending between 55 and 73 inches.

What frequently accounts for the confusion between an osprey and a bald eagle is that both birds are dark colored with whitish-colored heads. However, their color patterns are very different and easy to distinguish. Where both the head and tail feathers of a bald eagle are an unmistakable white, the upper head and tail feathers of the osprey are colored. The osprey has a distinct brown band through its eye and on the side of its face that easily marks it as different from a bald eagle.

In the Southeast, wherever there is water and fish, the osprey is almost always present. The osprey prefers to nest in the limbs of dead trees, on top of channel markers and atop telephone or electrical transmission poles. The nests are tall and wide, made of sticks and reused year after year. Ospreys add to their nests each season, so a long-used nest tends to be huge.

The osprey is one hawk that farmers generally don't mind having on their land, since a nesting pair will usually keep other hawks away. For this reason, some people have erected platforms to encourage the birds to nest in a particular area.

The female lays between two and four eggs that are white with brown splotches. The birds are very protective of their nests and, with loud screams, sometimes even dive-bomb intruders. Ospreys were among the birds damaged by the indiscriminate use of pesticides. Their populations are making a strong comeback.

The osprey, often mistaken for the bald eagle because the two often share the same territory, is easily distinguished by the brown streak behind its eye.

Hot Spots

Fish are the sole diet of the osprey, so it is always found near water—fresh or salt, inland or on the coast, wherever the pickings are good. Look for the big nests in tall, dead trees bordering any waterway; it's surprising how many nests can be found this way.

The **Savannah Coastal Refuges** where the Savannah River borders Georgia and South Carolina have miles of freshwater marsh and tidal rivers that are excellent osprey habitat. **Wassaw Island,** one of the famed Golden Isles, is a good nesting area. Access is by boat only. Contact the refuge office for information on how to arrange trips: (912) 652-4415. **Cumberland Island National Seashore,** which is limited to 300 visitors a day, has osprey nests. **Okefenokee NWR** has quite a few nests that are easy to find near the three access points.

Another good nesting area that can be seen only by boat is Florida's Gulf Coast **Chassahowitzka NWR,** near the city of Crystal River (the refuge headquarters) and the town of Homosassa. The water here is clear and fish-filled, which also attracts lots of anglers. Boats, either power or canoes, are readily available for easy exploration. It's not necessary to go into obscure winding waterways, because the ospreys like to be near the center of action, close to the main channel. The refuge office, open 7:30 A.M. to 4 P.M. weekdays, is located at 1502 Southeast King's Bay Drive, Crystal River; (904) 563-2088. The **Lower Suwannee NWR,** which must be explored by boat, has as many as 150 pairs of nesting ospreys, an unusually heavy concentration. Boats can be rented at the town of Suwannee or at Fowler's Bluff.

Anywhere along the **St. Johns River** is possible osprey habitat, but the nests are most easily seen while cruising the river. **Ocean Pond** in **Osceola National Forest** west of Jacksonville has frequent osprey sightings. In the region of the **Ocala National Forest,** it seems that every channel marker in the St. Johns is a nest. For land cruisers, drive State Road 19, which parallels the river. Ospreys are frequently seen along here in the trees that have been left for them in clear-cut areas. From land, an active nest is visible at **Blue Spring State Park** near Orange City. The **Lake Woodruff NWR** is a hotbed of nesting activity, but again it takes a boat to locate many of the nests.

Ospreys also nest in **Wekiwa Springs State Park** near Orlando, and in **Orlando Wetlands Park** near the town of Christmas on State Road 50 between Orlando and Titusville. From the viewpoint of a driver's seat, you'll probably do just as well at **Merritt Island NWR** near Titusville. Explore the maze of paved and dirt roads and you're bound to see ospreys.

Osprey nests are quite visible at **Myakka River State Park** near Sarasota. They are quite easy to reach at the **J. N. "Ding" Darling NWR** on Sanibel Island near Fort Myers. The combination of sheltered waterways, canoe trails and access to one of the richest fishing areas along the entire Gulf Coast make Ding Darling a sure bet. The wildlife drive (closed on Fridays) and canoe trails provide excellent access. Weekends tend to be extremely crowded. Call (813) 472-1100. Across the street from the refuge is **Sanibel-Captiva Conservation Foundation,** which has its own nesting ospreys. At nearby **Cayo Costa State Park,** ospreys nest year-round.

Continuing south on the Gulf side, **Briggs Nature Center** has ospreys near its observation deck. The center is located off State Road 951, the road to Marco Island. Although the **National Key Deer Refuge** on Big Pine Key is best known for its endangered deer population, ospreys are easy to find here as well. The birds favor the telephone poles that line the streets crisscrossing parts of the refuge. This is one spot where all the osprey viewing is land-based. Ospreys are also commonly sighted in **Everglades National Park.**

On the Atlantic Coast, look for ospreys at **John D. MacArthur Beach State Park** and **Loxahatchee NWR,** both near the Palm Beaches. **Wakulla Springs State Park,** on the crystal-clear Wakulla River near Tallahassee, is loaded with osprey nests best seen from the river cruise boats. Also near Tallahassee is **St. Marks NWR,** which has an estimated 100 osprey nests. **St. Vincent NWR,** formerly a private island that can be reached only by private boat, also contains a healthy osprey nesting population. The refuge headquarters is located in the town of Apalachicola, quite a distance from the refuge; (904) 653-8808. Alabama's **Little Dauphin Island** also has a number of active nests, as do the forks near the **Fowl River.**

29

May Shorttakes

Birding the Keys

The Florida Keys are a birder's paradise year-round, but the late spring and early summer months are especially good for viewing nesting birds of many different species. They include the mangrove cuckoo, magnificent frigatebird, Antillean nighthawk, reddish egret and many more. The National Audubon Research Department offers the most detailed guide available, *Birding in the Florida Keys*. Audubon requests a modest $2 donation to cover postage and handling. Write National Audubon Research Department, 115 Indian Mound Trail, Tavernier, FL 33070; (305) 852-5092. The booklet is also available at The Florida Keys Wild Bird Center at MM 93.8 in Key Largo.

A Great White Heron on the Florida Keys: One of many birds that commonly make their nests here.

Spotlighting Ghosts

Georgia's **Cumberland Island National Seashore** is loaded with ghosts, the sand-colored ghost crabs that are active at night and that can vanish into the sand as quickly as any wispy specter. Found all the way from New Jersey to Brazil, ghost crabs on Cumberland Island dig their burrows in the dry sandy areas above the high-tide line. The burrows are easy to identify by all the small pencil-point-size tracks that lead from the burrows, which may be a yard deep.

Ghost crabs, whose shells may be as much as $1^1/_2$ inches wide, have pronounced stalked eyes. They spend most of their time in their dry tunnels but must emerge several times every 24 hours to wet their gills in the shallows. Females lay their eggs in the surf zone.

Essentially beachbound vultures, ghost crabs will eat any type of carrion that washes ashore. Unfortunately, they also appear to have a fondness for turtle eggs whenever they encounter a logger-head nest, likely to be built in the same beach zone as the crab burrows.

With a good flashlight and bug repellent always ready, it's fun to hunt for the crabs at night, to watch them scurry away and zip into their burrows. Of course, they wouldn't be nearly as much fun to watch if they grew as large as a small dog or a cat. Then, the ghosts might be stalking *us*.

30

A Closer Look: Night Sounds

As the summer rains return in May, the amphibian chorus in the swamps and lowlands increases to its loudest pitch of the year. With the rain comes the mating time, and the evenings echo with the croaks and calls of earnest suitors.

But these sounds also spill over into the daytime, and the tiny frogs often prove more accurate at weather forecasting than the most sophisticated computers. They react to changes in humidity or barometric pressure even during the day. Impending rain sends the animals into a noisy state of anticipation that turns raucously delirious once the first drops start to fall. It takes only minutes for the cries to reach the fevered intensity of a wild political rally.

The thousands of froggy voices sometimes make it seem that every square inch of lowlands must be layered in piles of the animals, yet the cacophony of voices always drastically underrepresents the number present for it is only the males singing. Females are close to mute, and immature males also do not croak, *ribbit* or *quonk, quonk, quonk.*

There are more than 50 species of frogs living in the Southeast, many of them a variety of tree frog. Like male construction workers whistling to passing females, the frogs have developed the practice of calling for a mate because it is the safest way to avoid predators. Performing individually, in public, with a display like some other animals use, is simply too risky. Of course, the simple act of calling out also alerts predators, but there is safety in numbers, one reason the calls are issued as a chorus. The combined sounds also carry farther to distant females.

Tree frog vocalizations cover a tremendous array of sound. Some sounds are more like those of insects or birds than those normally associated with frogs. The names of some species in fact reflect their calls. Barking tree frogs bark, squirrel tree frogs sound raspy like a squirrel, bird-voiced tree frogs have a high-pitched birdlike whistle, and southern spring peepers peep peep. The green tree frog confuses the entire matter by issuing a tremendous variety of sounds that have been compared to a cowbell or a noise similar to *quonk, quonk, quonk,* among others. The size of a frog helps determine the pitch of its call. Larger frogs have a lower pitch, smaller frogs a higher one.

Tree frogs tend to be heard far more often than they are seen because the markings and coloration of many varieties closely resemble their surroundings. Furthermore, many are quite adept at hiding under tree bark, in knotholes or under leaves.

June

Notes

31

Reef Snorkeling

Florida has the only true coral reef system in all of North America, and the best reefs are located off the Keys, situated only 40 miles southwest of Miami. These fabled isles are often compared to the Caribbean, but their winter weather pattern is definitely not Caribbeanlike.

The calmest and clearest waters—barring a hurricane—can be counted on from May through September. The rest of the year the wind sometimes blows hard enough that dive boats don't even venture out because of the probability that everyone will get seasick. Furthermore, any time a winter cold front barrels down the Atlantic Coast, the Keys will feel it, just not as severely. Wintertime snorkeling often demands a full wetsuit too, since the water temperatures will be anywhere from the 60s to the 70s.

Without its coral reefs South Florida would be a far different place, and not nearly so enjoyable. Coral reefs are important nurseries for many gamefish as well as being the chief residence of bottom dwellers such as snapper, grouper and jewfish, not to mention hundreds of different species of tropicals.

Several factors, all due to geography, account for why Florida is the only state with a true reef system. Coral reefs are found in the world's warm ocean currents in a 3,000-mile-wide tropical belt around the equator. In the Northern Hemisphere these currents travel in a clockwise direction, so reefs are found only along the eastern coasts. This is why the Gulf of Mexico lacks the profuse reef system found on the Atlantic side, off of which the Gulf Stream flows.

Corals grow most favorably in water temperatures between 77 and 86 degrees Fahrenheit. They can survive within a range of 61 to 97 degrees, but extreme temperatures will kill them. Especially susceptible are the corals nearest the surface, which bear the brunt of any passing cold fronts.

Scientists have classified coral reefs into three categories. A *fringing reef,* one that is located mainly in shallow water adjacent to the shores of a continent, characterizes Florida's reef system. Such reefs tend to grow toward the surface and in the direction of the open ocean. Corals that grow toward the shore generally encounter unfavorable conditions, such as water temperatures that are too warm in summer. The two other reef types are known as *atolls* and *barrier reefs*. Atolls are normally found far from any mainland, rising

Florida's coral reef system, the only one in North America, is filled with colorful corals, sea fans and fish.

from a bottom thousands of feet deep. Barrier reefs, on the other hand, are separated from coasts by deep channels. Australia's Great Barrier Reef is the best known of its kind, but there are two other barrier reefs much closer to us: One is off Andros Island in the Bahamas and the other is off Belize in Central America.

Despite their massive size, coral reefs are relatively fragile structures. A thin, almost slimy, layer covers the corals. This soft tissue is what interconnects a particular colony of corals. Continual scraping of or contact with this tissue will damage it and open the coral to possible infection. This is why divers and snorkelers should never touch or otherwise come in contact with a reef. (Scuba divers are greater offenders than snorkelers.)

Because of their massive formations, the hard, stony corals are the types most easily noticed. However, there is another branch of the corals properly known as *octocorals* that derive their name from the peculiar fact that all the polyps of these soft corals invariably have eight rays, hence the name *octo.*

Growing among the rock garden of the stony corals, octocorals can be mistaken for underwater versions of trees, shrubs and cacti. It's easy for snorkelers to get the impression they're floating over a rolling countryside populated with specially crafted bonsai plants. In a current, soft corals sway and move with a seemingly controlled and graceful rhythm. Probably the best-known member of the octocoral family is the sea fan.

Coral reefs also serve as permanent anchoring points for the remarkable creatures known as sponges. Sponges are another species scientists debated over how to categorize—as plants or animals. It was only a hundred years ago that sponges were finally classified as animal forms.

One aspect that puzzled scientists for decades was how sponges feed. Technically, to be an animal they must capture food, but for years no one knew how they did this. It turned out that each sponge is a nonstop filter that continually absorbs water and nourishment through the microscopic pores covering its surface. In turn, water is expelled through the large openings, or *oscula,* on the upper part of the sponge. The surface of some sponges appear like moon craters; the oscula, especially, resemble volcanic mountain slopes. Some sponges, especially the vase type, have top openings so large that small tropical fish and the very flexible bristle starfish sometimes hide in them.

Both marine animals and residents of South Florida all have one thing very much in common: They greatly depend on the coral reefs for their well-being. Treat the reefs gently!

Hot Spots

Those unskilled in snorkeling and scuba diving can visit one of the oldest parts of Florida's coral reef at the **Windley Key State Geologic Site** located at Mile Marker 85.5 on the bayside. This fossil reef is a part of the Key Largo Reef Limestone formation that dates back an estimated 125,000 years. In the early 1900s, the limestone rock was quarried to help build the foundation for Henry Flagler's overseas railroad. Several trails meander through the formation that contains countless fossilized counterparts of the animals that still thrive offshore: brain corals, sea fans and more. Educational facilities are still under development, so the site is fenced off and locked. The key may be obtained at the **Long Key State Recreation Area** located at Mile Marker 67.5, 18 miles farther south. For information, call Long Key at (305) 664-4815.

The **Florida Keys** are visited by more divers and snorkelers than any other single place in the world. About 2 million dives are made here annually. Yet there is still some large and exciting marine life, including sharks. More likely to be observed are the moray eels, which stick their heads from small coral caves, plus loads and loads of reef fish. The prettiest fish snorkelers are likely to see is the rainbow-hued queen angel, whose yellow and blue borders appear like a fluorescent halo. Many Keys queen angels are quite tame and will stay with people for most of a dive, as pretty a companion as any high-fashion model.

Snorkeling is available throughout the Keys, though most dive shops are concentrated in the Key Largo–Islamorada section. Key Largo is also home to the **John Pennekamp Coral Reef State Park,** the nation's first underwater park, and the **Key Largo National Marine Sanctuary,** which extends offshore protection farther than the state's 3-mile limit.

One of the northernmost points off Key Largo is **Carysfort Reef,** easily identifiable by its 125-foot-tall lighthouse. It harbors acres and acres of shallow staghorn coral and tame tropical fish that sometimes can be fed by hand.

The **Key Largo Dry Rocks** is the location of the famed Christ of the Deep statue that stands in about 25 feet of water. The shallow water is ideal for snorkelers, who can prowl the tops of the reefs and still have a fine view of the 9-foot-high Christ, probably the most photographed underwater monument in the world. This statue is a duplicate of one by Italian sculptor Guido Galleti that was placed in the Mediterranean near Genoa in 1954. The upraised arms are intended to symbolize peace and understanding in the same way as do those of the Christ of the Andes in South America.

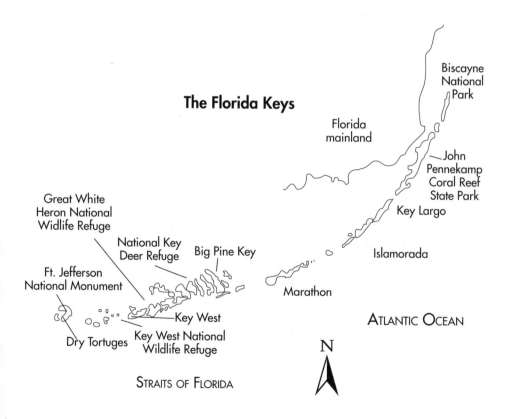

The Florida Keys

Magnificent brain corals, many of them unusually large, also abound at this site. Furthermore, there are huge stands of fire coral very near the surface. Fire coral is easy to recognize. It is mustard-colored with a white border. The sting from this coral can be vicious, as bad as from any wasp. Any part of the body scratched by the coral should be cleaned with soap and water to get rid of the mucouslike secretion, then treated with a first-aid ointment, household ammonia or a paste of baking soda.

Less than a mile southwest of the Christ statue is **Grecian Rocks**, which is partially awash at low tide. The dense stand of elkhorn coral runs north-south for a half-mile and is 150 yards in width. With depths of 4 to 25 feet, this is one of the better snorkeling areas.

Although part of it was damaged by an errant oil tanker in 1984, **Molasses Reef** is still considered one of the best examples of reef life anywhere in the Keys. The shallower north end is a favorite of snorkelers. Fish there are quite tame.

Pennekamp Park and the National Marine Sanctuary may receive most of the publicity, but there are many other good snorkeling sites to the south between Tavernier and Lower Matecumbe Key. **Alligator Reef**, marked with a 136-foot-high tower, is named after a warship that sank in 1825. A few parts of the vessel can still be found on the ocean side of the light that marks the spot. Depths go to 40 feet but are as shallow as 8. Another good shallow site is the **Coral Gardens**, with a good variety of marine life and depths ranging from 5 to 18 feet, making it easy to view the brain, lettuce and star corals.

Islamorada is perhaps the only place in North America where snorkelers can investigate a faithful replica of an ancient Spanish galleon. The **San Pedro Underwater Archaeological Preserve** is in only 18 feet of water off Indian Key. The *San Pedro* was part of the ill-fated 21-ship Spanish fleet of which all but one of the boats were destroyed by a deadly storm on a truly unlucky Friday the Thirteenth in July 1733. Wrecks were scattered for 80 miles over the Keys' bottom. The *San Pedro* site has seven concrete cannon replicas, ballast rock and even limited remains of the wooden hull. The 500-pound cannons were placed in their historically accurate position. A no-fishing policy is strictly enforced, so there is normally a tremendous amount of marine life around the *San Pedro.*

Many consider the **Looe Key National Marine Sanctuary,** 6 miles south of Big Pine Key, to have the finest coral and fish collection outside of Key Largo/Islamorada. The Looe Key Sanctuary, covering 5.3 square miles of federal waters, is named after the 44-gun British frigate HMS *Looe,* which sank on the reef in 1744. The sanctuary is situated off Big Pine Key; some boats leave from Marathon.

Six miles south of Key West is **Sand Key** and its 110-foot-tall lighthouse, which makes the reef quite easy to find. Depths start at 15 feet, so this is a good all-around spot for both snorkeling and scuba.

The best snorkeling of all, however, is another 60 miles south of Key West in the **Dry Tortugas.** A number of charter boats run dives here regularly from both Key West and Marathon. The trips can last as long as a week. The Tortugas reefs are protected, just like Pennekamp's, but they suffer none of the same overpopulation problems.

Because the Dry Tortugas are continually bathed by the warm, clear waters of the Gulf Stream, visibility underwater ranges 80 to 100 feet most of the year. Since it is so inaccessible and a rather long voyage, the reefs are for the most part as they were hundreds of years ago: virgin and unspoiled.

For complete information on Keys snorkeling operations, camping opportunities and accommodations, call (800) FLA-KEYS.

32

Gators Galore

Alligators are seen so frequently throughout the Southeast that it's sometimes difficult to remember how rare they are in the rest of the world. Alligators exist in only two countries: the United States and China. Everything else that resembles an alligator is actually a crocodile, a caiman or a gharial. The only place where the range of the alligator and crocodile overlap is on the tip of South Florida, in the Everglades and Upper Keys. It's quite easy to tell gators and crocs apart. Gators have blunt, rounded snouts, are black and usually inhabit fresh water. Crocodiles have pointed snouts, are green in color and prefer saltwater. However, the saltwater crocodile population is quite small, with only an estimated 400 animals surviving.

The nation's population of alligators is somewhere around two million, half of which live in Florida. The name *alligator* apparently comes from the corruption of the Spanish *el lagarto,* "lizard."

For most of our history, alligators have been plentiful. William Bartram, the naturalist who explored Florida in the 1700s, recorded that "they are so abundant that, if permitted by them, I could walk over any part of the basin and the river upon their heads, which slowly float and turn about like knotty chunks of wood log." It took almost 200 years and James Bond to finally accomplish this feat in the film *Live and Let Die.*

Alligators have evolved in many specialized ways that make them ideally adapted for survival. Although they look extremely primitive, their anatomy and living habits are ideally suited for their swampy, wet habitat. For instance, rather than deposit jellylike eggs in the water, as some other reptiles and amphibians do, alligators reproduce with hard-shelled eggs laid on land, which tends to assure a higher survival rate.

Alligators also possess very efficient four-chambered hearts, compared to the two chambers of other modern reptiles and amphibians. Four chambers is a definite asset when alligators spend extended time underwater. Once submerged, alligators hold their breath, and their blood is routed through the heart to bypass the lungs, which in turn makes more oxygen available for other organs. On warm days alligators can stay underwater for 45 minutes or more. In colder conditions, when their metabolism rate is lower, they can stay underwater even longer.

Their cold-blooded physiology permits alligators to live for amazingly long periods without food—up to six months, if necessary. Gator diets include a number of tough, potentially tooth-cracking

Okefenokee Swamp Park's system of boardwalks makes it quite easy to approach alligators any time of year.

tidbits such as turtles, but tooth loss is not a serious concern, at least for young gators. Gator teeth are sharp, hollow and grow from sockets in the jawbone. New teeth form under existing ones routinely in younger animals, but replacement does not always occur in older alligators. Although the teeth do differ in size, all are cone-shaped, and there are no molars for crushing.

When eating a small animal such as a turtle, a gator may crush the shell and then swallow it whole. When attacking a larger animal like a deer, gators will roll it underwater to drown it. Then they will guard the corpse for a couple of days, waiting for it to age so the meat can be more easily ripped apart.

Because their jaws are hinged far back, gators are able to open their jaws to impressive dimensions and to tackle animals as large as the white-tailed deer. The jaws are tremendously powerful—capable of as much pressure as 3,000 pounds per square inch. Once shut, an alligator's jaws are virtually impossible to pry open.

So how is it that some people are able to wrestle with alligators and live to tell about it? Simple. The muscles for opening the mouth are far weaker than for clamping down. Gator evolution never anticipated that a playful mammal would delight in clamping gator mouths shut for amusement. Humans can get away with this trick only because of our thumbs. You probably have never considered this, but the loss of a thumb normally nips short any gator wrestler's career. The difficulty is illustrated when you try to hold a dog or cat's mouth closed with only four fingers. It can't be done.

Alligators on land are usually slow, lumbering creatures. They walk for brief distances, dragging their tails, then flop for a moment to rest before continuing. Over short distances gators can move quickly by raising their bodies high off the ground, doing what's known as a "high walk." In the water, gators propel themselves by moving their massive tails from side to side. Gators can see quite well underwater thanks to their two sets of eyelids. One set, employed for underwater vision like a set of goggles, closes from side to side. The other eyelids are like our own and close up and down.

Gators can be very noisy creatures. Their springtime bellows can be heard for a half-mile or more. Some have compared the sounds to that of thunder, but the grating of an old washboard is probably more accurate. Gators do not have to open their mouths to bellow. They make the sound by vibrating air in their throats while on land or in the water. The bellows are not normally just single grunts but have a rhythm to them; the rhythm of the females is slightly faster. Alligators will bellow at any time of year but bellow most frequently during spring, in the mating season. This is one of several ways gators communicate.

During the mating season, gators also perform head slaps. This involves a gator holding its head and tail out of the water, then quickly opening the mouth and slapping the bottom jaw on the water. This usually brings the jaws crashing together. Gators also hiss when agitated.

The breeding season lasts from spring through early summer. Despite all the creature's ferocity, gator courtship is actually a quiet, almost tender ritual. A pair may swim together and sun together for several days before mating. During this courtship, the gators will lie in the water with their noses almost touching. The male may submerge and blow bubbles past the female's head. When the female is ready, she swims beside the male, holding her tail slightly above water. They both submerge, and the joining lasts about half a minute.

Females begin building their nests about two months after courtship. This usually occurs in mid- to late June, after the rainy season has started. Females tend to nest in the same vicinity year after year but seldom use the same nest.

Gator eggs will drown in high water, so nests may be as many as 15 feet from the water's edge. Females lay, on the average, about 30 eggs, which are placed in a cavity at the top of the nest and covered with vegetation for the 60- to 70-day incubation period. Gators do not sit on their nests but rely on the marsh grasses and cattails to maintain the proper temperature. The mothers don't usually wander too far away and are surprisingly diligent at discouraging intruders.

One old wives' tale about alligators is true: that the sex of the gators is determined by the temperature inside the nest during the first three weeks of incubation. Temperatures of 91 degrees or greater during this time will develop males; 85 degrees or less will develop females. Nest temperatures are higher at the top, which produces mostly males. Eggs placed in the bottom of the nest, where it's cooler, develop as females. Newborn female gators at the nest bottom sometimes cannot escape without their mother's help.

When emerging from the egg, a newborn gator may issue a grunting call. That will bring the mother if she is nearby, and she will begin to dig away the covering, grasp the youngsters in her mouth and take them to open water. Even when the mother isn't present, newborns instinctively head for water.

Newborn gators, which are about 8 or 9 inches long, begin appearing in September. They are able to fend for themselves but usually remain with their mother and siblings. This is very understandable: Just one grunt of distress will bring the mother running at full throttle, always a dismaying sight to potential eaters of young gators.

Young alligators feed on tadpoles, small fish, flies and other insects. Since they are born as winter approaches, gators in colder climes may feed a few weeks before going dormant for several months. In South Georgia, for instance, gators may not eat between October and March, a six-month period. Surrounding temperatures and the availability of food determine how quickly gators grow.

Like sharks, gators are known for sometimes having odd things in their stomachs, such as bottles, sand and wood. This is because gators have a two-part stomach, and the first part is essentially a gizzard where large bits of food are pulverized into smaller ones. Then the food is passed into the second stomach, where strong digestive juices break down much of the bone, scales or shell.

Male gators grow larger than females. In fact, any gator over 9 feet in length is likely to be a male. It's possible to estimate the length of a submerged gator by doing the following calculation. Estimate the number of inches between the snout and the eyes. That's how many feet long the gator is from snout to tail. In the wild, gators probably live about 30 to 35 years, with the males surviving longer.

During the wettest periods gators tend to roam freely. In dry conditions, when much of the land is drying up, many seek out their gator "holes," wallows the animal creates in soft mud or shallow water. Sometimes gators will dig horizontal holes that may extend for as much as 10 feet under a bank. In dry seasons gator holes are important food and water sources for other animals, particularly birds, but also for raccoons, bobcats and otters. Gators do sometimes share their holes with other alligators, but on other occasions the largest and strongest will drive the others away.

It's illegal for people to feed alligators, but it happens anyway. A people-fed alligator is one that loses its natural fear of humans, and the animal often becomes aggressive when it wants a handout. Gators and people already have enough problems sharing living space: In the summer months, state authorities may receive as many as 12,000 reports about nuisance gators that show up in swimming pools, on golf courses, on boat ramps, in public fountains and inside buildings. But for all their terrible reputation, gators are believed responsible for only seven human deaths in the last 22 years.

Hot Spots Just a few decades ago alligator numbers had declined to the extent that they were considered a threatened species. Thanks to the protection they received, the gator population once again is quite healthy. Some critics say *too* healthy.

The best time to see gators in hot weather is early in the day. In cool weather, the animals like to sun themselves at almost any time. They also have more time for relaxing in the sun during cooler months because they are not involved in other activities such as feeding and breeding.

Outside of commercial attractions, you can be as certain of spotting gators as you can of tomorrow's sunrise at the following locations. But keep in mind that in South Florida it's possible to see a gator any time near any freshwater marsh, lake, river, drainage canal—or golf-course water hazards.

On the Alabama coast, look in **Gator Lake** and any of the marshland along Mobile Street in the **Bon Secour NWR**. The three freshwater lakes at **Gulf State Park** are another sure bet for gators. The **Mobile Delta** is also loaded with them.

In Georgia, the 600-square-mile **Okefenokee Swamp NWR** houses between 10,000 and 20,000 alligators. Much of the swamp is freshwater marsh and deep forest swamps that can be reached only by boat. Rentals or tours are normally available at the refuge's three access points. The main entrance is on the east side. An easy half-hour ride from I-95 via State Road 40 will take you to the refuge's **Suwannee Canal Recreation Area,** the main refuge entrance, near Folkston. A visitor center offers exhibits (8 A.M. to 4 P.M.), and rental boats are available from 7 A.M. to 7:30 P.M. March 1 to September 10; from 8 A.M. to 6 P.M. the rest of the year. Call (912) 496-7156. The western entrance is near Stephen C. Foster State Park.

Your surest and easiest place to see gators is at the private, nonprofit **Okefenokee Swamp Park** 8 miles south of Waycross at the northern end of the 396,000-acre wilderness. The animals tend to be more concentrated here and don't require an extensive hunt to locate. It would be rare not to see several from shore or the boardwalk. The park is open from 9 A.M. to 6:30 P.M. June through August; 9 A.M. to 5:30 P.M. the rest of the year.

The year-round 72-degree water at **Wakulla Springs State Park,** just south of Tallahassee, has fostered an amazingly dense alligator population despite its northerly location. In fact, there are so many gators in the clear spring run that human swimmers are confined to one very limited area. Gators, not people, have the run of this place. The best way to appreciate this beautiful park is aboard one of the ranger-led wildlife cruises, the only good way to see the scores of gators that are scattered along the banks. The ranger's corny jokes will make this seem a lot like the Jungle Cruise at Disney's Magic Kingdom, except everything here has real teeth. On second thought, maybe this is more like *Jaws* at Universal Studios than the Jungle Cruise.

The gators aren't as obvious at nearby **St. Marks NWR,** although sometimes they cooperate nicely, for one or more of them may be floating in the pond in back of the visitor information center. Or they might be in the pond down by the lighthouse. Ask at the information center, since the hotspots will be determined by weather conditions.

One of the surest places to see alligators in South Florida is along the draining canals of the **Tamiami Trail (U.S. 41)** between Miami and Naples. Places where you can stop an auto and look are limited, which is probably just as well, considering all the gators. Driving the trail, you will also pass a number of airboat operations, some of them owned by members of the Seminole nation, who try to make a gator sighting the highlight of an airboat trip.

In **Everglades National Park, Shark Valley** is a sure bet. Located 30 miles west of Miami on U.S. 41 (the Tamiami Trail), adult gators frequent the canals while the newly hatched young are often found on the grassy banks that line the canal. The thing that is most impressive here is that there is no real barrier between you and the gators. In fact, you may have to be careful not to step on the baby gators in the grass.

Royal Palm Hammock just inside the Homestead entrance to Everglades National Park may attract as many as 200 alligators during the winter dry season. They disperse into other wetlands during the rainy period, which begins at the end of May and lasts through November.

Close to West Palm Beach is the **Loxahatchee NWR,** where you can just about bet money on finding one or more gators in front of the visitor information center. You won't see the number here that you will deeper in the Glades, but this is a good spot for a quick look if gators have been scarce elsewhere.

Orlando Wetlands Park, not far from Florida's main tourist city, is a man-made wetlands that boasts a sizable wading bird and alligator population. Of course, there are also several commercial gator attractions in the vicinity, but that's not quite as challenging as finding your own animal in the wild.

In Southwest Florida, Sanibel Island's **J. N. "Ding" Darling NWR** offers the opportunity for plenty of gator sightings from your vehicle as you drive the 5-mile-long road that cuts through the heart of the refuge.

33

Mobile Bay Jubilee

Visualize the following scenario: The ocean turns sour, forcing crabs, flounder, shrimp and other creatures to flee into shallow water. Conditions are so toxic that rather than endure the lethal seawater, the animals flop themselves onto shore, where they eventually die of asphyxiation.

Such a phenomenon sounds like something from a science fiction movie depicting the end of the earth, but it's hardly anything so dire. Instead, it's a greatly anticipated, highly prized phenomenon because of all the free seafood available for the taking. Imagine picking 12-pound flounder off the beach, or so many big blue crabs that they fill an ice chest. This summertime event, called a Jubilee, occurs annually and regularly on only one place on earth, the eastern shore of Alabama's Mobile Bay.

Ironically, the presence of Jubilees has nothing to do with the overall health of Mobile Bay, which is actually a very productive seafood-packed estuary. Jubilees have been recorded in Mobile newspapers since at least 1867. Stories told by local Native Americans also spoke of these happenings. It's likely they occurred for centuries, if not millennia, before the first European settlers arrived. Jubilees are not in any way a human-related event.

The conditions that generate Mobile Bay Jubilees are present in many other places around the globe. Mobile Bay just happens to have certain geologic and geographic peculiarities that bring the phenomenon to complete fruition. Triangular-shaped Mobile Bay is a semienclosed basin connected both to the Gulf of Mexico and the east Mississippi Sound. It is roughly 31 miles long with an average width of 10.5 miles. A very shallow body of water, the bay depth averages only 10 feet at mean high tide. Water temperatures are quite high during summers, ranging between 86 and 91 degrees Fahrenheit.

Mobile Bay also receives huge quantities of fresh water during the summer rainy season from both the Alabama and Tombigbee

Rivers, whose combined flow creates the sixth largest freshwater discharge in all North America. The rivers pour massive amounts of nutrients into the bay, particularly on the deeper eastern side.

During hot summer weather, the breakdown of these nutrients by bacterial action consumes considerable amounts of oxygen. At the same time, the high water temperature boosts the metabolic rates of bottom dwellers like flounder, crabs and shrimp, which all begin consuming greater amounts of oxygen. The result is that the dissolved oxygen content near the bottom drops dramatically, creating a dead zone over 5 to 10 percent of the bay.

This dead zone remains throughout the hot months, since the water in Mobile Bay, instead of blending together like water in a drinking glass, stratifies into different layers, like a cake. The hotter oxygen-rich water stays on the top. This prevents the depleted bottom layer from mixing with the oxygen-rich surface layer. Fortunately, this is only a seasonal condition. All it takes is several days of good brisk wind with the first storms of autumn to mix the water column and reoxygenate most of the bay.

Oxygen depletion and vertical stratification of the water column are not unique to Mobile Bay. Isolation of bottom waters occurs in many lakes, even fjords. It is known to take place, for example, in the Chesapeake Bay, but the water there is deep and the effects not as visibly pronounced.

In Mobile Bay, under even the worst circumstances, the bad water never extends over the whole bay but remains in the deeper half of the bay on the eastern side. A Jubilee occurs when the "puddle" of high-density deoxygenated water moves near shore. Two factors must be present for this movement: a rising tide and a wind blowing from the east. Both conditions need to happen at night, when there is no biological production of oxygen, only the consumption of it. In effect, the rising tide pushes the bottom water toward the eastern shoreline as the wind simultaneously shoves the healthy top-water layer to the western side of Mobile Bay. The bottom layer of water now rises closer to the top. What previously was a puddle of bad water is suddenly a vertical wall of deoxygenated water progressing shoreward.

Naturally, marine animals attempt to stay in front of the bad water. First, they migrate into the shallows. They will move onto land only if the oxygen-depleted water goes right up to the shoreline. Many of those that choose to remain in the degraded water may die, depending on how long the phenomenon lasts. Those that move onto shore (with the exception of the blue crabs) will most certainly die.

A Jubilee may impact an area of shoreline as short as a hundred yards or as long as a mile. The phenomenon can begin in a single area, then advance either north or south along the shoreline. A Jubilee generally does not occur in more than one area of the bay. And it is only a temporary event because it ends once the high-tide level begins receding or the wind stops blowing from the east. If just one of these two conditions occurs, the Jubilee ends as the zone of degraded water moves away from land and back to the bay bottom.

How many times Jubilees take place in a summer and how long they last depends on how frequently all the necessary conditions occur over the course of a summer. High-energy events, such as the winds of a tropical storm or a hurricane, alter the dynamics tremendously and make Jubilees far less likely.

Hot Spots Jubilees occur on the eastern side of **Mobile Bay** along Baldwin County, most often between **Bon Secour Bay** and the town of **Fairhope**. They normally occur quite late, or early, depending on your point of view. Jubilees often begin just before dawn and extend into the early morning hours, though sometimes they begin shortly after midnight. Mid-July to early September is the normal range of occurrence.

How many animals are driven shoreward depends on how the bubble of bad water is configured. If it is circular or egg-shaped as it approaches the shoreline, animals can escape laterally to the north or south. If it is more of a U shape, there will be far less opportunity for animals to avoid the bad water, and more of them will be shoved shoreward.

Technically, a full-blown Jubilee is said to occur only if the animals actually move onto shore. A good Jubilee is one that yields a lot of flounder, shrimp and crab, in that order. Eels and nongamefish are generally considered more of a nuisance than anything else, so they usually are left to rot.

Residents wise in the ways of the Jubilee phenomenon do not wait for everything to be handed to them. When the animals are in the shallows, close to land but not yet on it, they put on shorts and tennis shoes and wade out into the shallows with a shrimp net to claim their bounty. In the old days, people would show up with metal washtubs and wooden baskets to hold their catch. Today the favorite devices are a shrimp net and an ice chest. A gig is necessary to take swimming flounder and those flopping on shore.

The first indication of a Jubilee is a disturbance just offshore where crabs, fish, shrimp and eels can be seen swimming on the surface, trying to stay out of the bad water. The rippling action on an otherwise calm surface is always a dead giveaway. It is a matter of extreme last resort when the animals actually move out of the water.

Unfortunately, Jubilees are not precisely predictable. Old-timers say they are most likely to happen after periods of prolonged calm weather. The trick is to be there then, and to be prepared to lose some sleep.

34

Dolphin Watching

Ponder this question: Over the course of evolution, was the dolphin the first mammal ever to smile? And is this why the dolphin smiles so well, because it has had millions of years of practice?

If the dolphin didn't wear its perpetual, "Hi, how are you, buddy?" welcoming grin, would humans still be attracted to it as much? A dolphin without a smile would be like a world in eternal blackness: It's too uncomfortable to imagine. Besides, that happy-looking face perfectly reflects the dolphin's naturally playful nature, which is probably the real reason humans love these animals so.

Dolphins, which are actually whales of the small-toothed variety, are characterized by a beaklike snout and sharp conical teeth. For many decades, the popular name for the dolphin was "porpoise," which is totally incorrect because true porpoises are in a different family. The porpoise also has a blunt snout and chisellike or spade-shaped teeth.

To confuse the dolphin name further, the so-called dolphin fish (now called "mahimahi" on restaurant menus to distinguish it from Flipper) is not a porpoise or a dolphin. It is related to the mackerels. But that doesn't stop sportscasters from referring to the Miami Dolphins football team as "the fish."

The largest of all dolphins is the bottlenose, which is also the most common species found off Southeast coasts. The bottlenose is also the heavyweight of dolphins, reaching 9 feet in length and 440 pounds. Contrast it to the world's smallest dolphin, found in the Amazon, the buffeo, which rarely grows to even 4 feet long and almost never weighs more than 65 pounds.

A bottlenose dolphin eats as much daily as the buffeo weighs. Its primary food is live fish such as mackerel, herring and squid. In captivity it has to be trained to eat previously frozen dead fish. Consider what kind of shock such a diet change must be to a dolphin born in the wild. It could be like switching a person from cooked food to raw.

The bottlenose dolphin, which occurs worldwide, is an ocean-roaming creature. There are a few dolphin species that live in fresh water, including the Ganges River and several South American rivers. Some dolphin species travel in schools of up to 1,000 individuals, but the bottlenose is rarely found in groups larger than 100. Sometimes the bottlenose travel only as a family group, but it is rare to find a solitary animal.

More and more dolphins in the wild willingly approach divers every year. Sometimes the encounter turns into an underwater ballet.

The bottlenose is as streamlined as any torpedo. Capable of swimming continually at a speed of 18 mph, it may achieve bursts of 23–25 mph. The front flippers, which contain the skeletal remains of five digits, act primarily as stabilizers while the animal is swimming. The bottlenose, like all dolphins, propels itself through the water in the same manner as whales do. Its thrust comes from its tail, which is all flesh and skin, not skeletal. When dolphins ride the bow waves of ships—probably the most spectacular way to see them in the wild—they are not resting motionless, as they appear—they're riding the thrust of the ship.

As mammals, dolphins are warm-blooded and have a body temperature between 97.9 and 99 degrees Fahrenheit. They help maintain this temperature with a thick layer of blubber under the skin, another characteristic of whales. Dolphins must also breathe air, which they do through a specialized nostril, or blowhole, on top of the head. Dolphins usually breathe about every two minutes. They can hold their breath for several minutes longer and are able to dive as deep as 1,000 feet on a single breath of air.

In studies with captive animals, scientists have learned that courtship and copulation are confined only to the spring months. Gestation lasts 11 to 12 months. Only a single calf is born. It comes out tail-first, ready to breathe and able to swim within minutes. In captive animals, nursing lasts as long as 12 to 18 months.

Besides its smile, one of the fascinating features of the dolphin is its almost constant vocalization. It can emit two kinds of sounds. Some are clicks, produced so rapidly they resemble a buzz or ducklike quack. These sounds are used for the famous dolphin sonar, or *echolocation*, where echoes of sound allow the animal to detect other objects. Experimental studies have shown that humans echolocated by captive dolphins in close quarters often undergo some kind of therapeutic healing effect. Such studies are still highly speculative but also highly suggestive: It appears a dolphin recognizes that something is wrong with the person it echolocates. Echolocation is not something dolphins do to everyone who swims with them.

However, communicating with dolphins in any form of recognizable language is still more dream than reality. Scientists classify dolphins as smarter than dogs but not equal to humans in intelligence.

Yet it's still strongly held that the dolphin or the gorilla will be humankind's breakthrough in communicating with another species. But who cares about IQ when an emotional attachment is involved? Dolphins adapt readily to human companionship in captivity. Dolphins, whether as a family or as individuals, willingly seek out scuba divers in the wild. It would revolutionize the world if man learned the thoughts behind the dolphin's enigmatic smile. Would we like what it has to say about us?

Hot Spots The best places to spot dolphins are at the mouths of rivers leading into the Gulf or the Atlantic, in bays, in many of the wider sections of the Intracoastal Waterway, around inlets and around barrier islands. There is no guarantee, of course, when or where the animals will appear. Sometimes the most you'll see are the fins moving in and out of the water. (The over-and-under movement of a dolphin through the water is very different from that of a shark. A shark's fin cuts straight through the water and stays exposed for prolonged periods.) Other times, a dolphin may ride the bow wave of a boat. If that happens, don't slow down or stop. The presence of one dolphin usually indicates others are nearby. Binoculars will help you scan the water for more.

Dolphins are often seen in **Mobile Bay.** The ferry ride to **Dauphin Island** can be particularly good. **Pensacola Bay** and the waters surrounding the **Gulf Islands National Seashore** are often quite good in summer. **St. Joseph Peninsula State Park** frequently has dolphins swimming offshore. The inlet near the city of Destin can be a real hotspot most of the year. **Apalachicola Bay,** one of Florida's most important seafood producers, has regular dolphin sightings.

Continuing south down the Gulf Coast, look for dolphins on any boat trip through the **Cedar Keys** and around the mouths of the **Chassawitzka, Homosassa** and **Crystal Rivers. Tampa Bay, Sarasota Bay, Charlotte Harbor** and **Pine Island Sound** near Fort Myers are all good spots. So are the **Ten Thousand Islands** and the **Everglades' Wilderness Waterway,** near the western boundary of the park. The cuts, channels and offshore waters of the **Keys, Biscayne National Park** and **Biscayne Bay** all hold plenty of dolphins.

Moving into Central Florida, the **Indian River** and the **Banana River** have some of the state's friendliest dolphins. **Ponce de Leon Inlet** and the **Halifax River** near Daytona are more good sites, as are any of the many bridges on A1A from Anastasia Island and St. Augustine.

Northward check the waters around **Amelia Island** and the town of **Mayport** near Jacksonville where the St. Johns River flows into the Atlantic. Keep a sharp eye out for dolphins on any boat trip to **Cumberland Island.** The waters around Georgia's **Golden Isles** and the mouth of the **Savannah River** are more good places. Anywhere along Georgia's coastal **Low Country** offers plenty of dolphin-watching opportunities.

35

June Shorttakes

Nesting Ducks

Ponds of water, whether natural or man-made, always attract birds, and so it is that the **Welaka National Fish Hatchery** is the summer nesting area for mottled ducks and purple gallinules (also called marsh hens). Go south of the town of Palatka on U.S. 17 and turn on State Road 309. The best ponds have been about a mile east of the main office. For more information, call (904) 467-2374. The facility is open seven days a week from 7 A.M. to 4 P.M.

Summer Manatees

After spending the winter in clear spring runs, many manatees spend the rest of the year dispersed throughout the rest of the state in rather murky water. One exception is the **Wakulla River** just south of Tallahassee. This river is actually the spring run of a huge underwater fountain, **Wakulla Springs**, a protected state park. Manatees are often in the crystal-clear river or near the mouth, where it pours into the Gulf of Mexico. Simply follow U.S. 98, which parallels the Gulf, until it crosses the Wakulla River. A canoe rental outfit is located there. This is an exceptionally pretty canoe trip, with lots of sunning turtles and even a few alligators are almost guaranteed, even if the manatees aren't present. The Wakulla is one of the prettiest rivers in all Florida.

36

A Closer Look: Lightning

Florida is the lightning capital of the United States, if not the world. The only places where lightning may strike more frequently are in parts of Africa. In Florida, as many as a dozen people are killed and several dozen injured annually by the sudden bolts from the blue. The most dangerous places are open fields, beaches, under trees, in boats or on golf courses.

The state's lightning hotspot is the Fort Myers area, which averages 100 days with lightning every year. The region between Orlando and Tampa and south to Fort Myers and Lake Okeechobee is considered the state's lightning belt. Most of the activity is from June to October, with July and August the peak months. The explosive thunder that accompanies these storms are the shock waves created by the heating and expansion of air along the lightning's path.

For a naturalist, lightning is an easy problem to avoid. It occurs most often in the afternoons during Florida's almost daily summer thunderstorms. Animals are typically most active during the early hours, before the day heats up. This is the same routine people should copy in order to avoid lightning.

Lightning, essentially a large electrical spark in the atmosphere, causes an estimated 10,000 forest fires a year in the United States. In the Southeast, fires created by lightning are necessary for the propagation of certain seeds and the recycling of nutrients. The best example is the longleaf pine, which once covered hundreds of thousands of square miles throughout the Southeast. Fire is the only thing that will pop open the pine cones and release the seeds that replenish the forest. In the absence of fire, hardwood trees such as oaks will replace the pine, which is exactly what's happened through much of the region.

Pines and oaks are favorite targets of lightning because of their height and high starch content, which makes them good conductors. A hot lightning bolt, whose temperature is in excess of 25,000 degrees may make a tree burst into flame. A colder bolt may be no less damaging, because it may hit at a speed of 20,000 miles per second, causing the tree to explode.

One thing that makes lightning so dangerous is that it can occur when the sky overhead is clear. That sometimes lures people at the beach or on a golf course into a false sense of security because storm clouds may still be several miles away. Remember, if there is a thunderstorm anywhere in the vicinity, lightning strikes are possible.

A lightning bolt is visible only for a thousandth of a second, yet the wallop it packs is incredible. The temperature of a lightning bolt is usually around 30,000 degrees (but it can get as hot as 50,000 degrees) that is enclosed in a 1-inch corridor that carries a shock in the 6,000- to 10,000-ampere range. Thunderstorms normally have several different *cells,* which are considered separate electric entities. The life span of a cell is about 45 minutes. When one fades, another becomes active.

Cumulonimbus clouds with their distinctive anvil-shaped tops are the main producers of thunderstorms and the accompanying lightning. Such clouds form as the land surface heats up and *thermals* of warm air rise to the level of condensation. In order to produce storms, the thermals must contain adequate moisture, and the atmosphere must be conditionally unstable in conjunction with a larger-scale air circulation produced by something like a sea breeze. These conditions occur almost daily during the Florida summer.

Thunderstorms carry enough water that they sometimes prompt the weather bureau to issue flood warnings or flood watches, which may seem strange for a part of the nation that is so flat. Floods are usually associated with overflowing rivers or canyons and valleys that suddenly fill with torrents of storm water. In Florida, the warnings apply mostly to the roads, which may fill with water once the ground becomes saturated and the runoff has nowhere to go.

An old wives' tale claims that lightning never strikes twice in the same place. That is wishful thinking. Lightning strikes have been recorded as occurring in the same place, even on the same tree, more than 20 times.

One of the most striking accounts of the fury of a thunderstorm and its impact was recorded by naturalist William Bartram as he traveled through Florida and the Southeast between 1773 and 1778. Although the event he chronicles happened more than 250 years ago, the tale still has tremendous impact and demonstrates why these fiery acts of nature deserve so much respect. From the amount of devastation, it is likely that a tornado accompanied this particular storm. Bartram called this tumult a hurricane, but the event lacks many classic characteristics of a typical hurricane:

> How purple and fiery appeared the tumultuous clouds, swiftly ascending or darting from the horizon upwards! They seemed to oppose and dash against each other; the skies appeared streaked with blood or purple flame overhead, the flaming lightning streaming and darting about in every direction around, seemed to fill the earth with fire; whilst the heavy thunder kept the earth in a constant tremor ... such floods of rain fell during the space of half or three-quarters of an hour, that my boat was filled, and I expected every moment where I should see her sink to the bottom of the lake. ... All the buildings on the plantation, except his own dwelling house, were laid almost flat to the ground, or the logs and roof rent asunder and twisted about. ... He had nearly one hundred acres of the Indigo plant almost ripe for the first cutting, which were nearly ruined; and several acres of very promising sugar cane, totally spoiled for the season. The great live oaks which had been left standing about the fields, were torn to pieces, their limbs lying scattered over the ground: and one very large one which stood near his house torn down, which could not have been done by the united strength of a thousand men.

A convincing report. When a thunderstorm approaches, seek shelter.

July

Notes

37

Carnivorous Plant Bogs

What is it about a meat-eating plant that is so fascinating to so many children and adults? It must be because carnivores are so rare in the plant world.

As many parents know, carnivorous plants make perfect pets for children. Their bite doesn't hurt, they never have to be cleaned up after, they can't run away and they even feed themselves. Tidy and independent, carnivorous plants are ideal to share a home with.

Unfortunately, ever-increasing human expansion has not treated these plants well. Some authorities estimate that as much as 98 percent of the nation's carnivorous plant bogs have been destroyed. To thrive, the plants require wide open spaces with lots of sunlight, because they also engage in photosynthesis. The only way such habitat can be maintained is by periodic fires sweeping over the landscape. Since modern man considers wildfires one of his greatest threats, most former bog habitat is now shaded out. Many of today's surviving carnivorous plants grow wild only in national forests and other protected areas.

Carnivorous plants apparently evolved their animal-trapping techniques because they had a diet deficiency due to poor soil conditions. The plants live in a variety of habitats, such as sphagnum (or peat moss) bogs, swampy areas and even hardened soil that is seasonally flooded (plants in seasonally wet locations use dormancy mechanisms to survive the dry spells). Such places usually are poor in minerals, and mineral nutrients from their prey are what the plants benefit from most.

The most famous carnivorous plant is Venus's-flytrap. A member of the sundew family, Venus's-flytrap acts as a snap-trap, where the insect is trapped by a rapidly closing set of lobes. The plant closes once the animal touches certain sensory hairs. The contact promotes the growth of acid inside the lobes in less than a second, which makes the plant seem to snap shut.

There are more than 29 different kinds of carnivorous plants in the Florida Panhandle and along the Alabama and Georgia coasts. One of the largest and most spectacular looking—it would even make a fine ornamental plant—is the trumpet pitcher plant. Growing almost waist-high, it has green stems topped with a wine-colored circular top containing a flap or lid.

Smaller but also striking is the white-top pitcher plant, which grows about knee-high. It is distinguished by a white leaflike top laced with wine-dark veins. Another common species is the hooded

Because of wholesale habitat destruction, carnivorous plants like the white-top pitcher plant are normally found in protected areas.

pitcher plant, which favors bogs where the peat moss often grows more than a foot thick. These green-and-red or green-and-yellow pitcher plants, usually over a foot tall, are easy to spot because they typically grow in clumps of four, five or more plants.

All pitcher plants trap their prey in much the same way. Insects, particularly ants, are lured to the top of the plant by the sweet nectar on the overhanging flap. Ants that try to reach the nectar end up falling off the slick edge at the top of the funnel and plop into the plant. The insect cannot escape because of the downward-pointing hairs that make it impossible for the ant to climb back up the stem sides. Since the stem bottom usually contains water, the trapped insect eventually drowns and the plant then "devours" it with digesting enzymes in order to absorb the nutrients. Look inside the stem of a very old pitcher plant: There may be the remains of thousands of ants at the bottom.

In the wild, nature's law is Eat or Be Eaten, so it's only fair that there should be a few insects that like dining on insectivorous plants. Several kinds of mites, flies, moths and an aphid live on, and off of, pitcher plants; some of these animals are found only in pitcher plant bogs.

Very different in appearance from the pitcher plants are the butterworts, which favor wet ditches and powerline right-of-ways. Butterworts have a rosette of flat overlapping leaves about 2 inches in length that curl at the edges. The leaves, either pale green or purple, are sticky and textured because of their many secretory glands. The sticky leaves act like flypaper, trapping whatever insect lands on them. The insect is then digested by secretions from the leaf's glands.

Not to be confused with the similar-sounding butterworts are bladderworts, an aquatic form of carnivorous plant. One of the largest types is the yellow-flowered floating bladderwort, common throughout the Southeast. It relies on suction to trap its prey. A bladderwort functions somewhat like a "humane" animal trap: The animal enters through a door but cannot leave. The bladderwort, of course, is not designed to release what it traps.

A bladderwort's leaves, which are filled with air, float in a spokelike shape. The plant "inhales" its prey when some small invertebrate touches one of its sensitive hairs: The air-filled leaves suddenly suck the prey into a special digestive sac, where it is consumed alive. Unfortunately for hard-core voyeurs, the bladderwort's trapping action takes place out of sight, underwater, which is why many people do not associate bladderworts with other insectivorous species.

Hot Spots

Carnivorous plants grow only in freshwater habitat. In Georgia, one of the best places to find pitcher plants is in the **Okefenokee Swamp NWR,** at the Suwannee Canal access on the east side. Clumps of the hooded pitcher plants grow near the 0.75-mile-long nature boardwalk leading to a cypress swamp. Look for the pitcher plants in the open, sunny wetlands before the swamp.

In Alabama, the **Weeks Bay National Estuarine Reserve** is reestablishing a pitcher plant bog that at one time may have covered as many as 40 or 50 acres. The unnatural absence of fire allowed maples and other saplings to encroach on the bog and gradually shade the plants out. The bog, reduced to about 2 acres, is now being managed with fire. Hopes are that within a few years the bog may expand to as many as 20 acres. Weeks Bay is located on Highway 98 near Fairhope on the eastern side of Mobile Bay.

In Florida's **Blackwater River State Forest,** take the loop trail around the **Bear Lake Recreation Area,** where sundews, bladderworts and especially pitcher plants are right beside the trail. Another good spot for pitcher plants especially is the **Wire Grass Trail.**

The **Apalachicola National Forest** is probably the one best place in the entire state to see carnivorous plants: Four different species grow here. They are concentrated in the southwestern section of the forest along the Scenic Byway, Highway 379 and State Road 65, in patches along the roadside. Most concentrated in the **Post Office Bay Savannah,** the plants grow throughout hundreds and hundreds of acres along a stretch of road between 8 and 10 miles long, from south of Wilma all the way past Sumatra. The savannahs alternate with flatwoods and other types of terrain. Please be very careful in parking along the road to see the carnivorous plants. There is a rare lily

Apalachicola National Forest
West Section

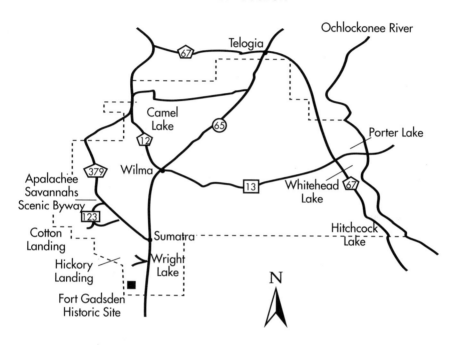

here that grows nowhere else in the world. It grows right beside the road.

Osceola National Forest has pitcher plants in wet areas scattered throughout the forest, especially in the transition areas between cypress domes and flatwoods. In the **Impassible Bay**—whose name accurately describes the dense fetterbush and greenbrier growth—is a true swamp where pitcher plants are quite common. There are a few openings into Impassible Bay, and old roads lead off into it from the primary Access Road 272.

Kanapaha Botanical Gardens in Gainesville also features carnivorous plants.

38

Lobstering

Like genuine Key lime pie and conch chowder, the spiny lobster belongs to the Sunshine State. This very tasty creature is quite distinctive in its absence of claws, a feature so prominent on its northern counterpart.

The lack of claws has both its good and bad points: It means the spiny lobster is easier to catch because a person doesn't have to worry about fingers getting mashed in a hearty handshake—but there's also less lobster to eat. The spiny lobster is so named because of the many sharp spines on its sides and its spiny-looking antennae.

Sometimes called a crayfish, the spiny lobster is found in Florida and throughout the Caribbean and Central America. In Florida, the best lobstering is from the Palm Beaches southward. During the day lobsters are found on reefs, around jetties and even on artificial reefs. Since artificial reefs are often visited only by line anglers, they can be well worth regular weekday visits, when this angling activity is lowest. However, thousands of lobsters typically migrate in the fall following spawning and molting, and after the first winter storm. They travel into deeper water in long lines, a moveable feast for the diver lucky enough to find them.

Snorkelers seeking lobsters in shallow water can cover considerable territory by dragging a person slowly behind a boat. When a lobster is sighted, the snorkeler can simply let go and descend to capture the animal. However, no one should tackle a spiny lobster bare-handed. Its spiny shell is sharp and most unpleasant to grab. Heavy gloves are a must.

The natural urge the first time you see a lobster is to grab it by the antennae. That's fine if all you want is a matched set of antennae: They are usually too delicate to put up with much manhandling and break off easily.

Lobsters, however, are fairly curious and not very bright, so if you haven't spooked one too badly, you may be able to lure it by cunning and guile. How? Simply beckon to it with your index finger while you keep the rest of your body motionless. The lobster may become curious enough about the movement that it will venture from its hiding place to within grabbing distance.

Suppose your lobster doesn't want to play games but wants instead to stay inside its home. How then do you get it out? The obvious answer is to reach in and grab it, but lobsters sometimes have roommates such as sea urchins, scorpion fish and moray eels. On the other hand, you may find two lobsters where you expected one. The safest procedure, in any case, is to indelicately grab a visible lobster by its head and pull, twisting at the same time to dislodge it.

If a lobster's hiding place has a sand or mud bottom, stir it up with your hand or an old broom handle. Then move back to the edge of the muddy water. The lobster will usually leave its cave. Lacking a dirt floor, you can try what's called "tickling" the lobster, though this really is a misnomer since it's doubtful a lobster feels anything through its shell. The tickle stick is about the only legal device you can use for taking lobster, because state law forbids the use of any mechanical device, hooks or spears. For tickling, place a blunted broom handle or stick into the hole and tap the lobster on

As the close-up of this tail section shows, the spiny lobster richly deserves its name. Divers who try to catch the lobsters normally wear gloves.

the tail. You shouldn't need to jab or gouge the lobster to get it to move forward. However, if the lobster is in a small hole, tickling won't work. The only thing to do then is make a grab for it.

If the lobster breaks free of your grip, don't consider it a lost bug. Although it may appear to be moving away at jet speed, this burst of energy typically occurs only once, and the path of flight is normally in a straight line. Swim after the lobster as fast as you can. Chances are you'll soon find it crawling along the bottom.

If things that go bump in the night don't bother you, twilight is a better time to hunt spiny lobsters, because they are more likely to venture forth in search of food after dark.

Hot Spots Regardless of when you go lobstering, there are some important legal requirements that need to be kept in mind. Laws governing the capture of lobsters are strictly enforced. Lobsters must remain whole, in one piece, until brought to shore. You can't simply keep the tail and discard the rest. Egg-bearing females may not be kept and should be released immediately. Lobsters are subject to strict size restrictions. The legal measurements are a minimum of 3 inches from the point between the "horns" to the back of the carapace. Measuring devices are available at all dive shops.

The regular lobstering season starts the first week of August and runs through March 31. However, a special sport-lobster miniseason is normally held one weekend at the end of July. Check locally for dates and the possession limit. A crawfish stamp is required.

The Keys are probably the most popular place for lobster diving, but the waters off **Miami, Fort Lauderdale** and **West Palm Beach** can also be quite good. Farther north, **Daytona** is another area where it's easy to find dive trips dedicated to hunting lobster.

The spiny lobster is not only a delicacy but delicate and should be kept cool after capture. Like crabs, lobsters can sometimes be kept alive for several days in an ice chest or refrigerator. Once a lobster dies, the tail should be removed immediately, or the digestive juices from the intestines and stomach may seep into the tail and body meat, causing contamination. Although the meat is concentrated in the tail, many divers like the taste of the leg meat even more, so don't just take off the tail and discard the rest of the animal.

Lobsters can be cooked in a variety of ways. Boiling is the easiest method: Drop a live lobster into boiling salted water head-first and cook according to weight. It takes about 7 minutes for a 1-pound lobster (the most common size), 12 minutes for 2 pounds, 15 minutes for 3 to 5 pounds and about 20 minutes for a really big bug going 6 to 10 pounds. Once cooked, the lobster should be placed under cold water for a few seconds, then served while still hot.

Broiling is good too, but too many cooks make the mistake of leaving the tail uncovered, which tends to dry it out. Baste the meat side of the tail shell with butter and paprika, then wrap it in foil. Place the foil about 6 inches from the heat and cook it for about 12 minutes on the meat side, another ten on the shell side. Brush the tail down again before turning. Serve with chilled white wine, garlic toast and a tossed salad. There aren't many better ways to end a day.

39

Endangered Red-Cockaded Woodpeckers

The red-cockaded woodpecker is the Southeast's version of the spotted owl, a highly specialized creature that relies on old-growth forests for its welfare. Red-cockaded woodpeckers live in mature forests of longleaf and slash pine where the trees range in age from 60 to 120 years or older. The birds excavate their nests in old living pines infected with red heart disease. This disease produces a white flowing resin that the birds place around their nest openings, possibly to discourage snakes. This woodpecker is the only bird that makes such cavities in live southern pines. This kind of specialization has placed the tiny woodpecker at a severe disadvantage, and its number has dwindled so greatly that it is now an endangered species. In this booming region, most mature pine forests have been cut down.

The outlook for saving the red-cockaded woodpecker is not favorable unless new steps are taken to provide it acceptable nesting space. On both public and private lands, trees are typically harvested on a rotation of every 20 to 40 years. Traditionally, the emphasis has been on harvesting to the maximum, even on public lands where income from timber has become increasingly important. The result is that wildlife is always at a disadvantage, even on lands that are intended to protect them. What is certain is that protection is likely to occur only within the boundaries of state and national forests and refuges. As a result, environmentalists in recent years have filed a number of lawsuits to alter this very short-sighted land management policy. The change has been slow to follow, but at least it has been happening.

The red-cockaded woodpecker, only 8 inches in length, is one of the area's smallest woodpeckers. The back and top of its head are black. It has ladderlike patterns of small white spots arranged in a horizontal pattern on the back and wings, and large white cheek patches. The red cockades of the male are not readily visible.

These very sociable birds live in clans of two to nine birds. They roost in a cluster of cavity trees called a *colony*, which may consist of only two trees or up to a dozen. Only one clan uses a colony, but not all trees in the colony may be in use. Some tree cavities may still be under construction, others will be in use and yet others may be abandoned. Although the woodpeckers may spend months and even years to perfect their tree cavities, other animals, including bees, bluebirds and other woodpeckers, often try to claim them. The main work on the tree cavities takes place following the nesting period, not before, and it's usually done in the morning.

Red-cockaded woodpeckers breed from late April through July and lay a clutch of two to five eggs. Nonbreeding family members serve as helpers in supplying food for the young, bearing fruit, beetles and other insects to the nest. They also incubate the eggs during the day, but at night the breeding male takes over. The eggs hatch in ten to twelve days. A clan normally requires a foraging area of a hundred acres or more. The birds feed at the base and limbs of pine trees that, ideally, are 9 inches and larger in diameter.

Plans are being discussed about providing man-made wooden boxes for the woodpeckers to nest in, which would offer the species a good opportunity to rebound. A similar program used for wood ducks since the 1940s has been a tremendous success.

Hot Spots

Most of the remaining red-cockaded woodpeckers (RCWs) live in the national forests. Their trees are easy to spot from a distance, for they appear to have been painted white by the flowing resin. The nests are about 30 feet off the ground in trees that are a foot or larger in diameter. The birds are visible any time of year because they are nonmigratory and sleep in the tree cavity. (Gopher tortoises and red-cockaded woodpeckers like the same kind of habitat, so be on the lookout for the tortoises and their burrows.)

The best times to see red-cockaded woodpeckers are early in the morning, just after sunrise, when they will be leaving their trees; and late in the afternoon, when they will be returning. They are quite vocal at both times with a high-pitched peep. They are often most visible during the nesting season when they are outside attending to their trees.

In bright sunshine, the resin of an actively used tree shines like the wax on a white candle. This is because the bird makes many small holes in the tree bark to create what are called *resin wells.* The white flow typically extends from several feet above the cavity to the tree base.

Blackwater River State Forest has RCW nests that are quite easy to spot from the road. **Three Notch,** which is in the **Coldwater Recreation Area,** is the most active place.

Apalachicola National Forest has the region's largest remaining population of red-cockaded woodpeckers in the stands of longleaf pine. It is distinguished from other pines by the fountainlike needles at the ends of branches that are supported by 1-inch-thick twigs, the largest produced by any pine species. It's possible to see numerous nests along the **Florida Trail,** which crosses through the huge, 557,000-acre forest. Easier still is driving along a number of forest roads.

Apalachicola is divided into both western and eastern sections. More RCWs live in the western half, in numbers large enough that the population is considered to be totally recovered. The highest concentration of nests is in the area called **Wilma,** near the intersection of State Road 12 and State Road 65. The trees are easy to spot from a car: All the active trees have white bands painted on them. Park, approach quietly and wait.

In the eastern section of the forest, some of the best spots are off Roads 376 and 373. The best map pinpointing the nesting areas is contained in the 1989 edition of Lane's *A Birder's Guide to Florida.* Nests are also sometimes seen as one drives through the nearby **Ochlockonee State Park,** west of the town of Panacea on U.S. 319.

Slash pine is dominant in the **Osceola National Forest,** but red-cockaded woodpecker nests can be found in the stands of longleaf pine by going east on U.S. 90 to Forest Road 236, the first paved road. Turn left and continue north to Forest Road 278. Go right, and you should find several nests over the next 6 miles. You can also hike to nests by taking U.S. 90 east past Forest Road 236 to the **Mt. Carrie Wayside Park.** Leave your vehicle here and start on the 1-mile trail. The nest trees are easily discerned.

Another spot is the area around the **Olustee Battlefield.** The nests are off the battlefield and in the woods, requiring a short walk. The **Florida Trail** extension going north from the battlefield passes a colony at about the first half-mile. Osceola National Forest, the smallest of Florida's three national forests, is located south of I-10 west of Jacksonville.

Osceola National Forest/ Red-Cockaded Woodpecker Clusters

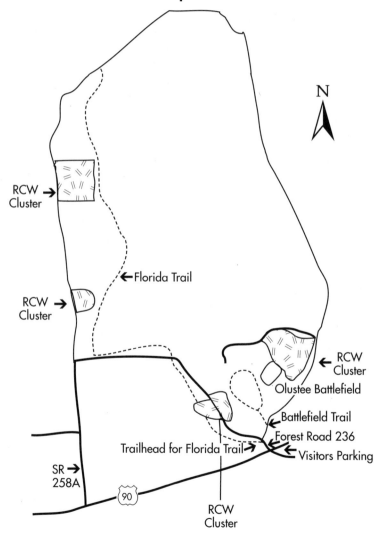

N

RCW
Cluster

←Florida Trail

RCW
Cluster

RCW
Cluster

Olustee Battlefield

Battlefield Trail

Forest Road 236

Trailhead for Florida Trail→

Visitors Parking

SR
258A

90

RCW
Cluster

North of I-10 is the **Cary State Forest,** where nests are far less common. Rather than search blindly, check with the ranger to see if he has a nest located. The forest is located off U.S. 301 about 9 miles north of I-10 and the town of Baldwin.

It seems to be almost a secret that **Withlacoochee State Forest** near Brooksville has one of the state's largest RCW populations—roughly 60 nesting sites, the third largest number in public ownership. They are located on the Croom and Citrus tracts of the forest, with the best area on the Citrus tract north of Forest Road 10. Some nests are visible from the car, but it's best to stop at the Brooksville headquarters for specific directions because the nests are widely scattered.

In the much larger **Ocala National Forest,** red-cockaded woodpecker nests are confined to the northern part, northwest of the Salt Springs Recreation Area. One of the best places to see them is on Forest Road 884.

Big Cypress National Preserve has one of South Florida's few good RCW populations, but getting to the colony requires some effort. Take the Florida Trail north from the Oasis Ranger Station, which is located on the Tamiami Trail about 50 miles west of Miami. It's about a 4-mile walk to the RCW colony. This is some of the prettiest and most remote RCW habitat in the state.

40

Plants That Walk?

If carnivorous plants can adapt to eating meat, then the ability to walk surely would be the next significant step in the evolution of flora. Just a few decades ago it was speculated that this had already happened. Red mangroves, with their long spindly legs, were credited with having achieved such mobility, though in a manner very different from that practiced in the animal kingdom.

The theory was based on the fact that the red mangrove, supposedly the most salt-tolerant of the three mangrove species, grows right to the edge of the water. Red mangroves were perceived as actively "walking seaward" because they accumulated sediment in the maze of their tangled roots. Once red mangrove roots had enough sediment, the plant would colonize a place and begin collecting more sediment so it could expand once more.

In some ways, this theory seemed quite probable. The red mangrove lacks a deep taproot, and its root system is shallow. In other words, red mangroves aren't all that securely planted to begin with, so the idea that they were always "walking" seaward became a popular one. Like a lot of intriguing theories, this one didn't hold up to close scrutiny for very long.

The walking theory was based on the concept that red mangroves actively were taking part in this advancement process by inducing a sequence of events that would eventually cause them to advance forward. But by the 1980s it was recognized that mangroves were not actively participating in, but passively responding to, external forces such as changes in water level and/or the shoreline. No walking trees ... yet.

But that hardly detracts from the importance and uniqueness of these extremely salt-tolerant plants. Mangroves are extremely important shoreline stabilizers. They often are the trees of choice for herons, ibis and other birds nesting along the coast this month.

There are three true species of mangroves in Florida: the red mangrove, the black mangrove and the white mangrove. The red mangrove is usually, but not always, closest to the water and has a maze of red interlocking roots that are almost impossible to penetrate. Red mangroves also have developed *prop roots* that grow from the lower part of the stem, as well as *drop roots* that grow from both the upper part of the stem and the tree's branches.

The black mangrove is best identified by its shallow cable roots that grow from the tree and produce *pneumatophores* that extend

Red mangroves and their twisted roots provide vital shelter for small gamefish, lobsters and crabs.

fingerlike above the soil. The third species, the white mangrove, has distinctive broad, flat, oval leaves.

The buttonwood, often classified as a fourth mangrove species, is not a true mangrove but a mangrove *associate*. Its root system lacks any modification for growing in saturated saline soil. Buttonwood, the most inland segment of the mangrove ecosystem, is better classified as a fringe element instead of a major participant in the mangrove community.

All mangroves are warm-weather trees. They do not survive where the annual average temperature is below 66 degrees. Freezing temperatures lasting just a few hours will kill the trees.

Although they grow on coastal shorelines, mangroves do not need salt water for vigorous growth. They utilize either fresh or salt water, whichever is available. And even though mangroves will grow well in nothing but fresh water, the plants are mostly found along the coast, apparently because the salt is harmful to other potential competing species.

Mangroves thrive best where there is low wave action. High powerful waves can destroy the root systems and wash away the anchoring sediment. Areas of Central and South America off the normal hurricane path grow mangroves that are considerably taller than those of Florida, where storms and freezes periodically devastate the mangrove community. Mangroves rarely grow higher than 20 feet in Florida but may tower as much as 100 feet above the water farther south.

Once blown down, mangroves are far from out. They are able to disperse over a wide region and establish new seedlings quickly. Mangroves produce brownish berries almost $1\frac{1}{2}$ inches long that begin to germinate while still on the tree and that grow an embryonic root as many as 12 inches long. Once the fruit falls, it drifts for weeks or months until it washes up on land. Once ashore, a new tree begins to grow almost immediately.

Nesting birds are not the only creatures who use mangroves as an integral element of their life cycle. The interlocking root system provides a safe haven for numerous small fish and invertebrates. Mangroves are also vital coastal nurseries upon which many of the most popular gamefish species depend.

Indeed, the variety and numbers of animals that use mangroves and associated waters is amazing: 181 species of birds; an estimated 220 species of fish, including tarpon, snook, mullet, bonefish and mangrove snapper; 18 mammal species, such as raccoons, black bear and river otters; and 24 species of reptiles and amphibians, including frogs, lizards, snakes and turtles. Invertebrates, for which no set number depending on mangroves has yet been formulated, include pink shrimp and the spiny lobster. The precise number of insects hasn't been established either, but on a still, hot summer evening it is all too evident that every saltwater mosquito species resides in mangroves, and that each tree houses enough of the biting insects to equal the population of China.

Hot Spots

Because of their warm-weather temperature requirements, extensive stretches of mangroves don't really begin until the Indian River section of the **Intracoastal Waterway** (ICW) near Ponce de Leon Inlet. Many of the spoil islands created to form the ICW have become dense with mangroves, but a boat is required to see most of them. South Florida stripped away many of its mangroves to allow shoreline development, but **Biscayne National Park** just south of Miami has 26 miles of unbroken mangrove shoreline bordering its eastern boundary. Located near Homestead, Biscayne Park has the longest unbroken stretch of mangroves remaining along Florida's east coast.

The **Keys** are rich in mangroves (many small islands are basically mangrove-covered, affording humans little chance of ever going ashore). The boardwalk nature trails at **John Pennekamp Coral Reef State Park** at Key Largo and at **Long Key State Park** near Layton cut right through thick mangrove forests. The edges of **Everglades National Park** and the **Wilderness Waterway** near the western park boundary have some of Florida's largest mangroves. The **West Lake Trail** located 30.5 miles inside the park on the road to Flamingo offers a good look at mangroves. The **Ten Thousand Islands** and some of the barrier islands off Fort Myers, including **Sanibel Island**, contain thick mangrove forests.

Remember, mangroves and mosquitoes go hand in hand. It's impossible to overstate how important it is to have a good insect repellent, especially at twilight.

41

July Shorttakes

Pelagic Birding Trips

One of Florida's greatest natural assets is something few visitors except fishermen ever see, the Gulf Stream. The Gulf Steam flows into Florida from the Caribbean, bringing with it many pelagic bird species that are rarely, if ever, viewed from shore. In the Keys, the Gulf Steam may be as little as 5 or 10 miles from land, but the problem is getting there: Organized pelagic birding trips are rare. The general attitude has been, With so much to see on land, why take the trouble to go offshore?

The answer is obvious: Because it's there, and you may see anything from masked boobies, to greater shearwaters to Cory's shearwaters, among others. Although the Gulf Steam continues due north along the entire Florida coast, the coastline shifts remarkably to the northwest, so that at Jacksonville the Stream is as many as 70 miles offshore. Trips from the Keys literally take only minutes, compared to hours elsewhere.

Unless one is wealthy enough to charter a boat of his or her own, the best way to get to the Gulf Steam is aboard a party or "head" boat filled with bottom anglers. You might as well bring along a rod with the binoculars. There are no guarantees of success, so a half-day trip is the best way to approach the matter. Party boats leave from **Islamorada, Marathon** and **Key West.** Farther north, it's possible to join party boats out of **Port Canaveral** and **Ponce de Leon Inlet.** Because of the much longer run to the Gulf Steam, these Central Florida trips last all day.

Pelagic bird trips are also possible on boats out of **St. Petersburg** and **Clearwater,** but in the Gulf it's necessary to go out at least 50 miles to have much success. In recent years, local Audubon Society chapters have scheduled birding trips to the **Dry Tortugas.** One is the Orange Audubon Society, P.O. Box 941142, Maitland, FL 32794-1142.

Blue Crabs

Blue crabs are a wonderful seafood delicacy, and this is the time of year to net them, trap them or lure them close to hand with a chicken neck tied to a piece of string. The best crabbing is often in the mouths of rivers flowing into the ocean. Especially good along all the Southeast coasts is the protected passage known as the **Intracoastal Waterway**. The easiest and most productive crabbing is done with crab traps, which can be put out in the morning and inspected at noon and in the evening. Check the local regulations on the number of traps permitted and where they may be placed. Crab traps are available at most marinas (which should also have copies of current regulations) and in major discount stores. A popular place in Florida for crabbing with chicken necks is **Turtle Mound**, an old Native-American shell mound at the northern end of **Canaveral National Seashore. Hickory Mound Impoundment**, located 18 miles west of Perry in the Big Bend region, is another good location for this crabbing method.

42

A Closer Look:
Animal Navigation

The sea turtles that crawl ashore on hot summer nights to nest in Florida and other parts of the Southeast have swum a long way. Most will have spent the winter months feeding in the Caribbean, thousands of miles away, on the rich grass beds there. Yet each sea turtle has returned not just to the United States but to the very same beach where she laid her eggs in previous years, the very same beach that she will continue to revisit season after season for as long as she lives to renew the species.

During the idyllic days of summer, manatees may roam up and down the Florida peninsula or even venture as far as the Carolinas or Texas. However, in winter they will die if they remain in water temperatures below 60 degrees for extended periods. So, come the first cold weather, the same groups of animals will return year after year to the comfortable 72-degree temperatures of certain spring runs and rarely to any other place.

In autumn, monarch butterflies and broad-winged hawks travel down the East Coast on their annual migrations. The monarchs are destined for their wintering grounds in the highlands of Mexico, the hawks to their winter roosts in Peru. As they are leaving, white pelicans are arriving from their summer breeding grounds thousands of miles to the northwest to winter in Alabama, Florida and Georgia.

Songbirds are another species that travel to far-off places seasonally but return not only to the same nesting territory but to the exact same nest year after year, as do pairs of bald eagles that have been separated over the summer.

How do they all do it? How do they accomplish their homecomings with such unerring precision?

We don't know, though we do have some clues. And what we've learned is quite remarkable compared to human navigation, dependant on the squiggly lines drawn by others on pieces of paper to find the way.

Much of what we know about animal navigation skills is based on studies with birds, especially pigeons. Among the easiest animals to track, pigeons recovered from great distances that bear simple leg bands can reveal a great deal. Animal migration seems to involve two elements. The first is orientation: The animal must know exactly where it is. The second aspect concerns navigation: The animal must be able to find precisely where it wants to go.

For birds, eyesight appears to play an important role in navigation. Local landmarks are employed for short flights when hunting or feeding. During long migrations, larger landmarks, such as coastlines and mountain ranges, serve as important navigational aids.

But like early mariners, birds apparently are skilled at celestial navigation, an important asset in heavy fog or at night. In fog, birds will often stay above the opaque layer to orient themselves by the sun. Planetarium studies with captive songbirds, which normally migrate at night, have revealed that these birds do orient themselves by the stars. And it doesn't need to be a completely clear night, either. If clouds obscure great portions of the sky, the songbird's navigational ability is still quite efficient.

Piloting by eyesight is something we all can understand, but what some species accomplish seems almost magic. Take the earth's magnetic field. To humans, it's as invisible as the phantom routes of migratory animals. We require a compass to detect the earth's magnetic field, but the latest research suggests that birds are able to sense it. It may be because they actually have rocks in their heads—in the form of magnetite, a magnetically sensitive type of iron oxide. This may be the secret of the homing pigeon, whose unfailing ability to find its way home made it the world's first airborne courier service.

What is more remarkable, some scientists claim that birds not only sense the earth's magnetic field but are able to see it. Such an ability would go a long way toward explaining the superb navigational ability of sea turtles, which have little in the way of visual landmarks. Like human swimmers, sea turtles are too low in the water to rely on any type of landmark even when a few miles away from shore. Besides, although sea turtles have good underwater vision, they are extremely nearsighted in the air.

If sea turtles use the earth's magnetic fields to guide them to the same beach each year, that would explain much. So would the suggestion that sea turtles are also able to follow a special taste or smell that's unique to each area of the ocean or perhaps even a coastline. This is not as far-fetched as it sounds, because the brain area that governs a sea turtle's sense of smell is very well developed.

Smell is known to be an important navigational sense for some birds, such as the petrel. For instance, a Leach's storm petrel at night in pitch blackness is able to find its own island burrow by the distinctive smell—but not if its nostrils are deliberately plugged. Fish too rely on smell to return to their spawning grounds. American shad, like salmon, apparently can detect minuscule levels of molecules in the water and identify their home river by its unique scent.

How much does smell aid the American eels born in the St. Johns River that make an astonishing journey once they reach about 10 years of age? Even landlocked eels have been known to cross fields wet with dew in order to reach rivers flowing seaward so that they may reach the Sargasso Sea, an area of dense seaweed located between Bermuda and Puerto Rico. It takes months to complete this journey, after which the eels spawn and die.

Some migratory birds seem to use hearing as yet another navigational guide. Birds may be able to hear low-frequency noises like wind and waves, sounds that may be detected for hundreds if not thousands of miles away. Changes in barometric pressure and the amount of ultraviolet light may also provide additional clues.

Of course, some scientists would argue that all this is merely instinctive behavior genetically encoded and, therefore, automatically programmed. These animals would never have developed these abilities if they didn't need to exploit various environments because of seasonal climate changes and the varying availability of food. Monarch butterflies, for instance, rely on milkweed for their main food source, and so when temperatures drop in the United

States in the fall, it's off to the milkweed and warmer climates of Mexico. All cut-and-dry, thank you.

Perhaps, but the stamina required for so delicate a creature as a monarch to travel from the fields of Canada to the tall trees of Mexico while also navigating unerringly along the way is a remarkable feat anyone would appreciate. What might it be like if we could read the earth like a road map, and we followed all our avenues in an unerring way?

August

Notes

43

Underwater Snowstorm

It has only recently been discovered that the week following the August full moon is an especially dramatic and active time underwater in the Florida Keys. On the eighth night following the full moon, the rarely witnessed phenomenon of mass coral reproduction takes place as several species of sexually reproducing corals erupt and fill the ocean with millions of BB-sized coral eggs and sperm packets. The mass spawning is like a huge underwater snowstorm as the eggs and sperm packets float to the surface and fertilize. The larvae that develop from the fertilized eggs eventually settle on the ocean floor to form new coral colonies.

Generally speaking, Florida's reefs are made up of colonies of similar types of corals, but what causes colonies to assume a particular shape—such as those of the staghorn coral or the huge boulderlike star corals—still isn't known. Genetic coding, probably.

For many years it was believed that corals were plants. Now they are recognized as animals, and their reefs are considered among the most spectacular natural wonders of the world. As solid and unyielding as any mountain, the massive reefs are built by animals no larger than a thimble, creatures that have labored together for millennia to form a structure as complex and intricate as anything man has yet devised.

Some of the intricate, elaborate forms are startlingly similar to many shapes found on land. It's as if some master sculptor, finding a design pleasing once, sought to duplicate it in a totally different environment. For example, the massive stands of elkhorn and staghorn corals richly deserve their names: These corals indeed mirror the racks of game animals with uncanny precision. Other corals resemble trees and shrubs and are sometimes so delicate in appearance that they seem far too fragile to exist, as if the slightest wave action would rip them apart.

Although the analogy may seem a bit grotesque, a living reef is much like a giant graveyard. The hard limestone exterior is actually a skeleton built on top of countless generations of dead coral creatures. This, in fact, is how the reefs grow: by accumulating more and more limestone layers that form only through the deaths of countless coral animals. This is why the growth rate of coral reefs is relatively slow. Their size increases only when one life cycle ends and a new one begins. Even then, growth is defined in terms only of inches per decade.

The small coral animals, known as *polyps,* normally hide inside the reef skeleton during the day. The polyps look much like squat sea anemones and in fact are closely related to them. It is primarily because of their tentacles that scientists once classified corals as plants. Polyps usually appear only after dark, when they emerge to feed. Polyps use their tentacles to send out small stinging threads to paralyze and kill minute prey. These venomous threads are so small and weak that larger creatures hardly ever notice them, with one important exception: fire coral, which has a richly deserved name.

When polyps are feeding, the reef changes dramatically in appearance. No longer does it look like a cold, dead rock garden. Instead, it becomes almost a tiny forest of waving filaments colored off-white, yellow, perhaps even bright orange. Looking at a reef when all the polyps are out can make one ponder the effects of overpopulation. Coral polyps live jammed together like the proverbial sardines in a can, and their tentacles almost intertwine like quilt threads. It does seem amazing that they could thrive so well in such a crowded condition.

Left to their own devices, the corals probably would not survive in such close quarters. However, they have worked out a remarkable arrangement with the microscopic plant life and algae that live in their tissue. As the polyps consume oxygen and give off carbon dioxide, the plant cells use up the coral waste and produce oxygen of their own as they photosynthesize. The result is a very stable and equally beneficial living arrangement for both plant and animal.

Continued enlargement of a coral colony can be brought about only through a steady reproduction rate. Not only do corals reproduce sexually, as when they spew eggs and sperm in August, but they can also reproduce asexually, through budding, where one polyp splits into two, which then grow and split, and so on.

Although the living corals are top on the totem pole for their particular colony, they often are forced to serve as the basement for a lot of other ocean inhabitants that sometimes walk over them, literally. Coral reefs are essentially a huge condominium complex for crabs, shrimp and other animals that live on the surface of the reef or hide in its crevices and overhangs. The corals are not always treated well by those they provide homes for. Parrot fish, for instance, graze on the corals with their sharp buck teeth. In the process of grinding up the coral skeleton and passing it off as waste, the parrot fish contribute new sand to the ocean floor.

Coral reefs also serve as permanent anchoring points for the remarkable creatures known as Christmas tree worms. When its gills are extended, the worm does look exactly like a tiny fir tree less than thumb high. When a Christmas tree worm is threatened, its gills disappear almost instantly into the worm's tubular casing, which sits atop a hard coral. Christmas tree worms sometimes cluster together in small colonies, looking like a small forest painted in fluorescent colors. The colors may range from pink to orange to purple to red to white. Flowering close together, the worm gills look like a painted forest Gulliver might have seen in Lilliput.

The varieties of worms and other animals that thrive on the coral reef system may be second only to those of the rainforest in terms of the diversity of life-forms. But it is the corals themselves that create the limestone foundation for all other life. It's definitely an unusual experience to swim through their reproductive soup.

Hot Spots The coral spawning phenomenon can be witnessed by snorkelers and scuba divers because the eggs and sperm packets float to the surface. Normally the event begins the eighth night after the August full moon, but this is still an unpredictable act of nature that also seems influenced by other elements such as wind and ocean currents. Although it is likely to occur, it's not guaranteed.

Several dive centers in the **Upper Keys** usually hold special programs during this time. **Captain Slate's Atlantis Dive Center** in Key Largo sets up an underwater oceanographic monitoring station for several nights as part of Project Reef Spawn, an international documentation program. Divers may participate as spectators or information gatherers. For information, call (800) 331-3483 or (305) 451-9240. The **Amoray Dive Resort** in Key Largo also holds educational sessions followed by a night dive for several evenings; call (800) 4-AMORAY or (305) 451-3595. In Islamorada, **Lady Cyana Divers** also offers ocean ecology lectures and night dives; (800) 221-8717 or (305) 664-8717.

44

The Snail-Loving Limpkin

Serious birders will want to add this species to their life lists, because in the United States the range of the limpkin is quite limited: It extends only from Georgia's Okefenokee Swamp and south through the Florida peninsula. The limpkin's range outside of North America is substantial, however—all the way to the southern end of South America.

The limpkin is a large bird, about the size of a long, slender goose. It is mostly dark brown with white streaks and spots, as if its feathers had been splattered by a wet paintbrush. Its bill is long, slender and downward-curved, ideally suited for probing vegetation for prey.

An important factor that appears to prevent the bird from extending its territory is its dependence on a particular type of freshwater snail, the pomacea, or apple, snail. Limpkins are able to dispatch a snail quickly, opening it with the expertise and speed of a two-handed oyster shucker. Besides snails, limpkins also eat aquatic insects and frogs.

Related to the cranes and rails, the limpkin is almost prissy-looking as it carefully and daintily places its long dark-olive feet on floating rafts of water lettuce or other floating vegetation bordering a riverbank. When walking quickly it appears to be limping, which may account for its name. As it takes to the air, it flies with jerky motions, like a crane, with legs and neck outstretched.

Primarily a nocturnal bird, the limpkin is easily spotted early or late in the day at the edges of marshes and flooded swamps. At night, the bird issues a very disturbing, shiver-down-the-back type of call that sometimes sounds like a young child in distress. Its loud, repeating *kerr-r-ee-ow* is one of the noises that makes swamps so eerie at night.

Nesting appears to occur year-round. Females lay between five and eight eggs in a nest made of matted water plants that is located just above the high-water line. The young can swim as soon as they hatch.

When not harassed, limpkins allow people to approach quite closely, making them ideal photo candidates.

The limpkin, which feeds on apple snails, appears to limp when it walks quickly. Its North American range is limited to Florida.

Hot
Spots

Canoeists tend to know limpkins well, since the birds are
common on the banks of many spring-fed streams throughout Florida. Anyone spending much time fishing or exploring the rivers and spring runs will find limpkins frequent
companions.

Places limpkins can be seen almost any day of the year include **Wakulla Springs State Park,** just south of Tallahassee,
with river cruise boats on hand for half-hour tours, and the
Alexander Springs Run in the **Ocala National Forest,** which
has a canoe concession at the spring headwaters. The very
crowded **Rock Springs Run** flows into the **Wekiva Springs
Run** near **Wekiwa Springs State Park** outside Orlando. Canoe
concessions are available at the park itself or at the Wekiva
Marina, just south of the state facility.

Limpkins have plenty of feeding territory on the banks of
the **St. Johns River** south of Lake George. The birds usually
stay in side bays, away from the main channel, which is often
crowded with power boats. Especially good is the area around
Lake Woodruff NWR.

Limpkins are quite common around the scores of lakes that
pockmark **Ocala National Forest**; get a map from one of the
ranger stations because it's easy to lose your way.

At **Loxahatchee NWR** the limpkin shares its bountiful
supply of apple snails with one of Florida's rarest birds, the
small Everglades snail kite. Search along the boardwalk or
rent a power boat or canoe to hunt the extensive waterway
system. Loxahatchee is actually a northern portion of the
Everglades.

Another reliable stretch of water is on the Gulf Coast at the
Lower Suwannee NWR, where the birds are fairly common,
especially in the tributaries. Again, a boat is a necessity.
One can be rented in the town of Suwannee or in Fowler's
Bluff.

On the Gulf Coast near St. Petersburg, **Sawgrass Lake Park's**
overlook tower should show limpkins working the shoreline.
Take U.S. 19 to 62nd Avenue north and turn east; go about

0.5 mile to 25th Street North and turn left. Follow signs to the park.

Look for limpkins at **Myakka River State Park** along the Bird Walk on North Park Drive. The park is located south of Sarasota; take I-75 Exit 37 and travel east on State Road 72 for 9 miles to the park entrance. **Corkscrew Swamp Sanctuary** near Naples has limpkins all year.

45

The Littlest Deer

One of the world's most endangered animals is the Key deer, nature's smallest version of the white-tailed deer. These animals, which weigh no more than a large dog, have a population almost as tiny as their size. Between 200 to 400 animals survive on a handful of landfalls in the lower Florida Keys.

Key deer are visible year-round, but August is an exceptional month. The bucks are particularly magnificent looking as they sport their new racks covered in velvet, the soft furry-looking vascular skin that envelops and nourishes the developing antlers. The bucks will rub off the velvet in early September, and the rut begins around the middle of that month. The rut peaks in October, then gradually decreases through November and December. The bucks will drop their antlers in February and March, and the fawns (weighing between 2 and 4 pounds) will be born from April through June.

In August the bucks have not yet begun to fight for territory, so they are still easily approachable. They are also an incredibly splendid sight. Their tawny-colored bodies and furry-looking antlers seem to glow in the diffuse, muffled sunlight just after dawn or prior to twilight. An added bonus this month is the opportunity to closely approach the offspring of last year's mating season. In August, the fawns still retain many of their spots (though those will soon disappear), and most have lost any shyness around humans.

Amazingly, you don't need to venture out into the 90-degree-plus heat to witness any of this. The deer readily present themselves along the sides of roads and usually pay little attention to cars that stop to observe them. This lack of fear poses one of the greatest threats to the herd's welfare: An average of one deer a week is killed by a car on Big Pine Key, headquarters of the National Key Deer Refuge. The main thoroughfare through the Keys, U.S. 1, is one of the roads that bisects the refuge, and about half the fatalities happen along this roadway despite a posted speed limit that is lower than on any other island. These collisions are just as apt to take place during the day as at night. Obviously, this is one instance where sharing the land isn't working at all well.

The problem is that only 40 percent of Big Pine Key is protected habitat. On a map, the island is revealed as a checkerboard of houses and businesses, and more development is planned. Some of the local developers would like to turn Big Pine Key into another Key West. That's a strange mind-set to understand, for a Key West style of life is not why people moved to this region to begin with. Furthermore, Key West is just another 30 miles farther south geographically, though it feels more like decades away psychologically.

Developers, interested only in dollar signs, and bureaucrats, who need a larger tax base to provide them with more power, are always an unholy alliance where protecting nature is concerned. On Big Pine Key, the two factions clearly deserve to count their money together—in hell.

If the status of the Key deer is still precarious today, at least it is far more secure than during the 1940s, when only an estimated 50 animals existed. Hunting and some habitat destruction had eliminated the rest. The establishment of the National Key Deer Refuge in 1957, coupled with strong law enforcement, saved the herd from extinction.

Traditionally, Key deer have been considered a subspecies of the Virginia white-tailed deer, which probably migrated from the mainland thousands of years ago during the last glacial period, when a land bridge existed. Then they were isolated as the sea rose to create the stepping-stone islands known as the Florida Keys.

Key deer are genetically small, not stunted because of lack of food. No matter how much you feed a Key deer, it won't grow larger than its relatives. The smaller size is believed to be an adaptation to ensure greater survival in a hot climate where there is limited food and water.

A shipwrecked Spanish explorer named Fontaneda recorded the first account of Key deer. The deer were considered a naturally occurring species by both Spaniards and Native Americans, who hunted the animals for food. Key deer were never very widely distributed throughout the region, due to the lack of fresh water. Today they range from Johnson Keys to Saddlebunch Keys, with about three-quarters of the herd centered on Big Pine Key and No Name Key.

In summer, the wet season, the females will sometimes visit keys that have limited amounts of water in order to fawn. One doe, in fact, was recorded swimming almost a half-mile to Big Pine daily for fresh water, then returning to her fawn on a nearby island.

To help increase year-round habitat on some of these outer islands, refuge personnel have dug water holes and put out "guzzlers," which hold 500 to 1,000 gallons of rainwater. Sometimes the deer have taken advantage of these improvements; sometimes

The Key deer, a dog-sized subspecies of the white-tailed deer, is quite easy to approach in many parts of Big Pine Key. It is illegal to feed one.

they have avoided them because something apparently was missing from the habitat (something we humans still can't identify).

Because much of the Key deer habitat is thick and spread out, it's impossible to come up with anything other than a boxcar estimate of their number. The count comes from road sightings, nighttime bicycle trips and spotting with lights at night. In addition, beginning in April, area residents are asked to report all the newborn fawns they see. Although the same fawn is apt to be reported more than once, by comparing each year's count with previous reports, it's possible to determine a general trend. The current trend, at least, is that the herd is stable and increasing in some areas. Just as important, the general health of the herd appears to be quite good in most sections.

The herd health is declining, however, near residential areas where a lot of feeding by people goes on—even though such feeding is illegal. Feeding by humans creates several problems. First, it causes the deer to concentrate in an area instead of dispersing through a wide variety of habitats, as they should. Furthermore, the normal Key deer diet is an extremely varied one that includes more than 150 different varieties of plants. There is no one food they nibble on more than others. In housing areas, the deer have only grass and a few sweet-tasting ornamental bushes to browse on. People add lettuce, cabbage, carrots and other store-bought foods that, in fact, may be too good for the deer. When the deer are concentrated in a limited area where the living is easy, parasites increase dramatically on their skin and in their digestive systems. In comparison, Key deer that roam more freely have few if any such parasites.

Deer that are accustomed to being fed will sometimes also eat out of trash cans. If they find something appetizing still in its plastic wrap, they sometimes consume both the food and the plastic, a true diet of death, because the plastic blocks the intestines and invariably kills the deer. Furthermore, the deer that stay crowded together are much more susceptible to contracting any disease that might break out in the herd. Nothing like this has yet happened, but what is of concern is the endemic deer virus the herd carries and that could become aggressive during a stressful period, such as during a drought or a hurricane. Although it may be common for white-tailed deer in other parts of the country to "gang" together, particularly during winter, Key deer normally stay fairly isolated from one another.

Key deer have evolved in other ways that are behaviorally, taxonomically, genetically and physically distinct from all the other white-tailed deer in North America. For instance, although fresh water is crucial to their long-term survival, the deer are able to drink fairly saline water—as much as 50 percent seawater—for short periods when necessary. They also eat mangrove leaves, which are very salty.

Key deer reproductive habits are unusual, too. The does very seldom deliver twins, and there are no records of triplets; northern whitetails commonly have twins, and triplets do occur. The ratio of males to females is much higher in the Keys, though what purpose this serves is not known. Bucks are the predominant roadkills.

Although Key deer do not gang up, they do live in extended families consisting of a doe and several years of her offspring. And occasionally two does will run together if they are related, whereas it's common for groups of five or six northern does to run together with their young.

The Key deer's only predator is man's best friend, the dog. Refuge officials have dealt with this problem effectively and efficiently by enforcing the county leash law. Even so, either through lack of cooperation or by mistake, dogs do sometimes get free, and a couple of deer are usually killed annually by canine pets.

Hot Spots The **National Key Deer Refuge** headquarters is located in the shopping center situated between Key Deer Boulevard and Wilder Road. Ask for the brochure *The Facts on Key Deer,* which has a map of the refuge. Remember, do not feed the deer! It's both illegal and bad for the animals. For more information, contact National Key Deer Refuge, P.O. Box 430510, Big Pine Key, FL 33043; (305) 872-2239.

Be careful when arriving on Big Pine Key. Many of the roadkills take place between Mile Markers 33 and 32, a broad curving stretch of road. The major intersection on Big Pine Key is at U.S. 1 and Key Deer Boulevard, which bears to the right. Proceed along Key Deer Boulevard, continuing past the shopping center on the right where the refuge office is located. Carefully observe the posted 35 mph speed limit. This road is regularly patrolled, and the speed limit is strictly enforced day and night.

Key Deer Boulevard extends for less than 5 miles. The best place to begin sighting deer starts at about mile three, though you may have to drive almost to the end to spot one of the animals. The best time to see a deer is during the two-hour period after sunrise and during the two hours before sunset. Because the deer lack any regular predators, they are very tame, perhaps too tame. If you see a deer eating on the side of the road, it's possible to park 20 or 30 yards away and approach it closely on foot to photograph it (a 200mm lens here is the maximum required).

In addition to the sides of the road, examine the field on your left at the Port Pine Heights housing development. Depending on how recently the grass has been cut, you may see as many as a half-dozen deer feeding in the field at one time. Farther down on the left is the old Lions Club building, which frequently has deer in back or across the street from it.

Adjoining Big Pine Key via a single road is **No Name Key**, most of which belongs to the refuge. No Name is reached via Wilder Road; where U.S. 1 intersects at the stoplight with Key Deer Boulevard, bear a sharp right onto Wilder Road. Currently there is no water or electricity on No Name Key, and the few people who live here rely on solar power and cisterns. No Name is sometimes better for observing deer at night than in the daytime.

46

Shifting Sands:
Sinkholes and Caves

Earthquakes are one of the few violent natural forces that have not had a hand in shaping Florida. So, instead of concerns about the ground trembling, the people of Central and North Florida have a different worry: The ground could swallow them up.

This uncommon but always annoying problem is created by sinkholes, giant maws in the ground that appear suddenly anytime, anywhere. In the past few years, they've opened under highways, apartment buildings and in the middle of nowhere. About 500 new sinkholes appear in Florida every year.

Florida's largest sinkhole, in the city of Winter Park near Orlando, claimed several expensive sports cars, a house, several trees and a road before it stopped gobbling up the earth. Today, the sinkhole is filled with water, resembling a placid pond. Several roads that were eaten away are now dead ends instead of through streets. A large, hungry sinkhole can never be filled.

Sinkholes are a sobering reminder of the awesome power of the Floridan aquifer, the huge underground river that flows beneath much of the state. The aquifer normally flows dozens of feet below ground level. Rising water sometimes pushes it toward the surface, causing it to bulldoze away tons of soil, which often produces a cave-in. Typically, these cave-ins happen incredibly fast and without warning. The unfortunate Winter Park woman whose house was swallowed up barely escaped before her home and yard slid into the huge pit.

Sinkholes, however, can also be created by the rainwater needed to recharge the underground aquifer, one of the state's most important sources of fresh drinking water. When Florida was covered by seawater thousands of years ago, living organisms deposited thick layers of limestone on the ocean floor. After the water receded, this limestone became the state's land base. Rainwater slowly seeped into the limestone, which dissolved to form many small caves, hollows and fissures. (Although rainwater is quite pure to drink, the drops become slightly acidic as they absorb carbon dioxide both from the air and from decaying vegetation. The mild acid is able to eat away and dissolve the limestone bedrock.) Eventually, the ground's surface may collapse to form a sinkhole or a crater-like depression. Limestone terrain that has been shaped by both rain and groundwater is known as *karst*.

Dry Sinks

Hot Spots

Leon Sinks are situated in the Woodville Karst Plain that extends from Tallahassee to the Gulf of Mexico. This plain is still active and evolving, which means new sinkholes are always a possibility. Located in the Apalachicola National Forest, Leon Sinks has three different walking trails that lead past both wet and dry sinkholes as well as swampland. The longest trail is three miles. On any of the trails, you'll have an excellent chance of spotting white-tailed deer, wild turkey, fox squirrels, gopher tortoises or red-shouldered hawks. One of the most interesting stops is the observation platform at Big Dismal Sink, which showcases over 75 different plant species perched on its steep sides. Plants that thrive around the sinks include longleaf and slash pines; ash, maple, beech and oak trees; wiregrass, gallberry and fetterbush form the underbrush. Leon Sinks is located off U.S. 319, 7 miles south of Tallahassee. For information, contact the Wakulla Ranger District, USDA Forest Service, Route 6, Box 7860, Crawfordville, FL 32327; (904) 926-3561. Leon Sinks is open from 8 A.M. to sunset.

The **Ocala National Forest** is one of the few places you can plumb the depths of a hundred-foot sinkhole and never get wet. Most sinkholes this deep are filled with water due to the state's high water table, but not the **Lake Eaton Sinkhole,** which is a huge depression that is 122 feet deep and 450 feet wide. Here, the water table happens to be too low. The trees that grow inside the sink itself are not common to Ocala's normal forest of scrub oak and sand pines. Instead, magnolia trees, live oaks, loblolly pine and sabal palms flourish in the heavy shade on the sides and bottom of this great pit.

The size of these trees and the small amount of organic material at the base of the sinkhole indicate that the sinkhole is probably less than a hundred years old. A wooden stairway, built to protect the pit against erosion, prevents anyone from standing in the deepest part of the pit. To find the Lake Eaton Sinkhole, from State Road 40 near Mill Dam, take Forest Road 79 and follow the winding road until the sinkhole sign appears on the right. The shortest path from the parking lot to the sinkhole rim is 0.5 mile.

Slightly larger than Lake Eaton is the **Devil's Millhopper,** an officially designated state geological site. This sinkhole is 120 feet deep and 500 feet across. A 221-step stairway leads to the very bottom of the sinkhole. From there, you can see or hear the water from the 12 different springs that flow down the sinkhole's sides. The intriguing name of Devil's Millhopper comes from the sink's funnel-like shape and the fossilized teeth and bones discovered at the bottom. In the 1800s, farmers who ground grain in grist mills used a funnel-shaped container called a hopper to hold the grain as it was fed into the grinder. Because of all the bones found here, this natural hopper was said to have been used to feed bodies to the devil; hence the Devil's Millhopper. This site is far more developed than Ocala's Lake Eaton. There's an interpretive center, and guided walks are offered Saturday mornings. Groups of five or more may be able to arrange walks at other times. Contact Devil's Millhopper State Geologic Site, 4732 Millhopper Road, Gainesville, FL 32606; (904) 336-2008.

Wet Sinks

Both of the following are popular sites for scuba divers, but casual sightseers should also find them interesting because of the remarkably different ways in which these two sinkholes were formed.

Devil's Den, only 30 minutes west of Ocala, is arguably the most impressive sinkhole in all of Florida. To reach the spring water that helped form it, you must descend an underground stairway to a wooden platform that places you at the center of an upside-down, scooped-out bowl that is almost 180-feet across and 30-feet high—all of it underground. Long lengths of vines and plants form a thick mat of jungle growth that hangs through the single jagged break in the limestone ceiling, making this a place of awesome, primitive beauty. Very visible overhead is a

Ocala National Forest

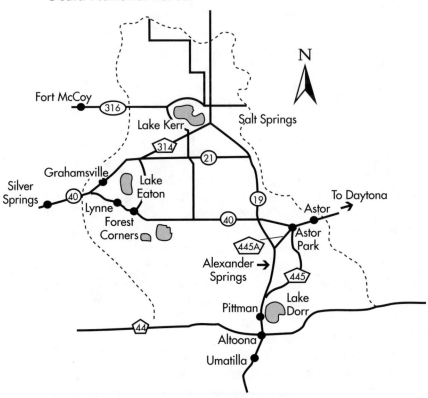

massive oak tree that leans over the opening, with half its tangled roots exposed. You may find yourself wondering if a single strong shove wouldn't topple the oak into the cavern—on top of you—but the tree is better anchored than it appears. The quiet underground pool is actually clear flowing water, part of the Floridan aquifer. At times, when it was at flood, the water was propelled almost through the earth's surface. If the water had eaten completely through the ground crust, Devil's Den would be just another hole in the ground.

Devil's Den received its name from early settlers who were understandably impressed by an extraordinary winter phenomenon: On cold days when the constant 72-degree springwater warms the cool air circulating in the huge cavern, great clouds of steam are generated. From a distance, this looks like smoke billowing from a huge underground fire; hence, Devil's Den.

Not far from Devil's Den is **Blue Grotto,** a very different kind of sinkhole formation. Blue Grotto is filled with water as much as 100 feet deep and is surrounded on all sides by steep dirt banks. As a true sink-syphon, it lacks the continuous, cleansing flow of a spring like Devil's Den, yet the water is still exceptionally clear. Unlike the sterile waters of Devil's Den, Blue Grotto is filled with fish, mostly bluegills.

Both sinks are located within a handful of miles of each other, just west of Williston on Highway 27A in North-Central Florida. This is about a half hour west of I-75. Signs prominently mark the respective turnoffs. Both are commercial scuba diving operations open from 8 A.M. to 5 P.M. daily. Contact Devil's Den at (904) 528-3344; Blue Grotto at (904) 528-5770.

A Walk Underground

Florida's most elaborate dry cave system open to the public is **Florida Caverns State Park** in the Panhandle town of Marianna. Most of Florida's limestone caves are flooded because of the state's high water table, so the dozens of dry caverns in this park are an unusual exception. Created over thousands of years, they contain a remarkable variety of rock formations: soda straws, stalactites, stalagmites, columns, rimstones, flowstones and draperies. Presently, you can explore only one of the caverns as part of a ranger-led tour that lasts about an hour. During heavy rains, the Chipola River may rise and flood parts of the cave system used during the tours. For information, contact Florida Caverns State Park, 3345 Caverns Road, Marianna, FL 32446; (904) 482-9598. The park is open from 8 A.M. to sundown.

47

August Shorttakes

Birding at Zellwood

One of the best places this month in which to spot great quantities and varieties of shorebirds are the muck farms at **Zellwood**, a vegetable-growing community just north of Orlando. In August the farmers flood their fields, which attracts shorebirds, ducks and wading species. These typically include white pelicans, terns, fulvous whistling ducks, sandpipers and many more. Because of the heat and the added humidity caused by the flooded fields, birding here should be done early. Take U.S. 441 from Orlando through the town of Apopka to the community of Zellwood, about a 45-minute drive. Ou the northern outskirts of Zellwood turn onto Laughlin Road and proceed about another half-mile. However, do not make this trip if it has been raining, for the roads can get as mucked up as the farmland. For more information, contact the Apopka Area Chamber of Commerce, (407) 886-1441. Zellwood is also the home of the tremendously popular sweet (white) corn festival in May. The corn is picked from the Zellwood fields the same day it is served to visitors—a taste as sweet as a candy apple.

Rare Schaus' Swallowtails

It was in August 1992 that nature destroyed the beautiful but rare Schaus' swallowtail butterfly. It was nature in the form of violent Hurricane Andrew, which literally blew the Schaus' swallowtail into extinction. At that time the species existed only in the **Keys** (especially Key Largo) and on selected islands in **Biscayne National Park** (primarily Elliott Key). Removal and development of the butterfly's native habitat (hardwood hammocks) had already made things very tenuous when the storm delivered the final crushing blow.

There are those who believe that in life timing is everything, and that is certainly true for the Schaus' swallowtail, now doing better than before nature destroyed it.

Just two months prior to Andrew, the Hurricane of the Century, a University of Florida butterfly researcher had visited the Keys and removed hundreds of egg samples from wild Schaus' swallowtail females to raise in the lab. The purpose was to expand the range of the butterfly in the Keys, not to restore it, but that's precisely what happened. The butterfly eggs were raised to the pupal stage, then returned to their natural habitat. The butterflies have flourished ever since and are more widely distributed than before.

The Schaus' swallowtail, a year-round Keys resident, has brown wings with dark yellow spots within a brown border. It also has a bold yellow band across the middle of the wings. The species' host plants are torchwood and wild lime. Look for the Schaus' swallowtail in shady hardwood hammocks. They are very approachable.

48

A Closer Look:
The Bugs of Love

Most wild creatures conduct their reproductive rites in private, but love bugs seem to have inspired the words of the old rock song, "Why Don't We Do It in the Road?"

Driving into a swarm of mating lovebugs is like accidentally sitting on an anthill at a picnic: It's annoying and messy and it ruins the whole day. At a picnic you can at least leave the ants behind, but lovebugs go home with you—usually all over the front of your vehicle. The scores of dead insects need to be removed as quickly as possible, because a mashed lovebug exudes a substance that will eat through car paint. Florida's lovebug love-in season happens twice a year, lasting between four and five weeks in May and then again in September.

Lovebugs are one of nature's more unusual oddities. They fly the skies united on one glorious unending honeymoon until parted by death. Formally known as Bibionidae flies, they are commonly termed lovebugs but are also called honeymoon flies and telephone bugs because they're always "hung up."

Except for their penchant for mating in the middle of roadways and getting mashed by motorists, lovebugs are considered harmless because they don't bite or sting. However, a heavy swarm of them can clog car radiators, sometimes causing overheating, so these mass suicides are definitely annoying.

A University of Florida entomology professor thought for a time he'd found the answer to the lovebug problem. He discovered that lovebugs have a sweet tooth, so he attempted to poison them by spreading a lethal mixture that included honey along the side of a road, a favorite congregating place of the insects. Lovebugs apparently aren't as dumb as we'd like them to be. They refused to dine on the deadly treat.

The lovebug population exploded in Florida in 1965 for reasons no one can quite explain. Most entomologists say the insects migrated down the Gulf Coast, apparently from Louisiana and Alabama, and first strongly established themselves in the Panhandle region. Since lovebugs tend to drift with the winds, sometimes traveling at altitudes of 1,000 to 1,500 feet, they could cover considerable distances fairly quickly, which allowed them eventually to reach all parts of the state. Other bug experts have disputed the migration theory and claim that the insects were here all along but that something in recent years happened to make them go haywire reproductively, and people are just noticing them more than before.

However they got here, the lovebugs, like mosquitoes, appear to be a permanent though annoying resident. At least there have been no reports of the insects attacking crop plants, or transmitting diseases, as mosquitoes do.

It appears the lovebug's only purpose in life is to reproduce itself. Both males and females are black-winged with orange heads. The female is considerably larger than the male. When a pair is mated in flight, the female is the one on top. With her larger size and strength, she virtually carries the male along.

The male dies when the two part. The female lives only long enough to deposit her eggs. Each female can lay as many as 350 eggs, which are normally deposited in moist decaying vegetation that the larvae feed upon. The larvae emerge as adults in the lovebug season immediately following the one in which they were deposited as eggs.

Not only are lovebugs offensive to humans, apparently few other creatures can tolerate them. With the exception of chickens, nothing in the world seems able to stand the taste of lovebugs. Like monarch butterflies, lovebugs give off a secretion that natural predators such as toads, frogs, lizards and birds have learned to avoid. Animals that try dining on lovebugs for the first time generally spit them out and don't return for seconds. This is why the surface of a lake littered with the insects remains undisturbed. Even fish won't touch them.

The only real enemies of lovebugs are cars and trucks. The insects are often at their worst on country roads, and they appear to sleep late. The greatest swarms are active from 10 A.M. until early evening. For whatever reasons, the bugs seem to be attracted to white-colored vehicles.

So whenever you encounter these aerial exhibitionists, control your irritation with the thought that you are witnessing one of nature's true mysteries—creatures overwhelmingly irresistible to one another, but to nothing else on earth.

Pesky lovebugs, which swarm in late summer and spring, are also known as telephone bugs since they're always hung up.

September

Notes

49

Migrating Hawks

Seeing a hawk in the wild is always a treat, but viewing a hundred or more in a single morning is one of the fall's greatest spectacles. September marks the beginning of the annual migration of hawks and falcons, a journey that for some species begins in Canada and ends as far south as Peru.

The most common hawk passing through Florida skies is the sharp-shinned hawk, whose large numbers make it possible to spot anywhere between 200 and 1,500 birds in a single day following a cold front. Sharp-shinned hawks are often in the company of the Cooper's hawk, which is larger but similar in appearance. Both hawks, birds of the woods, have a gray-black head, a slate gray back, a gray-and-black-banded tail and bands of light tan and bright rust on the chest and underparts. The two birds are also similar in their flight patterns: fast and erratic.

The broad-winged hawk, heavier than the Cooper's but around the same size, winters anywhere from Florida to Peru. The slower flying broadwing has a very obvious migratory characteristic that other hawks also adapt: It sometimes forms *kettles,* or groups, that will swirl in small flocks overhead rather than fly on a direct course, as the sharp-shinned and Cooper's hawks do. Hawks swirling in a kettle are actually circling tightly in an air thermal.

When a kettle of birds is tightly circling in a thermal, they look from a distance like something boiling in a cauldron, which may explain the origin of the word "kettle" to describe a thermaling flock.

Thermals are what the hawks rely on to assist them on their traditional migratory pathways, which are determined by both geography and weather patterns. The geographic features, known as *leading lines,* include mountain ridges, coastlines or lake shores. In parts of the Appalachians, the mountain ridges form nearly parallel lines. Wind following a cold front blows from the northwest, and it strikes these ridges at about a 90-degree angle. That deflects the breeze upward, creating a lift along the ridges that the hawks ride just like sailplane pilots. The birds also ride air thermals created by sunlight on roads and over fields and lakes. In essence, they repeatedly fly from one hot-air bubble to the next. How the birds are able to find these thermals is still uncertain.

Other hawks to look for include the marsh hawk, Mississippi kite, osprey, red-tailed hawk and the red-shouldered hawk, all in fairly small numbers.

The red-tailed hawk is one of several species which fill the skies over many refuges in the fall months.

One of the rarest and most sought-after migratory species is the endangered peregrine falcon, the great aerial performer that was used in the sport of falconry for thousands of years. The peregrine falcon, similar in size to the Cooper's hawk, has heavy stripes on its sides, a black-to-slate-blue coloration on its back and barred wing and tail feathers. Its head, smaller than that of a hawk, has a black cap. Once fairly common, this magnificent bird began disappearing in the 1930s when its eggs were decimated by egg collectors who pillaged nests in the remote breeding cliffs in the Northeast. Pesticides used following World War II affected the thickness of the bird's eggshells, which became so thin that they broke when a parent tried to incubate them.

The peregrine does not soar or glide in the air currents like many other migrating species. Instead, it relies on its own wing power to achieve the heights where it is able to survey the sky and land below. It will circle for a short period, then quickly wing to another survey station and wait for small ducks, starlings, pigeons and other game birds of a similar size to come into the open.

What made the peregrine so suitable for falconry is that these falcons prefer to seize birds that are in flight, instead of waiting for them to land. A peregrine will circle at a very high altitude until its prey is located. Then the falcon closes its wings and crash-dives into it.

Peregrines may be everyone's favorite, but the American kestrel, followed by the merlin, are the most commonly seen falcons during the hawk migration.

Hot Spots

The best time to view hawks is right after a cold front. In general, the birds follow the Gulf coastline toward Mexico and South America.

Different birds will often fly at different times of day. For instance, falcons and accipiters are most active from early morning to late afternoon, while buteos such as the broad-winged hawk fly mostly between 10 A.M. and 2 P.M.

The best hawk watching is on the **Gulf Coast,** sometimes on the mainland but typically more on the offshore barrier islands that parallel the coast. An important exception is **Guana River Wildlife Management Area and State Park** just north of St. Augustine, the best place for peregrine falcons in Northeast Florida. Both falcons and hawks should be present along the dune lines in October if there is a west wind or if a cold front has just gone through.

St. George Island near Apalachicola is another prime area for fall migrants, but perhaps the best place in all Florida to witness the fall hawk migration is nearby **St. Joseph Peninsula,** where 200 to 300 birds may be seen in a single day. The peninsula is Northwest Florida's most reliable place for peregrine falcons. At least one or more of these birds appears on the peninsula every fall.

What makes St. Joseph Peninsula such a hotspot is its narrow size, which averages only a third of a mile wide, which concentrates the birds together along a narrow funnel. Four places in particular are especially good. The elbow of the peninsula, while not attracting a huge number of birds, is the best place to see the peregrines. Hawks in large numbers can be sighted a half-mile north of the Sunland Center, since the birds tend to stay over land and not wander over the bay as much. Eagle Harbor is good in early morning before the birds begin flying out over the water, which puts them farther away. The single best place is the tip of the peninsula, where the hawks gather before flying to the mainland, several miles away. Keep in mind the hawks will be flying north—the exact opposite direction of their intended migration—because the peninsula runs north and south, with the southern end connected by a land bridge to the mainland.

St. Vincent NWR is also good for watching migrating hawks, and because it can be reached only by boat, it attracts only the most dedicated birders.

Paynes Prairie State Preserve near Gainesville is a December hotspot for redtails, marsh hawks and kestrels. The place to visit is the **La Chua Trail** on the north rim, at the observation platform about 3 miles in.

Miami's **Cape Florida State Recreation Area** is also a good spot in late September and early October at the old lighthouse. Sharp-shinned hawks are the most numerous here, but merlins and peregrines can usually be seen too.

Mid- to late October is Alabama's peak migration period. It's possible to see as many as 50 or 60 hawks in a day almost anywhere that's forested along the **Alabama Coast**. Kettles of hawks are usually seen after the weather straightens after a cold front. The main hawks seen in these kettles are the red-tailed hawk, red-shouldered hawk, broad-winged hawk, sharp-shinned hawk, kestrels, some Cooper's hawks and a fair number of peregrine falcons. The best places are at the **Bon Secour NWR** and **Dauphin Island**.

50

Spring Flings

Although scuba divers in their warm wetsuits can enjoy the many clear freshwater springs in both North and Central Florida any time of year, most mortals wait for summer to play in the cool, constant 72-degree waters. But regardless of season, there are plenty of springs to choose from: Florida has the largest system of freshwater springs in the nation.

Unless there has been an unusual amount of rain, summertime conditions are always perfect. Outside of a pool, there is no safer or better place to swim. Not only are the springs crystal clear, most are quite shallow. They have no waves or undertow to fight, and no sharks to fear. Furthermore, many springs are in state parks or near private campgrounds, ideal spots for weekend outings.

If you've never snorkeled before, Florida springs are ideal places to learn. You'll discover many springs are massive freshwater

Crystal clear springs that feed the St. Johns River often contain saltwater species, like these mullet. Mullet and blue crabs enter the St. Johns where it flows into the Atlantic just north of Jacksonville.

aquariums where bluegill, largemouth bass and even river otters can be viewed by simply floating facedown in the water.

Snorkeling is an activity that children take to instinctively. Give a mask and snorkel to any child and she or he will sightsee in the shallows for hours. It seems to matter little how much youngsters see or how far they explore. Instead, the ability to conquer another world and breathe freely in this new environment is reward enough.

Florida is blessed with its abundance of springs due to a vast underground river running most of the state's length. An important source of Florida's drinking water, this freshwater river is continually replenished through the heavy fall of rainwater, which passes through the porous sand and soil surface into the limestone beneath. At the same time, this filtering process cleans out impurities and accounts for the extreme clearness of the spring water.

The majority of Florida springs were created this way: Underground water (often under a considerable head of pressure) broke through the ground. The spot where the water emerged is known as the *spring boil.* Normally, there is too much water gushing out to be contained in an isolated pool, so rivers or *spring runs* are formed by the overflow. Because all of Florida's springs are fed by the same underground river, the water temperature is an unvarying 72 degrees every day of the year except in the Panhandle, where temperatures average closer to 68 degrees.

The world's largest limestone spring is the Silver Springs attraction near Ocala. The spring flow here is tremendous: 530,000,000 gallons of water and more than 430 tons of minerals every 24 hours. It's also the headwaters of the 7-mile long Silver River, actually a spring run. Silver Springs, locale for the pioneering underwater-adventure TV drama *Sea Hunt,* is a commercial operation closed to swimmers; to view its 30 varieties of fish you have to take one of the glass-bottomed-boat tours.

Silver Springs may be off-limits, but Florida does have 17 of the 75 *first magnitude* springs in the United States, more than any other state. A first magnitude spring spews out a whopping 100 cubic feet of water per second. Further, there are another 47 springs in Florida that rank as *second magnitude,* which put forth between 10 and 99 cubic feet of water per second. It's an unusual blessing indeed to have so many natural swimming pools. Descriptions of the most popular springs are available in *Fish and Dive Florida and the Keys.*

After Labor Day, fewer people visit the springs even though it's still quite hot. The spring basin at **Alexander Springs** in the Ocala National Forest can hold a platoon of snorkelers and divers, which it often does on weekends when scuba-training classes are held. However, you'll always find lots of empty water, for Alexander Springs has one of the state's largest spring basins. The shallow basin is home to numerous largemouth bass, panfish and even oceangoing mullet. The mullet enter via the 15-mile-long spring run that empties into the St. Johns River, which in turn empties into the Atlantic.

Entry to the spring basin is from a thin, sandy beach. The bottom remains sandy until you reach a grass bed that sits high over the scooped-out depression that marks the cave where the water flows into the basin. Staying on the edge of the grass, it's possible to see a hundred feet or more.

Fish are noticeably absent in this deep basin, so there is no compelling need to swim deep. Fish are absent at the spring boil because there is little oxygen in the water when it first comes from beneath the ground. Instead, the fish life is concentrated along the grassy shoreline to the right of your beach entry. You'll normally find a school of several dozen bream and occasionally a few largemouth bass. It's also possible a river otter might appear early in the day.

Alexander Springs offers canoeing, picnicking and camping. Canoeing the 15-mile-long spring run is an excellent way to see wading birds (especially limpkins), alligators and sunning turtles. Raccoons and gray squirrels are common too, but avoid overly friendly raccoons because there have been periodic outbreaks of rabies in the population.

To find Alexander Springs, go east on State Road 40 and turn south (right) on State Road 445 just before the town of Astor. The park entrance is on the right; call (904) 625-2520 for information. The canoe concessionaire is located inside the park.

Ichetucknee Springs State Park offers a totally different experience. Here the main activity is floating the crystal-clear, narrow Ichetucknee River, which is fed by nine different springs. The Ichetucknee, flowing for 6 miles before emptying into the Santa Fe River, passes through both a hardwood hammock and a striking river swamp. This is one of the most spectacular natural areas in all Florida. And a lot of people realize this, which is why the park has a maximum carrying capacity of 3,000 people per day. Without meaning to, a gaggle of tubers clogging the waterway can cause considerable damage to the vegetation and thereby increase the erosion along the riverbanks. The quota limit is usually approached only on hot summer weekends.

To help further minimize impact, park officials prefer that people canoe the narrower upper section of the river and take out just above U.S. 27, a distance of 3.5 miles. Tubers are encouraged to use the lower section. A free tram operates in summer to return tubers to their launching points so that no second vehicle is needed to shuttle back and forth. On a quiet weekday you can turn your float into a wildlife excursion. When crowds are absent, it's not uncommon to see limpkins, river otters and American swallow-tailed kites.

Huge truck inner tubes are available for rent outside the park, or you can tote your own float. Once you set out, you are committed for the duration; there is no turning back because of the current and the number of people following behind you.

The closest town to Ichetucknee Springs State Park is Fort White, located northwest of Gainesville. To find the park's northern entrance, take State Road 238 west from Fort White. The southern entrance is on U.S. 27 west of Fort White. For information, call (904) 497-2511.

51

Seafood Festivals

When residents of the small Florida town of Grant (population 300) send out dinner invitations each February, around 50,000 hungry people usually show up. It takes two days and several tons of loaves and fishes to feed a hungry army that happily waits in long lines for a heaping plate of fried fish, fried oysters, coleslaw, baked beans and hush puppies.

This kind of turnout is typical for the annual Grant Seafood Festival, because seafood festivals everywhere rival rock concerts and professional football teams in attracting big weekend crowds. Despite such acceptance, seafood festivals are a relatively new phenomenon in Florida.

Although many agricultural states can point to state fairs that began in the 1800s, most of Florida's seafood celebrations didn't begin until the 1970s and later. The first celebrations originated in small seaport communities that harvested oysters, shrimp or fish. Only locals attended.

Part of the problem was Florida's population makeup, which consisted largely of people born in other states who didn't know much about seafood or thought they wouldn't like it. It's hard to believe, but the old Department of Natural Resources (now the Department of Environmental Protection) even printed booklets explaining how best to cook the state's fresh local seafood.

Acceptance was slow and gradual. By the mid-1970s, even the most formerly landlocked migrant from the Midwest realized what he had been missing all his life. Today, most Floridians gladly pay more for fresh snapper than steak, and the booming popularity of the seafood festivals is a reflection of this.

Many festivals use only single cooking methods—frying is the most popular—in order to feed crowds quickly. The food is prepared in such a way that the natural, full flavor can be tasted, a change from the old Southern custom of burying everything under a thick batter that made everything taste the same. For instance, fish is often only thinly coated with flour, salt and pepper and then fried in oil at 400-degree temperatures for about five minutes. High-volume cookers can handle between 75 and 100 portions of fish at a time. All food is cooked on the spot—none ahead of time. That's what makes it worth standing in line for.

Most of Florida's seafood festivals are like county fairs. They're held outdoors and feature arts and crafts booths, rides, educational exhibits—anything that will give people an excuse to stay around and build up their appetite for another trek through the line.

Except during the summer months, there is always at least one major seafood festival somewhere in Florida. The big problem can be deciding which one to attend.

Following are the locations of the major festivals. Dates sometimes change, so always call ahead. Seafood lovers from all over the United States and Canada will be attending, and everyone is welcome. There's no way the locals by themselves could ever eat all they'll be fixin'.

Fall Festivals

Hot Spots

Since these events are often sponsored by volunteer committees, information is often sketchy until about two months before the festival is scheduled. So don't plan too early!

Pensacola, end of September. All types of seafood, particularly oysters, with a contest among the vendors for the best dishes, such as shrimp crepes in wine sauce. For time and place, call (904) 433-6512.

Panama City Beach, the beginning of October. The Indian Summer Seafood Festival, with oysters, shrimp, crab and local varieties of fish all prepared in different ways. Held at Wayside Park. Call toll-free (800) PCBEACH.

Niceville, the middle of October. The Boggy Bayou Mullet Festival offers mullet of every description, including sandwiches, but lots of other seafood is available, and some of it is cooked in both European and Asian traditional styles. Niceville is located in the Panhandle near Destin/Panama City. Call (904) 678-1615.

Cedar Key, the middle of October. Another small fishing community now almost equally a resort area; with fish, oysters, crab and shrimp served in conjunction with an art festival. The offshore pier is lined with seafood restaurants for visitors throughout the year. Call (904) 543-5600.

Apalachicola, the beginning of November. This small Gulf Coast fishing village boasts the state's oldest marine festival. Apalachicola traditionally has taken around 90 percent of the oysters and 52 percent of the entire shellfish harvest in Florida. In addition to oysters and shrimp and fish, oyster-shucking contests, the blessing of the fleet, live music and arts and crafts are featured. Call (904) 653-9419.

Inglis-Yankeetown, the middle of November. Gulf Coast anglers are familiar with the excellent fishing here, just north of Crystal River, but few outsiders are. This is an area that is still fairly traditional, one of the last to be swept into the modern day. Call (904) 447-3029.

Gulf Shores, Alabama, second week of October. This is a huge four-day shrimp festival that runs from Thursday to Sunday. In addition to loads of seafood booths, the event also includes musical entertainment, a children's art village and an arts-and-crafts show. Most tourists desert the beautiful beaches here after Labor Day, which is a big mistake. For information, call (334) 968-7511.

Winter-Spring Festivals

Islamorada, approximately the third weekend in January. Conch was once an important means of livelihood for Keys residents, but it's become so scarce that it's now illegal to harvest it. The conch here, which is served along with fish and other goodies, is imported from the Caribbean. For specific time and place, call (305) 852-0643.

Everglades City, usually the first weekend in February. Despite its location in one of Florida's more remote areas, the Everglades Fisherman's Seafood Festival draws good crowds to feast on stone crab claws, one of the state's most unusual delicacies. Oysters, shrimp, fried fish and traditional Seminole food are also offered, with rides for children, and arts, dancing and live bands for the adults. Call (941) 695-4100.

West Palm Beach, usually near the middle of February. Held on the mainland in Currie Park. The reefs off West Palm Beach are considered second only to those of the Keys for rich fish life. After eating, cruise along Ocean Boulevard on the island of Palm Beach for a look at the mansions of the rich and famous. Mar-A-Lago is Donald Trump's home. For date and time, call (407) 832-6397.

Grant, the middle of February. Grant is a small community 12 miles south of Melbourne on Central Florida's east coast. This festival has one of the most extensive menus: It may include shark meat, frogs' legs, lobster, Spanish mackerel, shrimp, oysters and clams, all served with a choice of potato or macaroni salad, and baked beans, coleslaw and hush puppies. It's no wonder 50,000 people clog the narrow streets here every year. Call (407) 724-0584.

Marathon, the middle or end of March. This two-day festival at Mile Marker 50 in the middle of the Florida Keys features crab claws, lobster, fried fish and shrimp. This event usually is heavy on entertainment, with children's rides, cloggers, glider rides, sky divers and bands. For the specific date contact the Marathon Chamber of Commerce at (305) 743-5417.

Mayport, located just north of Jacksonville, almost as far north on the East Coast as you can go and still be in Florida. Located right on the opening to the Atlantic. This has been an October event in recent years and is now moving to the spring. Call (904) 241-9591 for the current schedule.

Port Canaveral, toward the end of March. Port Canaveral, located at Cape Canaveral, is just south of the Kennedy Space Center. Dinners feature such items as fried whiting, calico scallops, corn on the cob, coleslaw, baked beans and hush puppies. À la carte booths offer rock shrimp, clam chowder, hot dogs and fennel cakes. For dates and directions, call (407) 454-2026.

Fort Lauderdale, the beginning of April. Like many other waterfront communities, Fort Lauderdale calls itself the Venice of America. Considering the hundreds of miles of canals here, this time it isn't much of an exaggeration. The festival is usually held at Bubier Park. Call (305) 463-4431.

Pompano Beach, near the end of April. Pompano Beach is one of the many communities that blend into one another along the Gold Coast. That places it in one of the best seafood regions in the state. For time and place, call (305) 941-2940.

Fernandina Beach, first weekend of May. The Amelia Island Shrimp Festival is one of the state's oldest and most elaborate celebrations. Besides shrimp prepared in every manner conceivable, a folk festival, beauty pageant, fireworks, beach run, pirate invasion and much more highlight the weekend. Everything in this small northeast resort community centers on shrimp, nothing but shrimp, during this time. Call toll-free (800) 2AMELIA.

Panacea, the beginning of April. This Panhandle community honors the blue crab during its weekend festival at Wooley Park. Come for crab cakes, crab fritters and steamed crabs. Floridians consider their blue crabs equal to those of Chesapeake Bay. Call (904) 926-1848.

52

Surf Fishing

The lure of the surf isn't confined just to muscle-strapped young men and women who ride the waves on their spear-shaped surfboards. Considering how much coastline exists in the Southeast (6,000 miles in Florida alone), the surf here is among the finest and most easily accessible places to fish year-round.

Besides being one of the least expensive ways to fish, surf fishing is one of the few angling activities that can include the entire family. Youngsters who tire of fishing can build sand castles, run in the surf or beachcomb for shells, driftwood and whatever else may have washed ashore. Furthermore, no expensive charter boat or guide is required. All you need is a comfortable stretch of sand, a rod rigged for surf fishing and an ice chest in which to place the catch. The surf is there to fish night or day, or both.

Except in the early morning, summer is often too uncomfortable for surf fishing, both for the angler and his quarry. Some species, such as bluefish, migrate north to spend the hot season in cooler waters, then migrate back to Florida in the fall.

The breaking waves offer an ever-changing smorgasbord, with the size and type of fish varying according to the time of year. Blues, red drum (redfish), whiting, flounder, sharks, pompano—the list is endless. But it does take specialized tackle to snag them, because the angler will be casting heavy bait and lead sinkers. A typical surf rod may be anywhere from 7 to 10 feet long, and some people even use sticks that extend out to $10^1/2$ feet. The bigger rods are used for throwing out heavy baits and for fighting large fish. Lighter rigs are appropriate in regions where the fish tend to run small.

When it comes to the big rods, it takes two hands to handle these whoppers. To cast, the right hand must hold the butt just under the reel while the left hand grabs the butt at the base. With either a spinning rod or revolving reel, the cast begins with the rod extended behind the shoulder but still lined up with the target area. Then the rod is swung up and forward.

When the rod reaches a vertical position, with the rod tip almost straight overhead, that's when the line should be released, and the swing should follow through as in golf. With a revolving-spool reel, be sure to keep a slight pressure on the spool after the line is released. Then apply full pressure when the line hits the water to prevent building a bird's nest, more commonly called backlash.

Small spinning outfits can also provide considerable sport. The

The 25-mile long beach at Canaveral National Seashore is especially popular with surf casters.

only problem is keeping sharp-toothed fish from fraying or breaking the line: A good 30-pound test monofilament leader should eliminate that problem.

Terminal gear for surf fishing is usually rigged in one of two ways. One method is to have the hook and leader attached directly to the line with a sliding sinker above the connecting swivel. Such an arrangement eliminates any resistance whenever a fish picks up the bait. Also common are rigs with two hooks. These normally consist of a 12- to 16-inch piece of heavy leader that has two small metal "arms" protruding from the side. A leader and hook should be snapped to each arm. The arms keep the hooks hanging away from the leader so they don't become entangled. Then a sinker (usually pyramid-shaped so it won't roll along the bottom) is attached at the end of the line.

It may be helpful to spray the swivels and any other shiny terminal hardware (except a lure, of course) with black paint. In their feeding frenzy, some fish may be drawn to the flashing metal instead of the bait dangling a few inches away. Since this kind of distraction isn't to an angler's benefit, it ought to be eliminated. Having a fish hanging on the line is one thing, but having it on a hook is even better.

Hot Spots

The biggest mistake a surf fisherman can make is to randomly select a spot on the beach and start fishing. Anyone who does this is simply counting on the law of averages to eventually work in his favor, that a fish some day, at some time, will wander by and maybe take a bite. It's just as possible to win $50,000,000 in a state lottery, but don't count on it.

There are better ways of approaching the surf. After arriving at the beach, scan the water with binoculars for birds feeding on the water or for any sign of baitfish activity on the surface. Of course, such nice Fish Here! markers aren't always evident, which means a little preplanning is required.

For surf fishing, one needs to know the lay of the land. This may mean a visit to the beach at low tide to study the terrain; because it's what's out front that counts. And out front of many beaches are channels and sloughs that run parallel to the beach. At low tide, you should be able to spot the surf breaking over a sandbar just offshore. That sandbar is the side of such a channel.

After breaking over a sandbar, the water rolls into deeper, darker colored water just inside, between the bar and the beach. That dark water is the place to cast, because game fish will be in these troughs feeding on the baitfish washed over or trapped by the sandbar.

Also worth fishing are the channels or sloughs that cut through the bars and lead out to the ocean. You can identify these by the receding waves curving and moving seaward through them. Game fish are likely to congregate here at high water, so this is another good spot to wet a hook.

The best surf fishing often is early in the morning or late in the afternoon during the first two hours of either an incoming or outgoing tide. A heavy surf caused by high winds and storms may make the fishing even better, for it will dislodge and churn up more natural bait to bring in the game fish. However, if the water becomes very dirty, the fish may not approach shore closely.

Generally speaking, the less developed the shoreline, the better the surf fishing. Among the places worth trying are Georgia's **Cumberland Island** and Florida's **Amelia Island**, both just north of Jacksonville. South of Jacksonville along the east coast there is one beach after another, all of which have their devotees: the **Talbot Islands**, which are state parks; **Anastasia Island**, another state park near St. Augustine; **Flagler and Ormond Beaches**, just north of Daytona Beach; **Ponce de Leon Inlet**, which dead-ends on A1A just south of Daytona Beach; **Canaveral National Seashore**, with 25 unbroken miles of beach; **Cocoa Beach** and **Melbourne Beach; Sebastian Inlet State Park**, Florida's most popular state park, offers beach, jetties and a bridge catwalk.

In the **Keys**, many of the old abandoned bridges that formerly were part of the Overseas Highway have been turned into free fishing piers. **Naples** has both beaches and a fishing pier, as does **Sanibel Island** just west of Fort Myers. In the Panhandle, from **St. George Island** and all the way to the Alabama border, the entire shoreline is one big surf-fishing coast that includes mainland beaches and a series of barrier islands.

Pensacola has also turned an abandoned mile-long bridge into a fishing pier, which it calls the longest fishing pier anywhere. Driving into Alabama, the beaches continue from the **Perdido River** to **Gulf Shores**, which has a fishing pier and over 30 miles of oceanfront.

Without doubt, the Southeast offers one of the longest stretches of surf-fishing coastline anywhere. Both the quality of fishing and the variety of game-fish species are unrivaled.

53

September Shorttakes

Fall Wildflowers

Prescribed burns in state and national forests will have changed the landscape considerably since last spring's wildflower display. The summer burns are also the places most likely to have the best fall wildflowers. Check at the following to see where the most recent burns are: **Apalachicola National Forest** (which has the nation's largest prescribed burn program, clearing 100,000 acres or more each year); **Blackwater River State Forest**, near Milton; **Osceola National Forest**, near Lake City; **Ocala National Forest**, east of the city of Ocala; **Withlacoochee State Forest**, near Brooksville (the Richloam tract and the flatwoods are usually spectacular) and **Wekiwa Springs State Park**, near Orlando. And don't forget **Paynes Prairie State Preserve**, just south of Gainesville: With more than 700 wildflower species here, something is almost always in bloom.

Sea Island Sojourns

The weather this time of year is normally glorious for boat trips to some of Georgia's less accessible **Sea Islands**, the local name for all the region's offshore landfalls. The following three islands, all major wildlife-viewing spots, can be reached only by boat. Fortunately, it's easily possible to get to all three even if you don't have your own craft. Although they are close in proximity, these islands differ significantly in their natural features.

Blackbeard Island, named after the pirates who once hid here, has 7 miles of beach and 20 miles of old dirt roads that pass through a wide variety of animal habitat, including slash pine, live oak, yaupon and palmetto. Look for alligators around Flag Pond. The only facilities on this 5,618-acre island are a boat dock, a wildlife refuge office, rest rooms and a picnic area. Access is from Shellman's Bluff on the mainland through a licensed charter guide from either Kip's Fishing Camp or Fisherman's Lodge Marina.

Sapelo Island is an interesting mix of humans and animals. One small permanent settlement includes a number of black families incorporating a mixture of both African and English customs that is known as the Gullah culture. The Gullah language, spoken on a few islands off Georgia and South Carolina, is not used anywhere else in the country. Sapelo Island is a blend of beaches, salt marsh, slash pines, live oak and laurel oak. Deer, wading birds, snakes, ospreys and turkeys are all present. The easiest way to get to the island is aboard the *Sapelo Queen* from the town of Meredian, at the Sapelo ferry dock. Reservations and advance tickets are required, and both are available at the Darien Welcome Center at the corner of U.S. 17 and Fort King George Drive. The ferry allows only a half-day trip and does not run every day of the week. Saturday and Wednesday are the normal days of passage.

Wolf Island NWR, just east of Darien, also encompasses Egg Island and Little Egg Island in Altamaha Sound. Wolf Island's interior is mostly salt marsh, attractive to various birds. The beaches are also good for birding, surf fishing and just plain old beachcombing. Access is from the marinas just northeast of Darien at Ridgeville, on State Road 99.

54

A Closer Look: Owling

The owl, more often heard than seen, is far more common than most people realize. Usually only those who remain outdoors through the purple murk of twilight hear their strange, sometimes startling calls.

Because owls hunt after dark, they are among the most invisible animals of the forest. Yet because they respond so well to sound—important to them for defending their territory and attracting a mate—owls will often respond to a tape recording of their species's calls. Not only will they answer it, it is not unusual to lure the owl to a nearby perch where it can be observed. This sport of enticement is known as *owling*.

In the Southeast, there are more than seven owl species, ranging from the great horned owl, with its magnificent 5-foot wingspread, to the uncommon burrowing owl, a Great Plains resident that has settled in several areas of South Florida. Other commonly encountered owls include the eastern screech owl, the barn owl and the barred owl.

The species that can be lured depends on the region and the habitat. The barn owl is more common in the Keys and South Florida in winter. A woodlands resident, it is strictly nocturnal and most easily seen by driving through farmland and keeping a sharp eye on posts and utility poles. Good areas include the **Overseas Highway** in the Keys and **State Road** 27 between Homestead and Everglades Park.

The barred owl prefers swampland, particularly the **Corkscrew Swamp Sanctuary, Highlands Hammock State Park, Wakulla Springs State Park** and **Mahogany Hammock** in Everglades National Park. It will respond to taped calls even during the day.

In Alabama, the boat landings along the coastal delta are all good owling spots. Barred owls, great horned owls, barn owls and screech owls all holler at the same time without too much trouble.

The burrowing owl favors open fields with good drainage, particularly the region north and east of **Lake Okeechobee**, the **Sombrero Golf Course at Marathon** in the Keys, and **Cape Coral**, north of Fort Myers. Burrowing owls can sometimes be seen in daylight and also are called "Howdy" owls because of their habit of bobbing and bowing repeatedly.

The great horned owl can live in many types of habitat, including forests and prairies, but it will also live quite close to humans.

The barn owl is just one of several species that can easily be attracted by recorded owl calls.

It nests in a variety of places, including abandoned eagle nests and the forks of trees. Its hoots can carry a considerable distance.

The eastern screech owl, also called the death owl, is one of the most common types and is well known for its quivering call. It can be found in orange groves, suburban backyards, pinelands and hardwood swamps.

Owling typically succeeds after midnight, but the best period frequently is the last two hours before dawn. Two other important factors make it easier to attract owls. As the old 1970s pop song advised, "moonlight feels right," especially a full moon. But wind and rain are definite handicaps, since owls typically stay silent when there is any significant breeze, even if it is not raining.

Although it's tempting to lure the largest owls first, it's better to start with the smallest since starting with the largest presents an unusual problem. Large owls have no compunction about killing and eating their smaller kin. Begin by attracting the largest owls first, and the smaller species will stay silent. A better order is to start by calling the screech owl and then progressing to the barred or great horned owl if all three are likely to be in the vicinity. If the smaller owls don't leave when you start calling the big ones, stop calling, or you could be inviting the larger owls to dinner. Better yet, call the large owls from a different location.

The noisy, boom-box approach may appeal to many humans, but owls are a bit classier. Instead of sounding the calls continually, it's better to play several repetitions of the call, then to get silent and listen. If an owl is nearby, it will probably answer, suspecting the presence of an intruder. When there is an answer, play a couple of calls and turn off the tape player again. And listen. With luck the owl will approach, but the only thing you'll see is a shadow overhead. If you've been sitting in your vehicle and intend to get out to photograph the owl, turn off the overhead light and do not slam the door.

Some owls, such as the screech owl, do not become alarmed easily and will sit at close range and endure the flash of a camera or the beam of a flashlight. Great horned owls usually don't like to become quite as familiar, though they will sometimes surprise you. Like people, some owls are more sociable than others.

As enjoyable—and challenging—as owling is, there are a few matters of protocol to keep in mind. Owling disrupts the owl's normal life. Once you've succeeded in attracting an owl, photograph it, admire it, and move on. Don't overly interfere. That means if owling is common in a specific area, be respectful—especially during breeding season, when the owls have more important matters on their minds. Owling is not only intrusive then but may also interrupt the animal's food-gathering or nesting activities. All of which are good reasons not to attempt owling during the breeding season.

Great horned owls are mating in January, barred owls lay their eggs between January and March, screech owls are pairing in March. Probably the best overall time for owling is late summer and early fall, not normal breeding periods for any owl species.

The key to owling is the quality of the tape. Often it will be necessary to acquire a general tape of bird calls and make from it your own tape of owl calls. Some of the better recordings include *A Field Guide to Bird Songs (Eastern and Central North America)*, which supplements the *Peterson Field Guide to the Birds*, and National Geographic Society's *Guide to Bird Sounds*, a complement to the Society's superb field guide.

October

Notes

55

Monarch Migrations

For many people, a butterfly's beauty is intensified by the creature's fragility. So it's all the more remarkable that some butterflies, like the monarch, migrate on a journey as long and arduous as those of many bird species.

The monarch's annual passage down the East Coast is a harbinger of the holiday season. Countless of the orange-and-black creatures east of the Rocky Mountains decorate fall trees like colorful Christmas ornaments as they move toward the Gulf Coast and Mexico. Butterflies west of the Rockies migrate too, but to the California coast, between Los Angeles and San Francisco.

Monarchs originally were a tropical species that gradually moved north after the last Ice Age to take advantage of an increased food supply in the United States. But after spending summer in the States, the animals depart until their staple food, milkweed, is available again the following spring. Monarchs remain a common sight

The fields adjacent to the lighthouse at St. Marks NWR are often filled with thousands of migrating monarchs in late October.

throughout the United States and Canada thanks to the continued abundance of the milkweed, the only food monarch caterpillars eat. This may seem like a very restricted diet, but there are over a hundred species of milkweed in the country, so its availability is anything but limited.

Milkweed is notorious for its digitalislike toxin that is harmful to many animals, including humans. As caterpillars, monarchs ingest these poisons, store them in their own tissues, and retain them through their metamorphosis to adults. Essentially, the monarchs are taking the plant's protection and using it as their own against predators such as birds.

A bird that eats a monarch will not die, but it *will* become quite ill. As a result, birds learn to avoid anything colored orange-and-black. Other nonpoisonous insects have adapted the same coloration since, in the animal world, orange-and-black acts as a universal Toxic: Do Not Eat warning.

Like many insects, the lives of monarch butterflies are broken into two phases: the immature stage, where the main job is to feed and grow, and the adult phase, where the insects disperse and reproduce.

Female monarchs deposit as many as 400 eggs individually on the undersides of plant leaves. Depending on weather, the eggs hatch in just one to four days. The caterpillars must go through five different moltings before turning into a pupa and emerging as an adult butterfly, a process that takes about two weeks. An adult monarch lives for only about 30 days, so the life cycle is repeated several times during a summer.

What seems to determine whether a monarch remains only a summer breeder or becomes a migrator are the juvenile hormones that increase as the days start to shorten and the temperature drops. When the hormones come into play, they extend the butterfly's adult life considerably, to a period of six to nine months. They also encourage the animal to migrate rather than reproduce.

The monarch migration is a generational one, which means it takes multiple generations for the migration cycle to become complete. This is very different from the migration of other animals, such as birds, where the same individual begins and ends the migratory journey.

Monarchs arrive in Mexico in November and stay until the end of March or the beginning of April. On their return to the United States, hormone changes kick in again and cause the butterflies both to become reproductive and to age quickly. Returning females lay most of their eggs once they arrive back in the southern states, then die. The adults that emerge from these eggs will continue the journey northward, although it may require another generation or two to complete the trip to the northernmost ranges.

Considering that the same butterfly travels from Wisconsin to Mexico, a distance of several thousand miles, it's a wonder the butterflies don't arrive in tatters. They probably would if they had to flap their way the entire trip. Instead, like birds, they use high-altitude air currents to carry them for a distance, then come down to feed, then take off again. Monarchs do not fly at night.

The millions of monarchs headed for Mexico will overwinter in an 80-square-mile area near Mexico City. All the winter sites are in relic fir forests in cool and moist mountain areas. The overwintering spots are small, each one only between 1 and 4 acres. Yet a single overwintering site may hold between 10 and 50 million monarchs that literally cover the trees. The butterflies, which individually weigh less than a penny, are sometimes so concentrated in one spot that they cause the smallest tree limbs to snap.

Monarchs do not feed while overwintering but, like bears, go into a state of hibernation and rely on the fat they stored during their migratory journey; the overwintering sites themselves have little food to provide. The butterflies will become active again only when the weather begins warming, usually in February.

When such a great portion of the entire North American reproductive population is concentrated in Mexico in only a handful of sites, the species as a whole is very vulnerable to disaster. Fortunately, only two species of birds have adapted to feed on Mexico's overwintering butterfly colonies, and they reduce the butterfly population by as much as 10 percent each year. It's estimated that marauding mice destroy another 5 percent.

There are greater threats to the monarchs than other animals. Monarchs are present in the high forests during the dry season, when the forest is most susceptible to fire. A fire that kills off all the butterflies in a single location may devastate as much as 10 percent of the entire North American monarch population. But the real problem has been freak snowstorms, which have occurred twice in the 1990s. One storm was estimated to have killed 70 percent of the monarch population when the colonies were covered with snow in December 1995. Later estimates placed the figure considerably lower. In any case, it will undoubtedly take a number of years for the monarch population to regain its former size.

Hot Spots

In Florida, the **St. Marks NWR,** near Tallahassee, is perhaps the best place anywhere to see large numbers of monarchs. On a good day, they are easy to count by the hundreds or thousands. Monarchs are present here between the first of October and the middle of November. How visible they are depends on the weather. When the sun is out, the weather fairly warm and the wind still, the sky is often filled with the creatures. On overcast windy days the butterflies cling to the trees and the goldenrod. Actually, it is easier to take portrait photographs of monarchs in the worst weather, when they are not moving.

Although the St. Marks refuge covers more than 60,000 acres, the butterflies usually pile up in one place: the old lighthouse, just a few miles past the visitor center. Monarchs are reluctant to fly directly across the water, so they bunch up at the lighthouse, located on a small tip beside the Gulf of Mexico. They tend to stay for a time because the food supply there is good at this time of year.

Special monarch butterfly programs are held at St. Marks in October. For specific dates, or to see how many monarchs are present at a particular time, call (904) 925-6121.

From Florida the monarchs filter along the Gulf Coast toward Texas. At Alabama's **Gulf State Park** near **Gulf Shores,** monarchs sometimes cover the oak trees or the sea oats on the beach. The **Bon Secour NWR** is another good spot, and a thousand or more butterflies can be seen here in a couple of hours. **Dauphin Island** is not only another migration stop but a place where a good number of monarchs overwinter. Dauphin Island's temperatures are usually mild enough that the animals have

St. Marks NWR

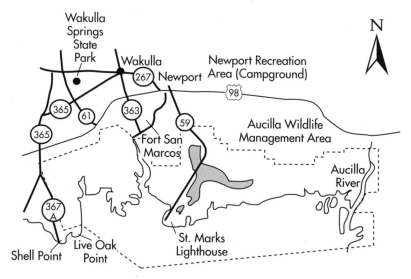

GULF OF MEXICO

little trouble surviving. One of the best places to see monarchs on the island is the old Native shell mound near the University of Alabama Dauphin Island Sea Lab. They are usually concentrated around the goldenrod near the west end, past the houses. Late October and November mark the best periods.

56

Stone Crabs and Crabbing

In most parts of the Southeast, *crabbing* refers to one species only, the Atlantic blue crab. In Florida the most highly prized crab is not the blue but the stone crab, whose lobster-sized claws can weigh as much as a pound! Although the stone crab is unknown to many people outside of Florida, its range is quite large, extending from the Carolinas to Mexico.

As crabs go, the stone crab is almost distinguished-looking. Adults are a reddish brown and have brown spots mottling their carapaces and claws. Their walking legs are also reddish brown. The body is oval-shaped and larger than that of other Florida crabs. Both of its black-tipped claws are big, though one is often larger than the other. The claws are used for crushing clam and oyster shells and for protection.

Stone crabs spend the summer months breeding in deep water. In the fall, as the water becomes cooler, the crabs migrate shoreward. A factor that appears to influence how many crabs make the annual migration is the abundance of octopi populating the deep water. Octopi may surpass humans in their love for stone crabs, so when the offshore octopus population is high, more stone crabs head for shallower water, apparently for better cover and protection.

Once close to land, the stone crabs move onto the shallow bay flats and around rock jetties. Female stone crabs will have recently laid their eggs and just have shed their shells before moving shoreward. It's possible a female's new shell will not yet have hardened completely. Any attempt to remove a claw while she is in this condition will probably kill her. Females with orange-colored eggs visibly protruding around the sides of the egg pouch must, by law, be released, if caught, with the claws still attached.

Many people take only the crab's larger claw. Removing both claws from a stone crab obviously makes it necessary for the crab to change for a time from its normal shellfish diet. Until their claws grow back, stone crabs appear to eat mostly vegetation, which some say acts as a stimulant to the growth of new claws.

Hot Spots

The restrictions regarding stone crabs should be followed closely. The season is closed between May 15 and October 15. The claws must measure $2^3/4$ inches. It is illegal to possess the whole crab. There is no trapping except with permission of the Department of Environmental Protection. The use of spears, grains, grabs, hooks or similar devices that can puncture, crush or injure a crab is illegal.

Commercial and recreational harvesting traditionally has been limited from the **Fort Lauderdale area** on the Atlantic coast to the **Cedar Keys** on the Gulf Coast, the region where the crabs are most plentiful.

Most stone crabs are caught in traps, and they often share their wire-mesh confine with blue crabs that have also been lured inside the traps. In comparison to blue crabs, stone crabs are downright rare, so expect the harvest to be a limited one.

Stone crabs can be sight-hunted by crabbers wading in shallow water. The best place is in water that is ankle- to knee-deep at low tide, a time when the crabs are usually hiding in their burrows. At high tide they're out hunting for food.

Find the stone crab's burrow and you have found the crab. In shallow bays, look for burrows on the grass flats. A burrow is easily identified by the white sand piled in front of it. Stone crabs slide into their burrows sideways, so the size of the hole opening is a good clue to the size of the crab inside.

Like a muscle-bound weight lifter who's hindered by his size, the stone crab is a slow mover, heavy and clumsy. The key to catching one is to prod it out of its burrow and into the open where it can be dip-netted.

Crabs are supposed to be ornery by nature, and the stone crab is no exception. If the crab is at home, the probe should feel like it's made contact with a rock. By gently prodding the crab, you'll irritate it enough that the animal will grab the probe with its powerful claws. Gently extract the crab from the burrow. If the crab lets go, its first inclination will not be to flee but to return to the safety of its burrow. Drop the prober and scoop up the crab.

Like blue crabs, stone crabs are skilled at tangling themselves in the mesh of a net. The only recourse is to dump the crab into a bucket and deal with it there.

Regardless of how the crab is harvested, it must be returned alive to the water. Once the crab is in the bucket, the recommended procedure is to approach quietly from the rear. There are two ways to accomplish this. One is to grab the crab from behind, placing your fingers under its body and your thumb on top of the back but toward the rear. Unlike blue crabs, which have a vicious tendency to shake hands by reaching under their body or over it, a stone crab's defense is more limited. It won't try to grab the fingers beneath its shell but will concentrate on squeezing the thumb on its back. A stone crab, fortunately, is unable to reach very far behind its head, something for which all crabbers should be thankful.

A second way of dealing with a stone crab emphasizes brute strength over cunning and guile. Again, you approach the crab from behind—and grab both of its claws at the same time. *At the same time* is very important. At this point, if there is any question whether the claw meets the legal limit of $2^3/4$ inches, someone with a measuring device will have to gauge the size for you as you hold the claws extended. With a claw in each hand, quickly rotate the body in one direction and the claw in the opposite to snap the claw off cleanly. In removing the claws, it's important that the crab not be hurt but will survive and grow new claws that can be harvested the following year. You need to make a clean break so that only hard, bony body is displayed after the claw is removed. If any of the body meat shows after the claw's removal, the crab will likely die.

57

Autumn Colors

Those living in other parts of the country may find this hard to imagine, but Florida natives who've stayed at home their entire lives have never seen the incredible array of reds, yellows and all the various hues in between that span the horizon and extend seemingly into infinity in so many other states.

And yet though autumn in Florida and along the Southeast coast may not be as dramatic, as ostentatious or as obvious as that in colder climes, yes, there is a definite and distinctive fall color change. The trick is knowing where to look. The most significant color changes take place in the swamps and certain parts of the Florida Panhandle where the foliage is more akin to the mountainous Appalachians than the flat Florida peninsula.

In cold areas where temperatures are often in the 30s and snow is a natural part of the winter landscape, color change is the striking preliminary to the shedding of leaves, which is often a survival mechanism to keep a tree from being killed by the extremes of winter. This is why leaves change color and are shed. Viewed in their most basic terms, leaves are food factories. Beneath their surface layer, or *epidermis,* are rows of specialized cells known as *chloroplasts,* which contain the chemical *chlorophyll.* Chlorophyll, chemically similar to the red pigment *hemoglobin* that is found in blood, is not only what gives leaves their green color in spring and summer but is what makes it possible for them to use the energy of sunlight to convert water and carbon dioxide into sugars. The pigments that will cause the leaves to glow bright in the fall are present from the outset, but the green chlorophyll masks them.

In sustained cold weather, leaves can become a fatal liability for a tree. The low humidity and high winds of winter will quickly dry out the leaves and through them the tree. To prevent the tree from becoming desiccated, the leaves must fall.

In autumn, as temperatures begin to drop, the food-making process begins to shut down in some tree species. Most of the chlorophyll is drawn into the twig or is broken down chemically. Sap no longer flows from the twig into the leaf stem, weakening the juncture where the two join. With the amount of chlorophyll now greatly reduced, the yellows and oranges that were hidden the rest of the year become visible. Just how vibrant they become depends on how much sugar is trapped within the leaves. The sugar in the now-isolated leaves undergoes chemical changes that will cause the leaves to turn their brilliant shades of red, bronze and purple. A tree must contain a specific gene for its leaves to turn either red or orange. In northern states, the only trees that do not shed their leaves are the conifers, whose needle-thin leaves are protected by a waxy coating.

In the low elevations of the Southeast, many of the native trees, such as the palms, retain their leaves year-round. The very common live oak gained its name because it is green year-round. There simply is no need in the South for the tree to shed its leaves. However, some hardwood species still undergo a modified color change, much subtler and often much later, and so drop their leaves. The color changes that begin in Canada in September may not peak in South Florida until November or December.

If leaf tints elsewhere are rainbowlike in their variety, in the Southeast they tend to mimic the sun's scarlet-and-gold at dawn and twilight. One of the most prominent trees to undergo a color change is the bald cypress. Its green needles often turn a striking reddish brown just before dropping. A gnarled, twisted cypress bearing reddish orange needles while draped in flowing white beards of Spanish moss is one of fall's most unforgettable sights, especially if there should be an alligator sprawled in the sun near the tree's thick, buttressed base.

Red maples are one of the few hardwood trees found both in Maine and in the thick of Florida swamps. The red maple seems to have adapted well to the alternating winter cycle of the South: warm weather followed by brief periods of extreme cold, then warmth again. However, each maple tree seems to function on its own very individual time clock, so that in the middle of February it's possible to see some maples still bearing red or yellow leaves while other maples nearby are totally bare.

Additional hardwoods adding color to the normally emerald Florida background include the hickory, with its mustard-gold colors, and the sweet gum, bearing yellow and burgundy leaves.

Hot Spots All the cypress domes throughout north Florida come alive with color, and some years are better than others. In addition to the orange cypress needles, sweet gum and black gum will be adding color as well. The best color tends to be in the areas of North Florida, from Gainesville to the state line.

Okefenokee NWR is loaded with color-changing cypress trees. At Florida's **Blackwater River State Forest**, colors are visible in many places, but the northwest end can be truly spectacular. Other good Panhandle locations are **Falling Waters State Park, Torreya State Park** and **Florida Caverns State Park.** The foliage in all three is more akin to that of the Appalachians than Florida.

In the **Apalachicola National Forest,** as one heads west on Highway 20, just after crossing the Ochlockonee River Bridge there is a corridor that fairly glows with all the primary Florida colors: red maple, sweet gum and black gum in addition to the bald cypress. The Scenic Byway that runs through the forest also has many cypress areas that hold the potential for good color.

The brightest autumn colors are found in the cypress swamps located north of Ocala.

U.S. 19/98 between Tallahassee and Chiefland often has spectacular colors right beside the road, as does the stretch between Chiefland and Cedar Key. Mixed with pines and other evergreens, this is often a remarkable sight in mid-November. **Ocean Pond** in the **Osceola National Forest** is surrounded by cypress trees. However, throughout much of the forest cypress trees are so common that they are visible from many points. **Fanny Bay,** off I-10, has some of the finest trees, but access is still somewhat limited. A boardwalk to the bay should be open within the next few years. **State Road 44** between I-75 and Inverness can be truly striking, especially around the Withlacoochee River bridge and the lakes just before Inverness. And the cypress swamps on the Richloam tract of the **Withlacoochee State Forest** near Brooksville can be quite beautiful in fall.

58

The Cedar Keys

Florida's most famous keys are the island chain that extends from south Florida toward Cuba and that contains such world-famous places as Key Largo and Key West. But Florida also has a second major batch of islands, virtually unknown and much less visited, collectively called the Cedar Keys, a group of 40 landfalls located in the Gulf of Mexico about midway between Tampa and Tallahassee.

The only one inhabited today is Way Key, a single square mile with a permanent population of less than a thousand. Most of the people here are commercial fishers or are descended from them. On Cedar Key, a rock garden in the backyard is most likely to be a pile of discarded oyster shells.

The offshore islands basically function as wildlife refuges that house dozens of varieties of birds along with a handful of amphibian and reptile species. Snake Key, for example, did not come by its name without cause.

But many of these could just as easily have been called "Bird Island." Most of the migratory species overwinter here, and most will remain until March or April. The number of waterbirds recorded here has been impressive: 238 different species. In spring the offshore islands become one of the largest heronries anywhere in the South. One of the nicest things about birding here is that the birds do not honor any boundaries, and many of the species that stay on the outer islands can be seen around Way Key.

So deserted are the Cedar Keys today that it's difficult to believe they ever were part of a tremendous economic boom. But in the 1800s, many more of the islands were settled, boasting such diverse enterprises as a lumber mill, an army hospital and even a detention camp for Native American prisoners. By 1885 the Cedar Keys had attracted 5,000 residents, and its busy port threatened to rival Mobile and New Orleans. Three sawmills shipped locally produced timber (lumber, railroad ties and cedar for pencils), fish, oysters, sponges and other commodities brought directly to

Cedar Key docks by rail and boat. In addition, both the Farber and Eagle pencil companies had large operations here to harvest the plentiful cedar supply.

In just five years it was over. The new port at Tampa had a much deeper harbor and took away considerable shipping business. Loggers had not bothered to selectively cut or replant the cedar forest, so the timber supply began to run out. The same rapacity in harvesting oysters, clams and stone crabs generated a simultaneous decline in the area's marine resources. As a result, by 1890 Cedar Key's population dropped to 1,200 from 5,000. In 1896 a hurricane destroyed the Cedar Keys' lumber mills, tore away all the wharves, damaged the railroad and swept away all bridges leading to Way Key. With the area's resources almost exhausted, there was no incentive to rebuild.

Eventually Way Key reestablished itself as a fishing community, a legacy very much evident today. Both sides of the road to Way Key are lined with shantylike oyster sheds on stilts. Empty oyster shells (excellent testimony to the richness of the resources) are piled so high at the base of some sheds that the shells obscure the original foundation. Close to the heart of Way Key is a small bay where the main fishing fleet anchors. When left unmanned, the boats are taken over by brown pelicans, which sit placidly, waiting for handouts.

Pelicans and other birds are common around Cedar Key, an old fishing village located in the middle of nowhere.

Most of Cedar Key's visitors today are drawn to the series of seafood restaurants built beside a semicircular roadway that loops offshore into the Gulf of Mexico. In addition to the usual seafood platters, they also serve mullet burgers, crab burgers, shrimp burgers, oyster burgers and a pâté made from mullet. Brown pelicans, either floating in the water nearby or sitting on offshore posts, are quite common here.

Hot Spots

The town of **Cedar Key** is located in the middle of nowhere. The nearest small town is Otter Creek, 22 miles away on U.S. 19. So out-of-the-way is Cedar Creek that there are just a few businesses along the stretch of State Road 24 that connects Cedar Key to Otter Creek. Only tall pines, cypress, cabbage palms and palmettos border the thoroughfare that eventually takes you 3 miles out into the Gulf and delivers you to Way Key and the town of Cedar Key.

The offshore islands comprise the **Cedar Keys NWR**, a satellite of the adjacent **Lower Suwannee NWR**. It's quite possible to visit both refuges while headquartered at Cedar Key. The Lower Suwannee is an excellent place for migrant shorebirds in March and April.

Only the sandy perimeters of the Cedar Keys islands are open to public access, and for very good reason. According to a number of studies, several of the islands are home to some of the world's greatest concentrations of poisonous cottonmouth water moccasins. One island alone is estimated to have 700 of the reptiles. There are said to be an average of 20 cottonmouths per acre on several other keys. However, the snakes and birds live in obviously good harmony, for both are so numerous here. The arrangement seems to have evolved this way: Snakes eat the rats that might rob the birds' nests, and the birds tend to leave the young snakes alone.

The numbers of nesting birds in the Cedar Keys is impressive: between 50,000 and 100,000, although the numbers have reached as high as 200,000. These include herons, brown pelicans, egrets, white ibis, cormorants and others. The white ibis is one of the dominant species, and the population estimated to be as high as 60,000 individuals. The island with the largest rookery is **Seahorse Key.** It is closed from January to June and is well patrolled to keep the curious away.

Summer can be very hot here, but there is usually a colony of almost two dozen roseate spoonbills present then. Beginning in October, waterfowl begin showing up. In winter, this is one of the few places where one can see both brown and white pelicans. The brown pelicans are easy to approach and eagerly seek handouts from fishermen. The white pelicans, on the other hand, tend to keep their distance and are best seen from a boat.

Information on boat tours or rentals is available from the Cedar Keys Chamber of Commerce: (904) 543-5600. Two books of note to look for in the Cedar Key bookstore are by local naturalist Harriet Smith: *The Naturalist's Guide to Cedar Key, Florida* and *Watching Birds in the Cedar Keys.* She also conducts tours to the islands; (904) 543-9339.

In addition to the Cedar Keys NWR, on the mainland is the 4,720-acre **Cedar Key Scrub State Reserve,** which highlights an entirely different kind of biosphere. Several walking trails skirt the perimeter of this thick brush (see Chapter 66).

Way Key may be becoming more modernized with condos and such, but fortunately the area around it is not far removed from the way it looked when John Muir decided at the age of 29 to walk here from Indiana in 1867, a considerable hike of about 1,000 miles. Details of that walk, along with many other interesting facts, are available at the **Cedar Key State Museum,** located at 1710 Museum Drive; follow the brown-and-white signs.

Those traveling south toward Tampa from the Cedar Keys should keep an eye out for the **Waccasassa Bay State Preserve,** an area most easily explored by boat and where it's possible to spot black bears, otters, raccoons, bald eagles and numerous wading birds. The best boat access is on the Waccasassa River at the end of County Road 326 west of Gulf Hammock and on Covass Creek, off County Road 40A near Yankeetown; the preserve telephone number is (904) 543- 5567.

59

October Shorttakes

Wild Whooping Cranes

Central Florida is home to the only wild whooping cranes east of the Mississippi. Although the birds are present year-round, October is a good time to visit their primary habitat at **Lake Kissimmee State Park** during the fall color change.

The Florida Game and Fresh Water Fish Commission began releasing whoopers into the wild in 1993. The large white birds are now established in several places, including the **Three Lakes Wildlife Management Area,** but the largest number of birds is normally visible at Lake Kissimmee State Park. Between 20 and 30 of the birds can usually be found along Overstreet Road and on either side of the Overstreet boat landing on the southeast side of the lake.

Genetically related to the common crane of Europe and Asia and distantly related to the sandhill crane, the whooping crane became extinct in Florida in 1935. The birds were never common here, with the highest estimates placing the peak population at between 3,000 and 5,000 whoopers.

Whooping cranes normally roost along the edges of the lake in water 8 to 10 inches deep; they cannot perch in trees. The cranes should not be approached closer than 200 feet during the last half-hour before sunset or any time after dark. Otherwise the birds could leave their safe roosts and move to other areas where they are likely to be killed. Bobcats, one of their primary predators, are relatively rare at Lake Kissimmee but common around other nearby lakes.

If a bird dramatically pumps its head up and down or begins vocalizing, that means you've approached too closely. Immediately back off. Whooping cranes are a protected species. Molesting or harassing them is subject to punishment. Lake Kissimmee State Park is located off State Road 60, 15 miles east of Lake Wales; (813) 696-1112.

Native Culture

Autumn is a good time to become familiar with many of the native plants and berries used for food by the Native Americans of the Southeast. A 5-mile trail, the Wiregrass Trail, in **Blackwater River State Forest** has many interpretive signs along the first mile. A brochure describes how to identify the plants and their uses; for instance the Yaupon, a holly with red berries, whose leaves were used to make the "black drink" emetic. The fruit of the shining (winged) sumac was once made into a sour drink similar to lemonade. An interpretive brochure and trail map are available at the state forest or from the Florida Trail Association: (904) 378-8823.

Exotic Bird-Watching

Normally it would be necessary to travel a lot of the world to see the many varieties of exotic birds that live in the Miami and South Florida area. As part of the alien invasion (chapter 60), thousands of exotic birds were once widely imported and sold, and some escaped in Florida and established breeding populations. They include the ringed turtledove, shell parakeet, red-crowned parrot, hill myna, canary-winged parakeet, spotted-breasted oriole, red-whiskered bulbul, blue-gray tanager, monk parakeet, fulvous tree duck, South American lapwing, Montezuma oropendola, rose-breasted cockatoo, Brazilian crested cardinal, Brazilian tanager, striped-headed tanager and a number of weaver finches, relatives of the familiar and widespread house sparrow.

Colorful exotic birds like these not only decorate the landscape, sometimes they ravage it. The monk parakeet, a native of Argentina, is such a menace to grain and fruit crops in its homeland that the Argentine government passed a law requiring property owners to destroy all the monk parakeet nests they could find. Although they may not all be welcome guests, the birds are here, so why not put them to good use? In South Miami, some of the best places to look are the parks. **Greynolds Park**, divided into two parts (the western section is considered to have the best birding), is also home to the famed but light pink "scarlet" ibis. These birds are the descendants of true scarlet ibis that mated with white ibis. Brighter-colored ibis are present from April to August, the nesting season.

Take U.S. 1 (Biscayne Boulevard) to Northeast 172nd Street. Cross to the west to reach the entrance to the park.

The community of **Miami Springs,** just north of the international airport, holds lots of exotic species. **Coconut Grove Bay Front Park,** on South Bayshore Drive, and **Parrot Jungle** are also good bird attractors. The open areas farther south at **Homestead** can also be productive.

The new round of storms and tropical fronts that come with every hurricane season can impact areas profoundly, as Hurricane Andrew illustrated. The best information on current exotic bird locations is the Naturalist's Office of the Dade County Parks Department (it's in Greynolds Park): (305) 949-3134. Also contact the **Tropical Audubon House** in South Miami; (305) 666-5111. Both organizations conduct field trips and seminars to acquaint people with the new birds on the block.

60

A Closer Look: Alien Invaders

Florida is rapidly becoming an alien nation populated by exotic animals, plants and trees that are in fierce competition with native flora and fauna for the same living space. Transported thousands of miles from their natural homelands, these exotics are far removed from the natural predators and disease that would normally keep them under control. Once exotics are free and reproducing in the environment, it is virtually impossible to remove them.

Too often, introduced species have been better competitors than the native ones for the same food, habitat, nesting space or breeding sites. No one really knows for certain how many different species are loose, but some estimates claim that at least a thousand alien species are now free throughout the Southeast but concentrated in Florida.

Similar to that of the Galápagos Islands and Hawaii, Florida's native fauna and flora developed in semi-isolation, allowing them to create a very fragile, highly specialized biological system. As a result, a newly introduced life-form is likely to do more harm in Florida than almost anywhere else in the United States.

New introductions can happen any place at any time; even the toughest regulations are powerless. For example, Hurricane Andrew's powerful winds did much more than level many buildings around Homestead in 1992. The storm's worst long-term effect may be the scores of new exotics that its winds liberated from Miami's Metrozoo: monkeys, parrots, pythons, baboons and more. And officials at Everglades National Park were not as concerned about the trees that were lost as they were about the new plants the storm may have added to the environment.

For the present, plants and trees, not animals, pose some of the greatest problems. Hydrilla, an aquarium plant, clogs many of the state's rivers and lakes, and little is being accomplished toward eliminating the noxious weed. The plant was released into the state's waterways by fish-farm owners and hobbyists who dumped unwanted or excess plants. Hydrilla was accidentally spread further by anglers moving their boat trailers from one waterway to the next. Mechanical harvesting of hydrilla is prohibitively expensive and chemicals are deemed impractical, so hydrilla will remain part of the Florida environment indefinitely.

Perhaps the worst alien invader is the Melaleuca tree imported from Australia in the early 1900s. Brought here both as an ornamental and "to forest the Everglades," an estimated six billion Melaleuca trees now infest South Florida. Not only have they spread like wildfire but each Melaleuca tree is like a straw sucking water out of the ground. The Melaleucas have seriously affected South Florida's water table.

Australian pines, which also easily crowd out native species, prevent sea turtles from digging on beaches used for nesting for perhaps thousands of years. The trees and their root systems have, in effect, erected a deadly barricade that effectively thwarts the turtles' delicate reproductive process.

In 1995 it was announced that the thorny soda apple weed that entered Florida in the 1980s had been spread to every part of the state by animals, farm equipment and packaged garden manure. Termed "the plant from hell," the soda apple weed crowds out important pasture grasses, which costs ranchers millions of dollars annually in lost productivity. The plant, which can grow a foot tall in 45 days, produces a tasty apple-smelling fruit that hogs, deer and cattle eagerly eat. Seeds from the fruit pass through the animals' digestive tracts unharmed, then are deposited in new areas or resown in old ones. Herbicides can control the weed, but the soda apple is now considered too widespread ever to be eradicated.

Exotic animal species, including birds, monkeys and fish, have had numerous opportunities to enter Florida. For decades the majority of birds, mammals and reptiles brought into the United States from all over the world came through Miami International Airport. Some creatures escaped right at the airport while others broke free from local pet stores or their new owners. This is why many Central and South Florida waterways are heavily populated with exotic fish that rightfully belong inside an aquarium. The poison rotenone, relied on in many places to eliminate undesirable fish species, isn't suitable for Florida. The southern part of the state is largely a system of shallow lakes and ponds joined together by drainage canals and natural channels so intricately complex that using rotenone could not succeed. This interconnected network also aided in the rapid expansion of the exotic fish species.

A prime example of how an exotic fish can dominate its new environment is the *Tilapia aurea,* or blue tilapia, a native of Africa that appears frequently on Florida restaurant menus. The blue tilapia, a member of the cichlid family, was imported into Florida in 1961 by the Game and Fresh Water Fish Commission, which thought it was importing a different fish, *Tilapia nilotica,* as part of a weed-control experiment. The misidentification was made by biologists at Auburn University who not only supplied the fish but had studied it for many years.

Three thousand blue tilapia were placed in phosphate pits at the Pleasant Grove Research Station in Hillsborough County, where their weed-eating ability could be closely monitored. News stories began circulating about how the blue tilapia was a fantastic game fish and an excellent food fish. The publicity prompted fishermen to raid the ponds and move some of the fish to other waters.

The press reports were dead wrong. Blue tilapia, with an elephant's appetite and a rabbit's reproductive ability, will not take bait and therefore cannot be caught on hook and line. They can be taken only by snagging or netting. There is still a wide variety of opinion about how tasty a food fish they are.

Another exotic fish that demonstrated good adaptability is the famous walking catfish. Capable of breathing air, the walking catfish is able to move across land by propelling itself on its pectoral and tail fins. Imported as an aquarium curiosity, walking catfish were not as popular as expected, and so the fish were left to grow unchecked in fish-farm ponds and crawl away into a local canal. From the Fort Lauderdale area the fish spread quickly into parts of South Florida. Fortunately, its expansion has been limited by its susceptibility to prolonged cold and fungus infections.

Not all exotic fish introductions have been a disaster. The highly aggressive and tackle-busting South American peacock bass has been introduced into waterways along the Gold Coast of South Florida, much to the pleasure of anglers living there. The fish was studied extensively before its release to be certain it would not negatively affect Florida's native fish or plant population.

Amphibians, and giant toads in particular, have also assaulted the Florida ecosystem. The giant toad, *Bufo marinus,* was deliberately set loose in South Florida in 1958 with the idea that it would eat more harmful insects than the smaller native toads. The bufo, which can attain a length of up to 30 inches, proved to be an effective insect eater—so good, in fact, that the native toad population decreased because the bufo consumed the largest share of the food supply.

A potentially very troublesome mammal is the nutria, a South American rodent once promoted like the chinchilla for get-rich-quick fur-raising schemes. People paid high prices for breeding stock, but few regained their original investments. Some disappointed owners let their animals go free. Nutria destroy native vegetation and weaken ditch banks through digging and building burrows. They live in Central Florida but have become a particular problem in Louisiana and Alabama marshlands, where they can destroy large amounts of vegetation.

A dangerous reptile now believed established in canals on Key Largo is the South American caiman, brought in to be sold as pets in place of the American alligator when alligators became protected by law. Most people were unaware that caiman were far more aggressive. Instead of killing the more vicious caiman, softhearted owners simply released their pets. There is concern about what could happen if the caiman becomes established in the Everglades, as it may have become at Key Largo.

Even insects have created very visible and costly problems. Take the fire ant—please! Established throughout Florida as well as in many parts of Alabama and Georgia, fire ants have built hundreds of thousands of large dirt mounds beside roadways and in pastures. These mounds, which look like miniature versions of African termite hills, are a threat to livestock, crops, pets and people when disturbed. If aroused, fire ants swarm angrily out of the ground like wasps, and their bites are just as painful and equally allergenic. Fire ants apparently entered the country from South

America through the port at Mobile in the late 1920s or early 1930s.

Fruit flies from the Mediterranean and the Caribbean have also threatened Florida's all-important citrus industry at various times. Of course, it only seems natural that there should be exotic citrus pests, for citrus itself is an exotic, introduced around the world from its native home in Asia.

The only way ever to end more introductions of exotics is to ban the importation of all foreign species. It's long past time that exotic animals were left in their natural habitats, where they belong.

November

Notes

61

Tracking: Sand Trails

Not long ago, every naturalist or outdoorsman worthy of the name was skilled at reading sign: deciphering the tracks, scrapes and even the droppings left by animals in the wild. Like Sherlock Holmes approaching a new mystery, these self-taught naturalists could draw upon a lifetime of specialized knowledge to deduce the meanings in the messages left on the ground.

The concrete and asphalt pathways of today's modern world aren't very conducive for initiating or maintaining this talent, yet tracking is one skill that can always be learned. And it can be practiced any time of year in the Southeast, in the soft sand that covers the Florida peninsula and the coasts of Georgia and Alabama. Snow, so essential for tracking elsewhere, isn't even a consideration.

At beaches, in forests and on national wildlife refuges (even backcountry roads) everything that lives leaves its imprint. Sometimes the story in the sand is as powerful and moving as any human drama. With every rain the storyboards are washed clean, so that the squiggles of a beetle are replaced by the plodding prints and dragging tail of a turtle, only to be later replaced by the plowing, sinuous furrow of a rattlesnake.

The first step in tracking is learning to identify the tracks of individual animals. A good field guide is essential. *Field Guide to Animal Tracks* by Olaus Murie, part of the Peterson series, is considered the classic work and includes mammals, birds, insects, reptiles and amphibians.

Learning to read tracks opens a whole new understanding of the world of animals. For instance, discovering the characteristic differences between cat and dog prints may have you regarding your pets in a wholly new light. Cat tracks—whether from a domestic cat or a wild panther—reveal that the animal is a stalker and a predator. To achieve a quieter walk, cats place their hind feet in the tracks of their front feet. They always walk in a straight line. They also walk with their claws retracted in order not to wear them down. Dogs, on the other hand, amble along with their claws displayed since they normally have little real need for them except in occasional digging.

Identifying sign is basic, but reading what it means is much more advanced. If you like to use your imagination, then you should enjoy unraveling all the clues: the depth, placement and condition of the tracks, plus their relationship to the terrain and the tracks left by others. It's not terribly difficult to uncover the universal pattern. For instance, here's how the arrangement of tracks helps identify an animal and also tell something about its habits: Animals that bound over the ground, such as rabbits, mice and squirrels, leave the same basic track pattern. The hind feet will always be paired (beside each other) and placed ahead of the marks left by the front feet. The direction of the hind feet also indicate the direction of travel.

Animals that rely on speed to escape their enemies or overtake their prey normally walk on their toes. These include dogs and cats, foxes, horses, pigs, sheep, deer, goats and cows. Was an animal in a hurry, or simply walking? The tracks will tell the story. If the tracks are close together, you can be fairly certain that the animal was not running. But tracks that are wide apart with the foot flared indicate rapid movement. The question then becomes: Who was chasing whom, and with what result?

Depending on the terrain, you may be able to follow an animal for long distances, perhaps even to its burrow or den. Many times, however, you will have to be content with less and limited to the tracks made by an animal as it crossed a forest road.

Animals that do not normally need to hurry, such as porcupines, tortoises and skunks, leave full-foot prints, placing both heel and toe into the ground. Bird tracks are equally informative, revealing whether a particular bird walks or hops or does both.

Good trackers know never to walk on the tracks they're following but always beside them. That makes backtracking easier and allows the possibility for restudying a section of prints.

Once you begin identifying tracks, so many mysteries in the sand will finally become clear. At the beach, for instance, you'll always know that it is the pointed feet of a crab that makes all those bands of dots in the sand. Or that it is a raccoon's hind feet that make tracks similar to the prints left by a human child.

If you wish to photograph tracks, either for illustration or for puzzling over later, you'll obtain the best detail when there is shadowing on the tracks. That occurs early and late, when the sun is low in the sky. Photographing in sand at midday is apt to produce overly bright pictures without many revealing features.

Mudflats, of course, are good for tracking, though many people don't like to muck up their feet for this purpose.

Good tracking opportunities throughout the Southeast exist year-round and are never hampered by lack of snow. Besides, as serious readers of the sand will tell you, the trails left by many animals who partially sink in all that cold white stuff often have all the charm and readability of pogo-stick holes.

Hot Spots In visiting beach areas, be sure to time your arrival for low tide, when tracks are most abundant.

Alabama's **Bon Secour NWR,** just south of Mobile, attracts not only many shorebirds but offers the chance for tracking fox, the endangered Alabama beach mouse and loggerhead turtle crawls (in summer only). The beautiful sands at **Gulf Shores** are excellent for distinguishing shorebird tracks at low tide.

Florida's **Santa Rosa Sound** at the Naval Live Oaks Visitor Center in the **Gulf Islands National Seashore** is rich in the bird tracks of great blue herons, willets and snowy plovers. The seashore is located in Northwest Florida near Pensacola. The Naval Live Oaks Visitor Center is located on the mainland near the town of Gulf Breeze.

St. Vincent NWR, an isolated island that can be reached only by private boat, offers 8 miles of Gulf beach and more than 80 miles of inland roads that crisscross the island. Wild turkeys, foxes, feral hogs, the usual shorebirds, white-tailed deer and the unusual Asian sambar deer are all easily trailed. The sambar were imported when the island was a private hunting preserve, many decades ago. A small sambar herd still exists. Thesdeer are easy to distinguish from whitetails because the sambar are larger and have distinctively flat, Mickey Mouse–like ears. They tend to favor the marshy areas. Primitive hunts are occasionally held here. The refuge office number is (904) 653-8808.

Another good area for bird tracks as well as those of foxes, bobcats and field mice is **St. Joseph Peninsula State Park.** The northern section is still a wilderness area that can be reached only by foot. Look for animal tracks in the dunes and upper beaches here. Also examine the beaches at **Eagle Harbor,** particularly at low tide, for tracks of snowy egrets, great blue herons, little blue herons and tricolored herons. The park is located south of U.S. 98 from the town of Port St. Joe. Take County Road 30A, turn west on County Road 30E and drive to the park entrance.

St. George Island State Park is surrounded by both Apalachicola Bay and the Gulf of Mexico. In summer you may be fortunate enough to spot the tracks of a loggerhead that nested at night along the 9 miles of pristine beach. You can always be certain of finding tracks of American oystercatchers, sandpipers, plovers, sanderlings, egrets and herons on the beach. The park is located across from the town of Eastpoint on U.S. 98. Take the causeway to the island and turn left. The park is another 8 miles to the east.

Florida's three national forests are among the best places to look for mammal and snake tracks. Skunks, gopher tortoises, rattlesnakes, black bears, deer, turkeys, lizards and many other animals can often be seen along the woodland roads. Early and late, you're also apt to see the animals still making tracks. The **Apalachicola National Forest** is located in the Panhandle, southwest of Tallahassee; **Osceola National Forest** is southwest of Jacksonville; and the **Ocala National Forest** is located east of the town of Ocala in Central Florida.

The mudflats at **Merritt Island NWR** and the 25-mile long beach of **Canaveral National Seashore** on the east-central coast near the town of Titusville are also good for tracking. Raccoon tracks are common, and the beach is good for loggerhead turtle tracks, particularly in June and July. Merritt Island NWR has over 100 miles of roads.

In Southwest Florida, beautiful **Cayo Costa State Park** has 7 miles of spectacular unspoiled white beach. The best tracking is on the Gulf side at **Johnson Shoals,** a cove that attracts black skimmers, plovers, gulls and American oystercatchers. The island can be reached only by boat. A ferry leaves from Bokeelia on Pine Island north of Fort Myers; for reservations, call (813) 964-0375.

On Sanibel Island west of Fort Myers, the **J. N. "Ding" Darling NWR** is home to over 30 species of mammals and more than 50 types of amphibians and reptiles. There is a route for autos and several footpaths. For information, call (813) 472-1100. The beaches of Sanibel are good for tracking.

Cumberland Island National Seashore, Georgia's southernmost barrier island, offers tracks of birds and mammals and of sea turtle crawls. Of the **Savannah Wildlife Refuges,** some of the most varied tracking is available at **Blackbeard Island,** where loggerhead turtles nest in summer, large flocks of shorebirds are found throughout most months and white-tailed deer walk the trails. Access is available from Shellman's Bluff, 51 miles south of the city of Savannah. Far easier to reach is the northernmost refuge island, **Pinckney,** which attracts many shorebirds at low tide.

62

Gopher Tortoises

If another race were to be held between a tortoise and a hare, the gopher tortoise ought to defend the title. The gopher tortoise is an industrious animal and a steady plodder. It can also cover an amazing amount of ground within a very short time.

The gopher tortoise, found only in the Southeast, is one of three true tortoises native to the United States. It is a good-sized creature, measuring between 9 and 14 inches in length. The elongated shell, which is round and domed, varies from brown to tan. The underside, or *plastron,* is yellowish. The head, a reddish tan, is rounded in front and small.

Like many other animals, the gopher tortoise mates in the spring and nests in May and June. A female may lay as many as three clutches, each consisting of anywhere between 2 and 14 eggs. Hatching occurs from early August to October.

Compared to the Florida box turtle, which may live well over a century, the gopher tortoise barely reaches middle age. Estimates vary between 40 and 80 years as a gopher tortoise's lifespan, and it may take one between 15 and 20 years to attain maturity.

The gopher tortoise's name comes from its underground ways: It digs very long burrows. A typical one is 10 feet deep and between 20 and 30 feet long, a notable excavation. The longest tunnel recorded was almost 48 feet. It went in a straight line and ended in a large chamber. Not surprisingly, a gopher tortoise's front limbs are ideally suited for digging: The toes are webless, and the foot is flattened. Its back feet are considerably smaller than the front. The preferred habitat for the tunnels is a dry, sandy area in grasslands, forests or in between. Not only is this good soil for the burrows, but the terrain supplies plenty of grass and leaves, the tortoise's primary food.

Like many other burrowing animals, the gopher tortoise often shares its living quarters with a variety of other creatures. Besides the tortoise itself, a nest might include snakes, frogs, toads, burrowing owls and even small mammals. It's quite a comfortable environment, too, where temperatures stay fairly stable.

Gopher tortoises are seen either as they sun at the entrances to their burrows on cool days or when they are out feeding, often in the middle of the day. Gopher tortoises can be extremely skittish. One that is at the mouth of its entrance should not be approached closely, unless someone wants to witness a demonstration of the animal's speed. It's best to observe one from a discreet distance (ideally behind cover) with binoculars. However, sometimes it is possible to closely approach a tortoise sunning itself well away from its burrow. As long as the tortoise doesn't feel threatened or crowded, it may stay quite still, almost as if posing.

Because so many other creatures depend on the gopher tortoise burrows for either temporary or permanent living space, the animal is considered a *keystone species*. Unfortunately, it is not doing well, so it also is currently designated a "species of special concern." There are two problems facing the gopher tortoise. Although it is illegal to kill one of the animals, people still eat them. In the Great Depression of the 1930s, gopher tortoises carried the nickname "Hoover's chickens."

But the gravest problem is a contagious respiratory disease similar to the one that is killing desert tortoises in California. Although

The gopher tortoise is found throughout the Southeast in well-drained, sandy soils. They are not always this approachable. The head of this one is covered with mosquitoes.

it is illegal to own or transport a gopher tortoise, it appears that people are spreading this infectious disease by moving tortoises from one area to another or by releasing captive tortoises. Overcrowding and stress also may be factors in the outbreaks.

Although the numbers of gopher tortoises have been steadily declining, they are still found in thriving numbers in a few large parks and preserves. Yet this concentration makes them very susceptible to infection. It appears doubtful that small isolated populations will survive over time.

The overall record for tortoises is not good: Twenty-three species of land tortoise originated about 60 million years ago. All but four are now extinct.

Hot Spots

Gopher tortoises were brought to **Dauphin Island,** Alabama, and released into the Audubon bird sanctuary there. They are also seen on the golf courses and in the pine woods on the mainland in Baldwin County. **Bon Secour NWR** also has a population of gopher tortoises.

Gopher tortoises are not as common in parts of Northwest Florida as they could be because—even though it's illegal—people still eat them. One place to look for them in the **Apalachicola National Forest** is at the Camel Lake campground on the western side of the forest. A colony of the tortoises lives on the north side of the lake, on a high, sandy ridge.

In **Osceola National Forest** gopher tortoises are quite common because of the sandy, well-drained terrain there. They are most common in the areas between Highway 90 and I-10, both of which run in a general east-west direction. A trail leads from the **Mt. Carrie Wayside Park,** across from the Columbia Correctional Institution. The trail passes several burrows that are impossible to miss thanks to the signs pointing right to them. At the southeast end of the **Olustee Battlefield** are several trails that have gopher tortoises living along them.

At **Paynes Prairie State Preserve,** take the Gainesville-Hawthorne Trail and seeing tortoises is almost guaranteed. Gopher tortoises are pretty much all over the sandy terrain of the **Ocala National Forest** in areas of longleaf pine and young

Bon Secour NWR

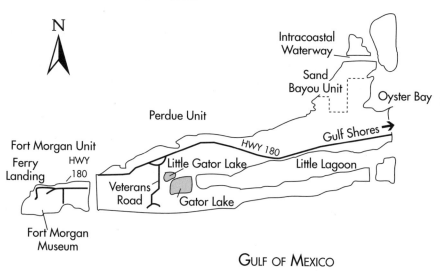

N

Intracoastal Waterway

Sand Bayou Unit

Oyster Bay

Perdue Unit

Gulf Shores →

HWY 180

Fort Morgan Unit

Ferry Landing

HWY 180

Little Gator Lake

Little Lagoon

Veterans Road

Gator Lake

Fort Morgan Museum

GULF OF MEXICO

scrub stands. Anyone who seeks out the red-cockaded woodpecker nests should see gopher tortoises, or at least their nests (see chapter 10 for directions).

Andrews Wildlife Management Area near Chiefland has gopher tortoise burrows in open areas with feed plots. Go north from Chiefland on U.S. 19 for almost 5 miles; turn left onto County Road 211. The entrance is less than a mile away. **Withlacoochee State Forest** near Brooksville offers two good opportunities for seeing the tortoises on two designated nature trails: the Colonel Robbins and McKethan Lake Nature Trails.

The Scrub Island Trail at **Boyd Hill Nature Park** near St. Petersburg passes through excellent tortoise habitat; take Exit 4 off I-275 and go east on 54th Avenue South to 9th Street. Turn left onto 9th Street and head north to Country Club

Way. The nature center will be on the right.

In Northeast Florida, gopher tortoises are usually seen at **Little Talbot Island State Park** and **Guana River Wildlife Management Area and State Park**. Both are located off A1A in the Jacksonville and St. Augustine areas, respectively.

Other coastal areas with good gopher tortoise populations include **Smyrna Dunes Park**, south of Daytona; **Canaveral National Seashore**, just a few miles farther south; the **Hobe Sound NWR** and **Jonathan Dickinson State Park**, both near Jupiter.

63

Barrier Islands

Thanks to the network of bridges that link many of the coastal islands to the mainland, it's easy to forget that many of the Southeast's best sand beaches are located offshore, on the chain of barrier islands that runs parallel to the coastline. These are some of the nation's finest beaches, known for their remarkably fine white sand that, at high noon, can be as blinding as snow but a lot warmer on the feet.

Florida's Panhandle has the best beaches in the nation, and most of them are located on barrier islands. Although for years Florida has claimed the best beaches in its advertising, the official confirmation comes from the annual rankings published by a Maryland-based beach geologist, Dr. Stephen Leatherman. Only one problem about enjoying these beaches, and it is a temporary one: Hurricane Opal clobbered the Panhandle in 1995, and it is expected to take between three and five years for the areas to fully recover.

The best season for visiting these (and any other) beaches are April and May, September, October and early November. The fall months are better for those who want to walk off the land and into the water, which will have had all summer to warm up (conditions will still be brisk in the early spring). Although Leatherman sometimes alters the rankings from year to year, the following almost always make the list of the Sunshine State's best sandboxes.

Everyone enjoys a fine beach, but from a naturalist's point of view sand strips are among the least interesting parts of a barrier island. Although the empty sand may make the entire island appear sterile and lifeless, undeveloped barrier islands are rich biological storehouses with a tremendous diversity of ecosystems. For example, the area behind the tall dunes is often a low-lying trough, possibly a wetland, that may host a rich variety of bird life. Inland from this trough is a field of smaller secondary dunes that sometimes cover the remainder of an island. More often though, the dunes yield to a hearty maritime forest or a field of scrub vegetation that grow on the opposite side of the island at the edge of a marsh.

Barrier island beaches are the creations of current, wind and wave, awesome powers that routinely demonstrate their strength during passing winter cold fronts. These islands, which tend to be long and skinny, are often separated from the mainland by bodies of water, or *estuaries,* that serve as important nurseries for fish, shellfish and crabs. In places where little development has occurred, wetlands often border the mainland side of the island.

Barrier islands frequently start life simply as a sandbar that slowly emerges from the sea and builds up over a long period of time. Once the bar extends for many miles parallel to shore, it is often sliced into separate cuts and inlets by storms and waves. Or sometimes a barrier island is formed when a long stretch of sand dunes on the mainland are cut away after the ocean floods the low back-lying areas behind the dunes.

Regardless of how they are formed, these islands tend to have very similar characteristics. Their seaward slope is gradual and gentle, perfect for swimming and other water-related activities. The beach's most dramatic feature is usually the primary dune, often the highest point on the entire island.

Creation of the dune field can be a long, slow process. The first dune often forms along the *wrack line,* the highest point on the beach that waves are able to reach. Waves deposit many kinds of suspended debris in the wrack line, including plant seeds. After the seeds germinate and the plants start to grow, their roots trap and accumulate enough sand to eventually create a mountain out of a mole-sized hill.

Foredunes may reach as high as 20 feet or more. In areas that are populated, these dunes are important dikes against hurricane storm-surge, which on average is 10 to 13 feet above the normal high tide. In Florida the foredune is often the tallest dune, but on Georgia's Cumberland Island the back dunes are larger. The primary dune eventually migrates inland to allow a new hill to form along the drift line. The process is repeated over and over until there is a field of dunes that extend across the island.

The plants that colonize the primary dune suffer harsh and varied conditions. Like desert plants, they must be highly salt- and wind-resistant and have adapted to conserve water. Some plants grow as mats of low-profile vegetation while others rely on small leaves with thick, waxy surfaces to retain water.

The long, graceful sea oat, actually a grass, is perhaps the most important plant for stabilizing the primary dune. Sea oats are universally protected by law and never to be picked. They not only tolerate salt spray well, but their growth is actually stimulated as they are slowly buried by sand.

Another common plant on primary dunes seems deliberately placed to protect the formation. This is the prickly sandbur, a pioneering grass that may grow as high as 12 inches. Its sharp tiny spurs often discourage barefoot trespassers, both human and animal.

Just behind the primary dune is a sheltered transitional zone rich in diversity. This more stabilized region contains endemic coastal plants not found anywhere else. Many are woody shrubs, which precede the dwarfed versions of common trees found farther inland. These plants must have long roots in order to probe deep to reach the small amounts of fresh water that accumulate beneath the dunes. These penetrating roots help stabilize the sand.

Trees that occupy the transitional zone of Northeast Florida vary significantly from those of Southeast Florida; the break occurs at Cape Canaveral. North of the Cape, the saw palmetto with its spike-shaped leaves grows in profusion, gradually giving way to a coastal scrub that includes smaller versions of live oaks, cabbage palms, wax myrtle and yaupon. South of the Cape, several types of grasses grow behind the foredune. They merge with a belt of Spanish bayonets and prickly pear cactus before yielding mostly to sea grapes farther inland. Sea grapes take their name from their grape-shaped fruit, which is green when unripe, purple when edible. In the fall, raccoons like to feed on the ripe fruit, which can also be turned into a delicious jelly.

The shallow depression between the foredune and back dunes is often well vegetated. Although somewhat protected, the bushes and trees in this interdune meadow will all appear to be leaning backward, away from the ocean. Their growth has been retarded by salt spray through a process known as *salt pruning*.

The plant growth behind the foredunes on the Gulf Coast is quite different from the Atlantic side. Grasses are dominant behind the foredune, whereas maritime forests of dwarfed shrubs or trees are strikingly absent. The absence of plant clutter tends to make the Gulf Coast dunes more photogenic.

Although the dunes may seem like very inhospitable places to live, the plants do provide enough shade and food to make the sand piles tolerable homes. Rodents, insects, the threatened Eastern indigo snake, the threatened gopher tortoise, spotted skunk, armadillo and many species of bird are among the dune dwellers.

Some of the animal-plant relationships have become highly specialized. The sharp-leafed Spanish bayonet, for instance, grows a creamy white blossom that is pollinated only by the yucca moth. The moth deposits its eggs in the flowers, and the larvae feed on

Sea oats have deep roots that help accumulate enough sand to create sand dunes.

the flower seeds. After the larvae mature, they drop to the ground to pupate. When the plant blooms the following spring, the adult moths emerge to start the cycle all over again.

Hot Spots Topping the list with the best beach of all is **Bahia Honda State Recreation Area** about two-thirds of the way down the Overseas Highway just north of Big Pine Key in the Lower Keys. There are actually two beaches, a larger one that fronts the Atlantic and is often seaweed covered in summer because of the prevailing winds. The seaweed is considered a natural phenomenon and is not removed. Another smaller, well-protected beach on **Florida Bay** is good for sunning and swimming. Call (305) 872-2353 for more information.

Grayton Beach State Recreation Area is about halfway between Fort Walton and Panama City on State Road 30A just south of Highway 98. A boardwalk leads across the high dunes to the mile-long strand. The water here, as along most of the Panhandle, is sometimes as blue as the Caribbean. There's a good nature trail that winds among the dunes and other habitats. Camping is available: (904) 231-4210.

St. Andrews State Recreation Area, yet another state facility, is 3 miles east of Panama City Beach, off State Road 392 (Thomas Drive) and south of Highway 98. An exceptionally beautiful barrier island, St. Andrews has 2 miles of fine sand beach that has always been popular with locals, and now tourists are finding it as the publicity has spread. With two fishing piers, a nature trail and good camping; (904) 234-2522.

Caladesi Island State Park is reached only by private boat or the scheduled ferries from both the city of Clearwater and Honeymoon Island State Recreation Area. People who come here to sun definitely feels it's worth the extra trouble. That little bit of extra effort has kept this area, one of the largest undeveloped barrier islands, in a remarkably natural condition despite its nearness to several large cities. The nearest town is Dunedin. No overnight facilities; (813) 469-5918.

St. George Island State Park is a barrier island accessible only by the toll bridge from Eastpoint, located just east of the town of Apalachicola on Highway 98. The long, slender beach extends for almost 9 miles. Boardwalks provide several access points. With all the expanse, this is an excellent place to get away from people, especially on weekdays. With several excellent hiking trails and lots of good camping. This also is one of the better fall hawk-migration sites; (904) 927-2111.

St. Joseph Peninsula State Park is on a barrier island near the town of Port St. Joe, located off County Road 30E, off Highway 98. The beach with its striking border of dunes stretches for many miles. Plenty of camping, rental cabins and several nature trails are available. This is the place to observe the fall hawk migration; (904) 227-1327.

Cape Florida State Recreation Area, located on the barrier island called Key Biscayne, near Miami, always has a traffic jam on weekends and sometimes is closed because it reaches its full carrying capacity. The beach is a mile long, wide and sandy and one place where swimming is comfortable year-round. But be prepared for people, lots and lots of them; (305) 361-5811.

Fort DeSoto Park is a county park located in the city of St. Petersburg. Spread over five islands, its 3 miles of beachfront often has many more shorebirds and wading birds than people on weekdays. With a good nature trail, and the camping is exceptional; (813) 866-2662.

Crandon Park, another county park, is located off U.S. 1 on Key Biscayne and can be reached only by taking the Rickenbacker Causeway. Besides the beach, the park offers as many activities as most amusement parks. Actually, it is an amusement park, with a skating rink, a zoo, rides and a ballfield; (305) 638-6414.

Delnor Wiggins Pass State Recreation Area offers swimming and fishing in a setting of sea grapes, sea oats, mangroves and cabbage palms. It is 6 miles south of Bonita Springs off County Road 901, which is off U.S. 41. The pass at the north end of this narrow barrier island is an outlet of the Caloosahatchie River; (813) 597-6196.

The following are not on the official list of bests, but that doesn't necessarily mean they're not good. **Honeymoon Island State Recreation Area,** originally named Hog Island, was renamed to attract honeymooners as part of a promotion in the Northeast in 1939. Besides the beautiful beach, there is a virgin slash pine forest (one of Florida's last), mangrove swamps and tidal flats. Lots of shorebirds and ospreys, too. It is located at the west end of State Road 586 north of Dunedin; (813) 469-5942.

Other Florida barrier islands noted for their beauty and recreational activities include **John D. MacArthur State Park** at North Palm Beach, (407) 624-6950; **St. Lucie Inlet State Preserve at Hobe Sound,** (407) 744-7603 and **Cayo Costa State Park,** near Boca Grande, (813) 964-0375. St. Lucie Inlet can be reached by private boat only. A passenger ferry service makes scheduled runs to Cayo Costa.

Cayo Costa, a state park located off Southwest Florida near Fort Myers, is one of the state's few remaining undeveloped barrier islands.

Georgia's **Cumberland Island,** a barrier island that can be reached by ferry from the town of St. Mary's, has an extensive sandy beach facing the Atlantic. Alabama's **Gulf Shores** beach on Mobile Bay's Pleasure Island extends for an incredible 32 miles. It is quite built up in many areas yet rarely seems crowded even in summer. After Labor Day the area becomes a ghost town, but the weather and the water are both at some of the year's finest. Good accommodations facing the water are offered at **Gulf State Park,** also an excellent area for viewing wildlife, including birds, alligators, migrating butterflies, hawks and more.

Dauphin Island, Alabama, is a Pleistocene hilltop. It is the oldest of the barrier islands in the Southeast, in existence for the last 20,000 years or so. All the rest of the Gulf barrier islands are much more recent. Dauphin Island has many intergrade species that are normally found elsewhere. Its cottonmouth is the Florida subspecies instead of the Eastern cottonmouth, and its pine trees are the same as those found on Big Pine Key in the Florida Keys. Wintertime temperatures are mild, averaging between 40 and 60 degrees. The coldest months tend to be January and February.

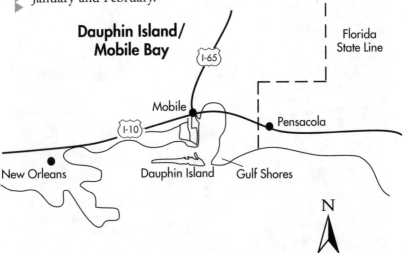

GULF OF MEXICO

64

Native American
Ceremonial Mounds

Some of the most attractive places for wildlife are old Native American mounds, which are now legally protected parks or historic sites, and which have been largely allowed to revert to their natural states. Not surprisingly, the mounds are located near the coast or large inland lakes, still among the richest places of all in terms of natural resources—and of wildlife viewing, especially birds and butterflies. Since most of the visible wildlife has already been covered in depth, it's only proper to take a look at the sites themselves and what they were used for.

Florida's Native Americans are probably the least known of any in the United States. Even many longtime residents know almost nothing about tribes like the Tocobagas, the Calusa, the Ais, the Timucuans and others. This modern ignorance is not due to lack of interest but rather to lack of individuals. By 1800, all of Florida's Native peoples were dead, killed either in battle or by infectious diseases imported by Europeans and against which the Natives had no natural immunity.

The Seminoles who live in the Everglades today are more recent transplants. They are descendants of the Creek Indians who moved from Georgia and the Carolinas into Florida in the late 1700s and intermarried with escaped slaves. They were not mound builders.

Ironically, reminders and remnants of Florida's first people are scattered all around the state in hundreds (if not thousands) of mounds once used for ceremonies, burials or just plain garbage dumps. These mounds, and the artifacts uncovered at some of the sites, are all we have. Florida's first people have no surviving oral or written history, no cave drawings with which to taunt us, nothing but these mounds, too many of which were destroyed to provide roadfill or were bulldozed to ground level for modern building projects. Fortunately, several of the larger mound complexes around the state have become historic sites so that it's still possible to take a peek at the people who lived here first thousands of years ago.

Early peoples first moved into Florida as long as 12,000 years ago, when the climate was far different from that of today. Florida was drier and cooler as the last Ice Age was drawing to an end. Prehistoric bison and mastodons still existed. The people of this Paleo period were primarily hunters, and the artifacts they left behind are points and knives made from stone.

As the climate grew warmer, fishing and shellfishing became more important for human survival. The native peoples began piling up their discarded shells in *middens* along the coasts. Broken pottery and everyday trash were also thrown into these shell piles.

The most elaborate mound building started relatively recently, around A.D. 1000, a direct influence of the Mississippian Culture that originated in Ohio. In the Tampa Bay area, it was the Tocobaga who built flat-topped mounds on which to hold ceremonies and as places for their chiefs to live; in Southwest Florida it was the Calusa.

Although they may seem to have little more than curiosity value, shell middens can actually provide scientists considerable data about a people. Archaeobotanists can not only determine the Indians' diet from the bones, but by boring into the shells they can determine what season of year the shells were collected and the salinity of the water they were gathered from. Archaeobotanists can study seeds and charcoal and identify their sources.

Just as our modern landfills will help reveal our culture to investigators of the future, so these ancient trash dumps are one of our most important ways of looking at the past. Of course, it is impossible to preserve every mound site, but it seems a crime that more can't be done to save these remaining vestiges of Florida's pre-Columbian past.

Hot Spots The cooler months are best for exploring the Native mounds, many of which are on or near the water. In summer, water and mosquitoes often go hand in hand.

Cumberland Island, Georgia, has numerous accumulations of oyster shells. Locally called "middens," they are in the form of big mounds or shell rings. Although many of the mounds were destroyed to build roads, dikes and dams, shell rings still exist in the island marshes. The many oyster piles were built by the Timucuan people, who lived here for more than 3,000 years.

At the northern entrance of **Canaveral National Seashore** is **Turtle Mound,** a 35-foot-high hill that is one of the highest points on Florida's entire east coast. A quarter-mile self-guided trail leads to the top of the 2-acre shell pile that was created by oyster-eating Indians between A.D. 800–1400. In the 1500s, Spanish explorers found the mound overgrown with grass, but local tribes still used it to watch for invaders. This thousand-year-old shell mound now has a good deal of thick vegetation (more than 100 species of plants) growing on it. These and the animals that live in them are described in detail in a trail guide available at the seashore.

One of the most important mound sites in Florida is the **Crystal Rivers State Archaeological Site,** near the town of Crystal River. This is one of the few mound sites that has a museum to provide information about the mound(s) in question. This 14-acre compound contains impressive structures that were begun as many as 2,200 years ago. The site was used by at least four different cultures over that period.

The most impressive site is the huge temple mound made of oyster shells. It was first described in 1859: "It is on all sides nearly perpendicular, the faces covered with brush and trees to which the curious have to cling to effect an ascent. It is nearly forty feet in height, the top surface nearly level, about thirty feet across, and covered with magnolia, live oak, and other forest trees, some of them four feet in diameter." This mound originally had a ramp leading to the top, which has been replicated by a staircase. Thick underbrush still covers most of the sides. Among the most intriguing aspects of the Crystal River site are two stelae made of limestone, each about 4 feet high. Dated to A.D. 440, one of them has a human face carved into it. No final determination has been made yet of their purpose. An estimated 1,000 burials were made in the burial mounds here. Despite the impressive amount of work done by the Native builders and the richness of Crystal River, this site was abandoned before Europeans arrived in 1500.

To find the Crystal River mounds, take U.S. 19 north of the town of Crystal River. Turn west at the prominent sign reading Crystal River Archaeological Site. This is one of the best presentations of Native culture in the entire state.

Spanish Point Mounds near Sarasota consists of four separate mounds that indicate humans lived here as long ago as 2150 B.C. Looking at these mounds in another context, the pyramids of Egypt were only several centuries old when mound building began here. The site was abandoned around A.D. 800, about 1,200 years ago. More than 400 burials were found here; all of the remains have been removed. Among the stranger findings were four dogs, an alligator and a human femur that had been drilled to make a flute. An interpretive center and museum is at the site, one of the few anywhere in the state. To find Spanish Point Mounds, a 30-acre preserve on Little Sarasota Bay, take U.S. 41 just north of the town of Osprey.

Pinellas County and the Tampa Bay region were a major center of Native activity over the centuries. There are many impressive mounds still remaining, but the most interesting to visit is the **Philippe Park Temple Mound and Middens,** just north of the town of Safety Harbour. This was the center of the Tocobaga, a name derived from an old Chahta Native word meaning "place of the gourds." The underbrush has been cleared from this site, so it's possible to determine the true shapes of the structures. The main temple mound is 20 feet high and measures 146 by 162 feet at the base; 49 by 99 feet at the top.

The society that last existed here is called the Safety Harbour Culture, after the name of the nearest modern city. This was the last important Native culture here before the Europeans arrived. Temple towns similar to this one had between 200 and 300 residents, and as many as 7,000 Natives may have lived in the Tampa Bay area when the Spanish arrived. This was a relatively complex society that included not only hunters and warriors but teachers, healers, elders and advisers and artisans.

To locate the Philippe Park Temple Mound and Middens, take the Philippe Parkway, north of Safety Harbour, which leads right to the park. Exhibits are at the Safety Harbour Museum, 329 South Bayshore Boulevard. For a description of the other area mounds, consult *Indian Mounds You Can Visit,* by I. Mac Perry.

Two of the most important sites are farther north than Perry's book goes. **Lake Jackson Mounds State Archaeological Site** in Tallahassee contains the remains of a ceremonial center that existed between A.D. 1200–1500. There are a total of six mounds here, three of which are within the protected location. Archaeological finds made here are on display at Tallahassee's **Museum of Florida History,** near the Florida State Capitol. The mounds site is 2 miles north of I-10 on the southern end of Lake Jackson. Open daily 8 A.M. to dark; (904) 562-0042.

Museum and mound are located side by side at the **Indian Temple Mound Museum** at Fort Walton Beach, between Panama City and Pensacola. The mound, constructed about A.D. 1400, is accompanied by a temple replica. The museum contains one of the Southeast's largest collections of woodlands pottery. It is located at 139 Miracle Strip Parkway. Hours vary by season; (904) 243-6521.

65

November Shorttakes

Florida Burrowing Owls

The burrowing owl looks like it got its legs caught in some stretching machine. The legs are unusually long, apparently because the owl spends most of its time on the ground and needs the added lift to see what's going on around it. The animal, only 9 inches tall, is also unusual in that it lacks the ear tufts of other woodland owls. Its bright yellow eyes are incredibly striking.

Unlike other owls, the burrowing owl is active both day and night. It roosts and nests in burrows 4 to 8 feet long located 1 to 3 feet underground. Nesting occurs between March and June, and the female lays 3 to 8 eggs that hatch after an incubation period of about four weeks. The young emerge from the burrow when they are about ten days old. They eat grasshoppers, beetles, frogs, lizards and rodents. When approached closely, the owl displays its agitation by bobbing and bowing (hence the nickname the "Howdy owl") and by making a clucking or chattering noise.

The owls live mostly from the Orlando/Brooksville region and southward to the Keys in open, treeless areas. One of the surest places to see the owls is in the **Cape Coral** area north of Fort Myers. Many of the vacant lots there have owls, and the burrow's presence is marked by a stick. From Cape Coral Parkway, the main street, take Santa Barbara Road just after crossing the Cape Coral Bridge. Santa Barbara has many undeveloped lots. It's possible to see more burrowing owls in Cape Coral than one might ever have imagined.

Withlacoochee State Forest has burrowing owls on a new tract of land recently purchased on the Rital-Croom Road, but it will be necessary to stop by the Brooksville office to have the location pinpointed. **Lake Kissimmee State Park**, east of Lake Wales, has a good burrowing owl population, as does the Prairie Lake Unit of **Three Lakes Wildlife Management Area**, near Kenansville. Look in elevated canal banks and berms, for the owls may be difficult to see. **Indian Prairie** north and west of Lake Okeechobee is prime burrowing owl habitat. Take State Road 70 to the area, but use a turnoff to look for the owls: C-721 is particularly good. Just look for dirt mounds, and an owl should be somewhere nearby. Also, take State Road 78, which runs along the northwest shore of the lake between Moore Haven and the town of Okeechobee. Burrowing owls live in the dry prairies punctuated with palm hammocks between Indian Prairie Canal and Fisheating Creek. In the **La Belle** area, take State Road 29 south for about 6.6 miles; the owls nest on the east side. From the Gold Coast city of Hollywood, take Hollywood Boulevard west to the intersection of David Road. Owls are on the grounds of both the **South Florida State Hospital** and **North Perry Airport**.

River Otters

These seemingly playful animals are always present but not always easily seen, except in the colder months when alligators are less active. By Thanksgiving the days are usually much cooler and alligators are becoming dormant and are not feeding. That's when river otters move more freely about the lakes and ponds. Look for otters at **Okefenokee NWR** in the lakes and boat trails. Sunrise and sunset are usually the best times to see river otters at **St. Marks NWR**, near Tallahassee; **Ichetucknee Springs State Park**, near Fort White; **Alexander Springs** (both the boil and canoe trail) in the Ocala National Forest; **Wekiwa Springs State Park**, near Orlando; **Blue Cypress Water Management Area** west of Vero Beach; and the **Corkscrew Swamp Sanctuary** east of Naples.

66

A Closer Look: Scrub Country

What is scrub? Pulitzer Prize–winning author Marjorie Kinnan Rawlings set her famous novel *The Yearling* in the Ocala National Forest, also known as The Big Scrub. However, her best description of Florida scrub came from a different work, *South Moon Under:* "The Florida scrub was unique. ... There was perhaps no similar region anywhere. ... The soil was a tawny sand, from whose parched infertility there reared, indifferent to water, so dense a growth of scrub pine. ... that the effect of the massed thin trunks was of a limitless, canopied stockade. ... Wide areas, indeed, admitted of no human passage."

Many of the trees and plants found in the Florida scrub also grow as far north as Virginia and as far west as the Mississippi, but in no other state (with the exception of a tiny area in Alabama) do such dense thickets of evergreen scrub oaks, rosemary, holly, hickory and bay grow.

The sandy soil of scrub areas seemed bereft of life to early settlers and scientists. One naturalist in 1822 complained that "nothing could be more sterile than the soil; and these tracts are, in fact, concealed deserts ... too poor to admit of cultivation and afford nothing that is fit even for the browsing of cattle."

Indeed, scrub soils lack clay, silt, organic matter or any substantial form of nutrients. The soil tends to be well drained and composed of derivatives of quartz sand. Yet there are at least 13 endemic plant species federally classified as endangered or threatened that grow on scrublands and that are not found anywhere else. Federally listed threatened animals include the Florida scrub jay, the sand skink and the blue-tailed mole skink.

Overall, scrub is generally considered Florida's most distinctive ecosystem. An amazing 40 to 60 percent of the state's plant and animal species are not found anywhere else. Not the most aesthetically pleasing type of terrain, perhaps, but still a very special one.

Mixed in with the Florida scrub are *pine islands* comprised of very tall or *high pines* that tower above the scrub and can be seen from great distances. High pine once composed the great forest that dominated the Southeast, extending from Virginia to Texas. Compared to the impenetrable scrub, moving through the open forest of the high pine was easy, even for mule-drawn wagons. To-day, over 90 percent of the South's high pine forest is gone.

Although scrub also occurs on the coast, the largest tracts left today are all inland, much of them in and around the Ocala National Forest in north-central Florida. Ocala also contains the world's largest surviving forest of the tall, leaning sand pine, whose presence is the traditional test for defining true scrub. Compared to other pines, sand pines are short-lived, typically lasting only 50 or 70 years before literally falling apart, snapping like matchsticks even without the assistance of a powerful wind. The skinny trees sometimes lean every which way, so the canopy appears almost tornado-tossed.

Scrub is maintained by high-intensity fires that may occur any-where from once a decade to once a century, depending on the amount of fuel accumulated on the ground. Yet scrub is not all that easy to ignite. Sustained periods of hot dry weather are needed for a fire to take hold. In fact, scrub is so fire-resistant that it some-times serves as a natural barrier to flames that originated in some other vegetative system. But when a scrub fire really gets going, it can be of awesome proportions. In 1935, the fastest-spreading for-est fire ever recorded until that time occurred in the Ocala National Forest. It burned more than 34,000 acres in just four hours, and spot fires broke out as much as a mile in front of the main fire.

Ironically, as fire-dependent as scrub is, some of the rarer plant species do quite well without fire and actually thrive better where the soil is disturbed mechanically instead. That means some of the scarcest plants of the scrub system are among the easiest to find along the sandy roads that crisscross an area, and adjacent to the fire breaks.

Controlled fires in scrub must be carefully managed to leave various stages of maturity in different parts of the scrub, which reflects the natural ecosystem. The blackened trees and dirty soil left by controlled fires are unsightly, though definitely necessary.

It doesn't take long for the soot and ash to disappear, for the scrub to rejuvenate, and the landscape becomes a vibrant green once more. It's the natural order of things.

When systems like the scrub developed and certain survival patterns were established, the fact that such a pyrogenic ecosystem might be criticized by people as ugly, disturbing or, at best, unsightly was hardly a consideration. What works best is what counts most in nature. And what works best for nature will definitely happen, regardless of human preferences. The uncontrollable Yellowstone fires certainly should have proven that.

December

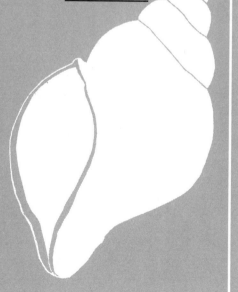

Notes

67

Winter Bird Counts

One particular change in the past hundred years demonstrates the remarkable shift in humankind's relationship with wildlife: Far more people these days are hunting birds with binoculars and cameras than with guns. For example, in the state of Florida, where less than 3 percent of the population now purchases hunting licenses, millions of people travel here from all over the world to stalk birds roosting or nesting in the state's mangroves, marshes, fields and forests.

Ironically, the annual Christmas Bird Count (CBC) sponsored by the National Audubon Society began as an alternative to the Christmas tradition of sending teams of hunters afield to shoot anything that moved, edible or not. The team with the largest bag of birds at the end of the day was the winner. Good sport, as long as you weren't a bird.

In 1900, one of the early giants of American ornithology, Frank M. Chapman, instituted a substitute activity. He and two dozen others spread out in varying parts of the northeastern United States to see who could claim the biggest bag of bird sightings. This was the origin of the CBCs, which today involve more than 40,000 people every year in every U.S. state, every province of Canada, in Guam, Colombia and even the South Pole. The annual count is always held on a single day during the last two weeks of December, or during the first week of January at 1,600 different count sites. Each site encompasses a circle 15 miles wide.

Birders take to the field for a 24-hour period and count all the different species as well as the total number of birds. In some winters the count has gone as high as 190 million birds in North America alone.

It takes a lot of people to work a 15-mile-wide circle, so new eyes are nearly always welcomed. The counters, all of whom are volunteers, begin their day before sunrise, looking for owls in the forests, along backcountry roads and in parks. Since the holiday season is also a time of good cheer (the kind that comes in bottles), more than one birder has been questioned by a rookie cop suspicious of anyone calling to owls in the cold, dark early A.M.

Serious birders can be a curious sort. Some enjoy their activity alone and in solitude while others prefer the camaraderie of the group. Regardless, they all take unparalleled delight in spotting any new species, no matter how distant or how small the subject may be, and a few of them are as competitive as any major league baseball player in striving for the most hits.

The CBCs are competitive to a certain degree, because individuals in count groups may strive against one another, while the various groups within a state are competing for the highest count of individual birds, species totals or the best list of rarities. The individual-bird counts are sometimes the greatest challenge: Pity those who have to count acres and acres of coots!

Data from the CBC is published annually by *American Birds,* the national magazine of the Audubon Society. The amount of data is encyclopedic: The telephone-book-sized volume contains detailed facts and figures from each of the count sites. This annual tally, the longest and most continuous information source on North American winter bird populations, has become a valuable reference for scientists. It reveals hints of many different kinds of trends, from the status of wintering red-tailed hawks to the range expansion of songbirds.

The Audubon CBCs have now been joined by another program, known as Project FeederWatch, which is sponsored by the Cornell (University) Lab of Ornithology in Ithaca, New York. This endeavor differs from the CBCs in that all counts are done by observing bird feeders, and many of the counts are done as classroom projects.

Project FeederWatch has observers in all 50 states and 12 Canadian provinces and territories. In 1994, more than 12,000 backyard bird-watchers were enrolled in FeederWatch, including 1,000 educators and their classes. The program is an ideal way to interest youngsters in the study, appreciation and conservation of birds, attitudes too often lacking in our ever-urbanizing society. A recent grant from the National Science Foundation should take the FeederWatch program to schools throughout the nation.

Hot Spots

The opportunity for joining a CBC in Florida and along the Alabama and Georgia coasts are excellent, for there are numerous counts held throughout this region. If you know little about birds but want to learn more, this can be a wonderful opportunity as long as you're honest about your field experience. Typically, those with limited birding abilities are teamed with more experienced counters.

To find those in charge of the nearest CBC, contact your local birding club, science museum or nature center. Or write directly to the Audubon Society, asking for a list of the count sites and contacts in your area: Christmas Bird Count Editor, *American Birds,* National Audubon Society, 950 3rd Avenue, New York, NY 10022.

As this is written, there is a $5 fee to join a CBC to help cover the cost of printing the accumulated data. Be prepared for a full day outdoors, and realize that it may be much warmer in the afternoon than it was at daybreak. Dress in layers so that clothes can be shed when necessary. Always be prepared for rain.

The Cornell Laboratory of Ornithology charges $15 to join Project FeederWatch, but you also end up with lots of goodies: data forms, complete instructions, the project newsletter and a bird calendar (plus special materials for teachers). With a credit card, it's possible to enroll over the phone by calling (800) 843-BIRD. Or write Project FeederWatch, P.O. Box 11, Ithaca, NY 14851-0011.

The great white egret is unique to South Florida. Once considered a separate species, it is actually a white phase of the great blue heron.

68

Shelling Winter Beaches

In many parts of the nation, winter beaches are lonely, bone-chilling deserts where the plaintive-sounding calls of shorebirds stir only faint recollections of warm, sunny days long past. Winter beaches, especially those that front the Atlantic, are not friendly places.

Beaches that front the Gulf of Mexico, as those of Florida and Alabama do, are another matter. Many of these sand strips are quite crowded in winter, populated by people who seem to need chiropractic care because of their constant bent-over posture.

Walking stooped over with one's eyes focused on the ground is so common on one Southwest Florida island that the posture has a special name of its own: the Sanibel Stoop. People of all ages in this position are hardly in need of medical assistance. Instead, they are scouring the beach for sea shells washed up by winter storms.

Sanibel Island has long been considered one of the world's best shelling beaches. It, like other areas along the Gulf, enjoys several characteristics that explain why shelling here is far superior to the Atlantic side.

It's due to the geology of the Gulf, where the bottom drops off gently, an average of 1 foot for every mile. Shells on this shallow plateau are pushed gently shoreward, not hurled ahead as they are in the more tumultuous, deeper Atlantic. Shells on the Gulf Coast that are shoved landward by tides and storm surge are far more likely to be intact. Essentially, they're being delivered on a sand platter.

Although shells can be found every month, the best time for shelling is during a low tide and full moon following any winter storm. That's when the latest arrivals will be on display at the edge of the sparkling surf line, ready for the taking. Of course, if the hurricane season has been active, shelling season could open as early as August or September.

Archaeological records reveal that sea shells have been valued by humans for thousands of years, because shells have been found at ancient burial sites in many parts of the world. In our own time, shells often have been popular additions to women's fashions.

Searching for sea shells can have many purposes. Some people like to collect as many as they can find, almost without regard to the specimen, to make lamps, fill glass jars or to create a haphazard accumulation. Others prefer to collect as many different specimens as possible, saving only the finest.

Whatever the goal, for fun or scientific study, a good guide for identifying different specimens is essential. One guide specific to Florida that illustrates shells in both color photographs and black-and-white drawings is *A Field Guide to Shells of the Florida Coast,* by Jean Andrews.

The ethics of collecting shells with animals living in them as opposed to "dead" shells is something every collector needs to determine for himself. It should be noted that it is illegal to take live shells at Sanibel Island, where a substantial part of the economy is based on returning shell collectors. The community wants to be just as attractive to collectors 50 years from now as it is today.

Fresh dead shells without the animals and their soft parts are easier to deal with than live ones. Some shells "play possum" by not moving when picked up. Any bivalve that is closed or that has soft parts present should be considered alive, and therefore left alone.

The horse conch is one of the richest prizes any shell hunter can realize. But only collect dead shells, not the ones still containing a living animal.

Shells are actually the exoskeleton of members of the invertebrate phylum Mollusca, composed of approximately 50,000 species. Not all mollusks have shells, which tend to be a characteristic of more primitive orders that need the hard barrier for protection and support. The phylum Mollusca, which means "soft-bodied," also includes the octopus and the sea slug, both of which lack an adult shell.

Despite the varieties of shapes, sizes, colors and designs mollusks come in, their bodies can be divided into three distinct parts, a segmentation no other animals have. These include the head, the sensory feeding area; the foot, which provides locomotion and the visceral hump, or body mass.

Shell collecting in Florida requires minimal equipment. Old shoes that are comfortable when wet and a plastic bucket are the only items many people use. The most serious collectors outfit themselves with small pill bottles and cotton for exceptionally small shells, a strainer for sifting the sand and plastic bags for messy or smelly finds.

Once the shells have been collected, how should they be stored? First, they may need to be cleaned. A stiff-wire brush will accomplish the basics, but a nut pick or something similar may be required to remove stubborn lime deposits.

A shell's luster can be restored by rubbing it with a greasy substance like mineral oil, baby oil or petroleum jelly; avoid vegetable oils, which can become sticky over time. However, shells treated with any kind of oil tend to collect a lot of dust unless they're stored under glass or in drawers.

Hot Spots

As many as 600 different shells can be found on the Southwest Florida barrier island of **Sanibel,** one of the world's premier shelling areas. The best shelling conditions are a low morning tide during a full moon just after a major winter storm when the wind blew from the northwest.

Shells can be found anywhere on Sanibel, but the beaches fronting the Gulf are clearly the best. These beaches include Lighthouse Point, the end of Fulger Street, the end of Tarpon Bay Road, Bowman's Beach, Turner's Beach at Blind Pass and the end of the Sanibel-Captiva Road. In summer, when shelling on the Gulf side is often disappointing, wading the bay side can produce some real gems, such as horse conchs and large whelks. It is against the law to collect live shells, sand dollars, sea stars and sea urchins on Sanibel. The penalties are tough: $500 fine and 60 days in jail for a first offense.

Shelling on Sanibel is so good that some people work full-time as professional shelling guides. These guides and their boats typically visit **Cayo Costa** and **North Captiva Island,** offshore islands that can be reached only by a vessel. Names and phone numbers of shelling captains are available at the Sanibel Chamber of Commerce, located immediately on the right where the causeway reaches Sanibel.

Sanibel recently opened the nation's only museum dedicated entirely to mollusks. The **Bailey-Mathews Shell Museum,** which features fresh- and saltwater shells from all over the world, also contains the largest science library on mollusks in Southwest Florida. It is open Tuesday through Sunday, 10 A.M. to 4 P.M.; (941) 395-2233.

Other areas on the Gulf that have acceptable shelling include **Naples; Venice** (though it's best known for its large prehistoric sharks' teeth); **Caladesi Island;** the barrier islands of the **Panhandle;** and Alabama's **Dauphin Island, Bon Secour NWR** (Mobile Street beach access road and the Fort Morgan Peninsula) and **Gulf State Park** (Alabama Point after storms, especially since sandbars in the Gulf stop the shells from coming up on the beach readily).

Shells, of course, can also be found all along the Atlantic beaches, but specimens collected there usually aren't as good because the sea conditions are more severe. Serious shell collectors prefer the Gulf side.

69

Winter Waterfowl

It's no accident that people who migrate South every fall are called "snowbirds," since they're imitating the same pattern that's been established by wintering waterfowl for probably thousands of years.

One of the principal places to view the myriad ducks and coots is the national wildlife refuges that are strategically located on the coasts, along rivers and in other wetlands areas that are particularly attractive to waterfowl. Not only are the refuges intended to attract waterfowl, but these facilities are designed to live off them, heavily funded by the sale of duck stamps to hunters. This is why on the "refuges" the seemingly incongruous sound of hunters' shotgun blasts are common in November, December and sometimes into January.

This is part of the multiple-use approach that opens the refuges to a lot of different activities that sometimes seem at odds with their main role of protecting wildlife. Besides hunting, over 90 percent of the refuges around the country have been open to such uses as fishing, boating, logging, oil and gas drilling, grazing, trapping and even military bombing practice.

It makes good sense for anyone interested in waterfowl conservation to buy a federal duck stamp. Not only does it help support the national wildlife refuges, it also acts as a refuge entrance pass and negates the need to pay any admission fee.

By February, waterfowl spotters have replaced the ranks of shooters at the refuges, and most of the waterfowl are still present. How many depends partly on how cold the weather is up north. In severe winters, when large bodies of normally open water freeze over, the counts south will be much higher.

Because many of the refuges are near the coast, strong breezes will often be a factor in determining which parts of a refuge will have the heaviest concentrations of birds. Waterfowl typically like to stay in the lee, out of the wind, to avoid having to roller-coaster-ride the big waves or be buffeted by a strong breeze.

Alabama's **Mobile Bay** is an important wintering estuary for migrating waterfowl, particularly the lesser scaup, or bluebill, which is the dominant species; between 20,000 and 50,000 may be present in a single season. Red-breasted and hooded mergansers are also common but not nearly in the same numbers.

Wakulla Springs State Park near Tallahassee can always be counted on for wood ducks, scaup, widgeons and coots, but the numbers are far more impressive at nearby **St. Marks NWR,** which attracts as many as 80,000 ducks each year, including redheads, buffleheads, scaup and ringnecks. Waterfowl are found both in the refuge pools and in Apalachee Bay. Between St. Marks and the city of Perry is the **Hickory Mound Impoundment,** part of the **Big Bend Wildlife Management Area.** The impoundment, enclosed by a 6.5-mile-long dike, usually holds many species of ducks, as well as wading birds. Hunts are held here Mondays, Wednesdays and Fridays until noon from September through January. Call ahead for any changes; (904) 838-1306.

Paynes Prairie State Preserve near Gainesville is one of the few inland sites where waterfowl congregate in good numbers. The wet prairie is just as attractive as the coast or a series of lakes. The birds are most easily visible from the observation platform located about 3 miles along the La Chua Trail at the park's north rim. **Sunnyhill Restoration Area** in the upper Oklawaha River attracts wood ducks, teal, ringnecks and a host of other species. However, access to the property is only through advance-reservation group tours. Call the St. Johns Water Management District: (904) 821-1489. The area is located 6 miles east of Weirsdale on County Road 42.

Lower Suwannee NWR will need to be explored by boat to see the goldeneyes, ruddies, scaup and ringnecks that arrive in good numbers by November. **Chassahowitzka NWR** near Crystal River must also be explored by boat, but far more birds are more easily visible at St. Marks, and **Merritt Island NWR** has over 100 miles of driving and walking roads and trails. It's quite easy to move around and see the huge numbers of waterfowl always present at Merritt Island NWR in winter. Many

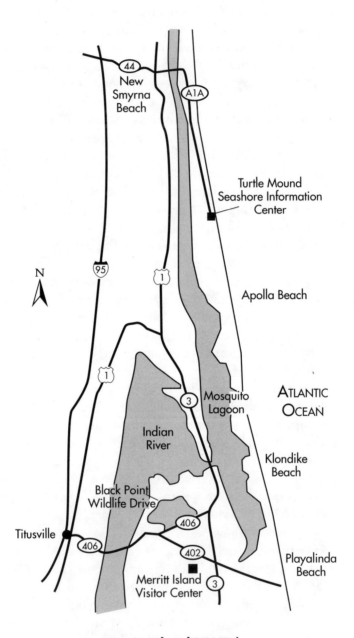

**Merritt Island NWR/
Canaveral National Seashore**

people come here to photograph the birds because of the easy access.

Savannah County Recreation Area, just south of Fort Pierce is a large freshwater marsh with nature trails and an observation tower. Green- and blue-winged teal, hooded mergansers, and ringnecks are common visitors. From the intersection with A1A, go south on U.S. 1 for 5.5 miles to Midway Road (C-712). Turn left and go almost 1.5 miles to the entrance.

Loxahatchee NWR near West Palm Beach has an easily accessible area where as many as 17 species of ducks winter. **J. N. "Ding" Darling NWR** on Sanibel Island is another good place for photographing waterfowl thanks to a 5-mile-long drive through the mangrove swamps. This road is closed on Fridays.

Savannah Coastal Refuges has counted as many as 3,000 wood ducks in the winter months. Scaup and mergansers are common around **Pinckney Island,** but it's the former rice fields from the Colonial era that are the real hotspots. The fields have been impounded expressly for waterfowl management, and as many as 20,000 ducks of 12 different species winter here from November through February.

70

White Pelicans

American white pelicans are not normal year-round residents of the Southeast but impressive winter visitors that, in color pattern at least, take the place of the white geese that no longer commute to Florida or much of the Southeast.

The white pelican, which has black wing tips, yellow feet and a large yellow bill that usually rests on its chest, overwinters mostly in coastal lagoons of Central and South Florida and Mobile Bay. It is considerably larger than the brown pelican, with a wingspread of almost 10 feet and a body length of 58 to 60 inches. It breeds during the summer in the Northwest and moves into the Southeast from about December to March. Nonbreeding white pelicans will sometimes remain behind in spring when the more mature birds depart for the traditional nesting grounds.

White pelicans are much more wary of people than are browns, so they are usually seen from a considerable distance. The best way to approach them closely is by boat. That is also the best method for witnessing their impressive cooperative feeding method. The birds will often form a straight line in the water, then herd fish into shallow water by beating their wings. Once the fish are within reach, the birds scoop them up in their bills. The water has to be drained from the pouch before a bird can swallow its catch. It does this by lowering its bill to let the water drain out.

Hot Spots White pelicans typically overwinter in Florida between December and April, though there will be odd birds at either end of the season.

Between 100 and 200 white pelicans normally winter at the **Chassahowitzka NWR** near Crystal River. Both the Chassahowitzka and Homosassa Rivers flow through the preserve, providing some of the richest waters anywhere in the country. **Lake Harney,** located off Highway 46 between Sanford and

Mims in Central Florida, also attracts white pelicans, as does **Orlando Wetlands Park,** between Orlando and Titusville off Highway 50. The park is actually a man-made wetlands that appeals to many types of birds and animals. **Merritt Island NWR,** just east of Titusville, one of the prime winter waterfowl areas in Florida, usually hosts a good population of white pelicans as well.

In Northeast Florida, white pelicans can appear in any of the lagoons beside A1A between Fernandina and Daytona. Several of the state's large bays—**Tampa Bay, Florida Bay** and **Pine Island Sound**—often attract white pelicans as well. Several hundred of the birds normally winter at **J. N. "Ding" Darling NWR** on Sanibel Island in Southwest Florida.

Since white pelicans normally nest anywhere from the Great Salt Lake to Canada, it is unusual that any of them should also be nesting in **Mobile Bay** on **Gaillard Island,** as a small colony has started doing recently. It is another island that can be reached only by boat, and wildlife authorities are being very protective of the birds and do not allow people to approach them too closely.

The white pelican is one of the outstanding winter visitors. They are much less approachable than brown pelicans.

309

71

December Shorttakes

Wilderness Canoe Tours

The best way to experience nature is to live with it for several days. Georgia's **Okefenokee Swamp NWR** and Florida's **Everglades National Park** both offer standout opportunities to canoe through miles and miles of wilderness waterways with overnight camp stops. Trips can be self-guided or with an outfitter. Because of limited camping facilities, there is a daily carrying capacity to prevent overcrowding. Okefenokee NWR has a pamphlet about wilderness canoeing: send $1 to U.S. Fish and Wildlife Service, Okefenokee NWR, Route 2, Box 338, Folkston, GA 31537. Before tackling the Everglades Wilderness Waterway (it takes seven to nine days to complete this 100-mile trip one-way), obtain a copy of *Guide to the Wilderness Waterway of the Everglades National Park,* by William Truesdell, the bible for canoeing this region. December through April is the best time to canoe the Okefenokee, from December through March the Everglades. Heat and mosquitoes tend to make it a hellish experience the rest of the year.

Fox Squirrels

The Shermans fox squirrel is a large squirrel easily identified by its black head. Fox squirrels like forested areas that are fairly open so that when they're feeding on the ground they can spot predators at a distance and have plenty of time to escape up a tree. Fox squirrels are another species that is declining due to habitat loss. Fox squirrel nests, usually built in the crooks of branches of turkey oaks and similar trees, are easiest to spot in winter, when the forest canopy is less thick. The nests are made of sticks, pine needles and tree leaves. Chewed pinecones at the base of a tree are evidence of the squirrel's presence. Look for fox squirrels at **Wekiwa Springs State Park** near Orlando and **Lower Wekiva River State Preserve** near Sanford. Also try the three national forests, **Apalachicola, Osceola** and **Ocala.** Other places to look for fox squirrels include **Mike Roess Gold**

Head Branch State Park near Keystone Heights; **Tosohatchee State Reserve** near the town of Christmas; **Withlacoochee State Forest** near Brooksville (anywhere in the sandhills of the Citrus or Croom tracts); **Jay B. Starkey Wilderness Park** near New Port Richey and **Boyd Hill Nature Park** near St. Petersburg. The nests will be in areas of pine flatwoods.

The best time to look for fox squirrel nests is in winter, when turkey oaks and similar trees shed their leaves.

72

A Closer Look:
Save One for the Lion

The best way to capture memories of the natural year is through still or moving pictures. Conditions, however, are extremely varied in the Southeast. In a single morning they can alternate from bright sunlight at the beach to the dark interiors of a cypress swamp.

In bright, open areas, including fields, prairies and beaches, the best times to shoot are early and late in the day, the same periods when animals are most likely to be active and visible. At both times the sunlight slants at an angle, highlighting the detail on a subject. Animal hairs and plant filaments, which tend to get washed out at midday, are prominent in subdued light. Shooting an animal during the first three or last three hours of sunlight, especially with the sun positioned behind the subject, will also emphasize feather texture, animal fur or highlight the veins of a plant.

Take time to study the animal pictures in the National Geographic Society's magazine and TV series. The detail is so remarkable because of the low angle of the sun in most of these pictures.

Some creatures like to avoid sunlight and stay in the shade, and they are most active before sunrise and after sunset. Shooting still photographs in subdued light calls for a fairly fast film, such as 400 ASA. Video cameras have an advantage in that they are often able to record animal movements when impatient still photographers may have to wait for brighter conditions. Providing a tripod for the still camera helps equalize the situation.

For animal photography, a lens in the 300mm range is about as large as anyone can use without the aid of a tripod. A good rule of thumb is that the camera's shutter speed needs to equal or be greater than the size of the lens. For instance, a 200mm lens requires a shutter speed of $1/250$ of a second. A 300mm lens demands $1/500$ of a second. This is a situation where fast film is again an asset. A telephoto lens can also be made "longer" by adding either a 2x or a 1.5x extender. A 2x extender, for instance, doubles the focal length of the lens, so a 300mm lens immediately becomes a 600mm, but at greatly reduced cost.

On many autofocus cameras extenders work best for scenics and close-ups, because a lens with an extender must usually be focused manually. An extender also takes away one or two f-stops, depending on its power. A tripod is often needed when an extender is added.

One very important point about photographing animals in state parks and on national wildlife refuges: Many animals, waterfowl in particular, allow people to approach very closely as long as they stay inside their vehicles. As soon as someone opens the door and steps outside, waterfowl in particular often seem to drift away; actually, they're swimming away. Shoot from inside your vehicle, with the window down and the motor off, in such situations. It's the same technique used on African photo safaris, because many wild species don't seem to associate vehicles with people. But once a person steps outside and is fully revealed—even if he moves slowly and doesn't perform any threatening motions—the game becomes spooked and moves away. Those who feel they must leave their vehicles should remove their keys to silence any buzzers and leave the door open. Some creatures react to the sound of a door slamming as if it were a gunshot.

Bright sunlight, unfortunately, is usually more of a hindrance than a help for photographers. The best pictures have rich, saturated colors, but in dazzling sunlight many colors tend to glare brightly. To compensate, underexpose by one-third or two-thirds of an f-stop. Bracketing with these two exposures will reveal what works best for a particular camera.

When trying to shoot objects under the water, especially very clear water like that in the Keys, the use of a polarizing filter will help "see through" the surface glare. The glare on the water is like light reflected on a mirror. Depending on the angle of the light, it may not be possible to avoid the reflection. A polarizing filter is the only way to work around it. A porpoise or manatee, for example, becomes much more visible when surface glare is reduced.

Close-ups of strange-looking insects and plants are among the more unusual photo opportunities in the swamplands. Unless the situation poses some kind of problem (such as deep water preventing the photographer from getting closer to the subject), the best type of lens to use is one that allows the photographer to move within a foot or so of the subject. Within that range it's possible to capture a life-size image, referred to as a reproduction rate of 1:1.

When photographing such subjects in the subdued light of a swamp (or even on a cloudy day), it's often necessary to rely on a strobe for illumination. Otherwise, detail and color are apt to be too muddied. Unless the strobe is designed for close-up work, it will probably be necessary to underexpose the picture by one-third or two-thirds to keep the flash from overpowering the subject. Once again, a tripod is a valuable asset.

Taking close-ups of large round objects, such as the hood of a carnivorous pitcher plant, is best achieved with a wide-angle lens, such as a 28mm or even a 20mm. A wide-angle lens provides tremendous depth of field so that more of the subject ends up in sharp focus. Contrast this to a 1:1 closeup lens, where only the first layer of the subject is sharp and clear.

Using a telephoto lens to take close-up pictures often presents the same problem. The closer a telephoto lens is to a subject, the less detail is in focus behind it. Of course, this can work to a photographer's advantage if the background is cluttered and distracting.

Sunset silhouettes are always a popular way to end a presentation. The key is not to shoot too soon or too late. Here's a good technique to employ: Hold a fist at arm's length with the thumb aimed straight up and the bottom of the hand lined up with the horizon. If the sun is above the thumb, it's too early for good silhouettes. Once the sun drops below the thumb tip, start shooting.

A good way to enhance a dull sunset is with a light orange, yellow or purple filter. The filter color can be made darker by underexposing between one-third or even a full f-stop.

During Florida's summer rainy season, weather can change very quickly. A day that starts clear could easily end up wet. Photographers should always be prepared to protect their equipment: A plastic garbage bag big enough to encase both the camera and the camera bag is good cheap insurance. Many professional photographers keep a thick garbage sack stored in a camera bag compartment.

And if it does rain? Well, those days can provide unusual and dramatic photos. They can be taken—while keeping the camera safe and dry—by placing the camera inside a clear plastic bag that's designed to roast turkeys and keep them moist. Such a bag is clear enough for acceptable pictures when the lens is held so tightly against the bag that there are no folds or creases. A thick rubber band will secure the bag tightly over the lens.

Never, ever, expose all the film until the shooting day is completely over. Keep at least one shot for that unexpected opportunity that will, without question, present itself once the film is gone. As they say on African photo safaris, "Save one for the lion."

Appendix A

Wildlife Habitats

In addition to the specific places mentioned at the end of each chapter, look for animals in many other places around the Southeast. Find the appropriate habitat, and the animals should be present. Beaches, salt marshes and other coastal elements are not included.

Vegetational Communities					
Cypress Swamp	Cypress Pond	Flag Pond	Prairie	Hardwood Transitional	Pine Flatwoods
Mammals					
Black Bear •				•	•
Bobcat •				•	•
Cotton Mouse •				•	•
Eastern Mole •				•	•
Eastern Spotted Skunk •	•	•	•	•	•
Florida Panther •					
Fox Squirrel					•
Gray Fox •				•	•
Gray Squirrel •				•	•
Hispid Cotton Rat •				•	•
Marsh Rabbit •					
Marsh Rice Rat •				•	•
Nine-Banded Armadillo •				•	•
Opossum •	•	•	•	•	•
Raccoon •	•	•	•	•	•
Red Bat •				•	•
River Otter •	•	•			
Short-Tailed Shrew •				•	•
Southern Flying Squirrel					•

	Cypress Swamp	Cypress Pond	Flag Pond	Prairie	Hardwood Transitional	Pine Flatwoods
Striped Skunk	●				●	●
White-Tailed Deer	●					●
Birds						
American Bittern	●	●	●			
American Kestrel						●
American Robin	●					
American Woodcock	●	●	●			
Anhinga	●	●	●			
Bald Eagle	●	●	●	●	●	●
Barred Owl	●	●	●			
Belted Kingfisher	●	●	●			
Black-Crowned Night Heron	●	●	●			
Black Vulture	●	●	●	●	●	●
Blue Jay	●	●	●		●	●
Boat-Tailed Grackle	●	●	●			
Bob-White Quail						●
Brown Thrasher	●	●	●		●	●
Brown-Headed Cowbird	●	●	●		●	●
Brown-Headed Nuthatch						●
Cardinal	●	●	●		●	●
Carolina Wren	●	●	●	●		●
Catbird	●	●	●		●	●
Cattle Egret	●	●	●		●	
Chuck Will's Widow	●				●	●
Common Crow	●	●	●	●	●	●
Common Grackle	●	●	●			
Common Moorhen	●	●	●			

	Cypress Swamp	Cypress Pond	Flag Pond	Prairie	Hardwood Transitional	Pine Flatwoods
Common Night Hawk	●	●	●	●	●	●
Double-Crested Cormorant	●	●	●			
Downy Woodpecker	●				●	●
Eastern Kingbird	●	●	●			
Eastern Meadowlark						●
Fish Crow	●	●	●			●
Glossy Ibis	●	●	●			
Great Blue Heron	●	●	●			
Great Crested Flycatcher	●	●	●	●	●	●
Great Egret	●	●	●			
Great Horned Owl					●	●
Green Backed Heron	●	●	●			
Ground Dove						●
Hairy Woodpecker	●				●	●
Hermit Thrush	●	●	●		●	●
House Sparrow						●
Killdeer	●					
Limpkin	●	●	●			
Little Blue Heron	●	●	●			
Loggerhead Shrike						●
Long-Billed Marsh Wren	●	●	●			
Mockingbird	●	●	●	●	●	●
Mottled Duck	●	●	●			
Mourning Dove						●
Northern Flicker	●	●	●		●	●
Northern Harrier	●	●	●	●	●	●

	Cypress Swamp	Cypress Pond	Flag Pond	Prairie	Hardwood Transitional	Pine Flatwoods
Palm Warbler	•	•	•			
Pied-Billed Grebe		•	•			
Pileated Woodpecker	•	•	•		•	•
Pine Warbler						•
Prairie Warbler	•	•	•		•	•
Purple Martin	•					
Red-Bellied Woodpecker	•	•	•		•	•
Red-Eyed Vireo	•	•	•		•	•
Red-Shouldered Hawk	•	•	•	•	•	•
Red-Tailed Hawk	•					
Red-Winged Blackbird	•	•		•		
Roseate Spoonbill	•					
Rufous-Sided Towhee	•	•			•	•
Screech Owl	•	•	•		•	•
Sharp-Shinned Hawk					•	•
Snowy Egret	•	•	•			
Song Sparrow	•	•	•	•		
Starling						•
Swallow-Tailed Kite						•
Swamp Sparrow	•			•		
Tree Swallow	•	•	•	•	•	•
Tri-Colored Heron	•	•	•			
Tufted Titmouse	•	•			•	•
Turkey Vulture	•	•	•	•	•	•
White-Eyed Vireo	•	•	•		•	•
White Ibis	•	•	•			

	Cypress Swamp	Cypress Pond	Flag Pond	Prairie	Hardwood Transitional	Pine Flatwoods
Wilson's Snipe	●	●	●	●		
Wood Duck	●	●	●			
Wood Stork	●	●	●			
Yellow-Bellied Sapsucker	●	●	●		●	●
Yellow-Crowned Night Heron		●	●			
Yellow-Rumped Warbler	●	●	●	●	●	●
Yellow-Throat Common	●	●	●	●	●	●
Yellow-Throated Warbler	●	●	●			
Reptiles						
American Alligator	●	●	●			
Black Swamp Snake					●	●
Brown Water Snake	●	●	●			
Chicken Turtle	●	●	●			
Coral Snake	●				●	●
Corn Snake					●	●
Dusky Pigmy Rattlesnake	●	●	●	●	●	●
Eastern Cottonmouth	●	●	●		●	
Eastern Diamond-back Rattlesnake	●	●	●	●	●	●
Eastern Garter Snake	●	●	●		●	●
Eastern Glass Lizard					●	●
Eastern Hognose Snake					●	●
Eastern Indigo Snake	●	●	●	●	●	●
Florida Box Turtle	●	●	●		●	●

	Cypress Swamp	Cypress Pond	Flag Pond	Prairie	Hardwood Transitional	Pine Flatwoods
Florida Brown Snake	•	•	•		•	•
Florida Cooter	•	•	•			
Florida Crowned Snake	•				•	•
Florida Green Water Snake	•	•	•			
Florida Kingsnake					•	•
Florida Mud Turtle	•	•	•			
Florida Pine Snake					•	•
Florida Red Bellied Turtle	•	•	•			
Florida Softshell	•	•	•			
Florida Water Snake	•	•	•			
Gopher Tortoise						•
Greater Siren	•	•	•			
Green Anole	•	•	•		•	•
Ground Skink						•
Island Glass Lizard					•	•
Mud Snake	•	•	•			
Musk Turtle	•	•	•			
Rough Green Snake	•	•	•	•	•	•
Scarlet Kingsnake	•				•	•
Six-Lined Racerunner						•
Slender Glass Lizard					•	•
Snapping Turtle	•	•	•			
Southeastern Five-Lined Skink	•				•	•
Southern Black Racer	•	•	•	•	•	•

	Cypress Swamp	Cypress Pond	Flag Pond	Prairie	Hardwood Transitional	Pine Flatwoods
Southern Ribbon Snake	•	•	•		•	•
Southern Ringneck Snake	•	•	•		•	•
Striped Mud Turtle	•	•	•			
Striped Swamp Snake	•	•	•			
Yellow Rat Snake	•	•	•	•	•	•
Amphibians						
Barking Tree Frog	•	•	•	•	•	•
Cuban Tree Frog	•	•	•	•	•	•
Dwarf Salamander	•	•	•		•	
Eastern Narrow-Mouthed Toad	•	•	•	•	•	•
Eastern Spadefoot Toad	•	•	•			
Florida Chorus Frog	•	•	•	•	•	•
Florida Cricket Frog	•	•	•	•	•	•
Florida Gopher Frog	•	•	•	•	•	•
Greenhouse Frog	•	•	•			
Green Tree Frog	•	•	•	•	•	•
Little Grass Frog			•	•	•	•
Oak Toad	•	•	•	•	•	•
Penninsula Newt	•	•	•			
Pig Frog	•	•	•	•	•	•
Pinewoods Tree Frog	•	•	•	•	•	•
Southern Leopard Frog	•	•	•	•	•	•
Southern Toad	•	•	•	•	•	•
Squirrel Tree Frog	•	•	•	•	•	•

Appendix B

National Wildlife Refuges

Coastal Alabama
Bon Secour NWR
P.O. Box 1650
Gulf Shores, AL 36542
(334) 540-7720

Coastal Georgia
Okefenokee NWR
Route 2, Box 338
Folkston, GA 31537
(912) 496-7836

Savannah Coastal Refuges (including
Wapello District, Savannah District,
Pickney Island, Harris Neck and
Blackbeard Island NWRs)
1000 Business Center Drive
Savannah, GA 31405
(912) 652-4415

Florida
Arthur R. Marshall Loxahatchee NWR
10216 Lee Road
Boynton Beach, FL 33437
(407) 732-3684

Cedar Keys and Lower Suwannee NWRs
Route 1, Box 1193C
Chiefland, FL 32626
(904) 493-0238

Chassahowitzka, Crystal River, Egmont
Key and Pinellas NWRs
1502 SE Kings Bay Drive
Crystal River, FL 34429
(904) 563-2088

Florida Panther and 10,000 Islands NWRs
3860 Tollgate Road, Suite 30
Naples, FL 33942
(941) 353-8442

Great White Heron and Key West NWRs,
National Key Deer Refuge
P.O. Box 430510
Big Pine Key, FL 33043
(305) 872-2239

Hobe Sound NWR
P.O. Box 645
Hobe Sound, FL 33475
(561) 546-6141

J. N. "Ding" Darling NWR
One Wildlife Drive
Sanibel, FL 33957
(941) 472-1100

Lake Woodruff NWR
4490 Grand Avenue
P.O. Box 488
DeLeon Springs, FL 32130
(904) 985-4673

Merritt Island NWR
P.O. Box 6504
Titusville, FL 32780
(407) 867-0667

St. Marks NWR
P.O. Box 68
St. Marks, FL 32355
(904) 925-6121

St. Vincent NWR
479 Market Street
P.O. Box 447
Apalachicola, FL 32329
(904) 653-8808

Appendix C

State Forests, Parks, Reserves and Wildlife Management Areas

Florida
Northwest Florida

Andrews Wildlife Management Area
Route 1, Box 741
Trenton, FL 32693
(352) 493-6020

Big Bend Wildlife Management Area
Route 7, Box 440
Lake City, FL 32055
(904) 838-1306; (904) 758-0525

Big Lagoon State Recreation Area
12301 Gulf Beach Highway
Pensacola, FL 32507
(904) 492-1595

Black River State Park
Dead Lakes State Recreation Area
P.O. Box 989
Wewahitchka, FL 32465
(904) 639-2702

Blackwater River State Forest
Route 1, Box 77
Milton, FL 32570
(904) 957-4201

Blackwater River State Park
Route 1, Box 57-C
Holt, FL 32564
(904) 623-2363

Falling Waters State Recreation Area
Route 5, Box 660
Chipley, FL 32428
(904) 638-6130

Grayton Beach State Recreation Area
Route 2, Box 6600
Santa Rosa Beach, FL 32459
(904) 231-4210

Henderson Beach State Recreation Area
17000 Emerald Coast Parkway
Destin, FL 32541
(904) 837-7550

Perdido Key State Recreation Area
c/o Big Lagoon State Recreation Area
12301 Gulf Beach Highway
Pensacola, FL 32507
(904) 492-1595

Rocky Bayou State Recreation Area
4281 Highway 20
Niceville, FL 32578
(904) 833-9144

St. Andrews State Recreation Area
4415 Thomas Drive
Panama City, FL 32408
(904) 233-5140

St. Joseph Peninsula State Park
Star Route 1, Box 200
Port St. Joe, FL 32456
(904) 227-1327

Big Bend Region

Econfina River State Park
Route 1, Box 255
Lamont, FL 32336
(904) 584-2135

Florida Caverns State Park
3345 Caverns Road
Marianna, FL 32446
(904) 482-9598

Lake Jackson Mounds State
Archaeological Site
1022 DeSoto Park Drive
Tallahassee, FL 32301
(904) 922-6007

Lake Talquin State Recreation Area
1022 Desoto Park Drive
Tallahassee, FL 32301
(904) 922-6007

Ochlockonee River State Park
P.O. Box 5
Sopchoppy, FL 32358
(904) 962-2771

St. George Island State Park
HCR Box 62
Eastpoint, FL 32328
(904) 927-2111

Three Rivers State Recreation Area
7908 Three Rivers Road
Sneads, FL 32460
(904) 482-9006

Torreya State Park
Route 2, Box 70
Bristol, FL 32321
(904) 643-2674

Wakulla Springs State Park
1 Spring Drive
Wakulla Springs, FL 32305
(904) 922-3633

North-Central Florida

Devil's Millhopper State Geological Site
4732 Millhopper Road
Gainesville, FL 32606
(904) 336-2008

Gainesville-Hawthorne State Rail-to-Trail
Region 2 Administration
4801 SE 17th Street
Gainesville, FL 32601
(904) 336-2135

Gold Head Branch State Park
6239 SR 21
Keystone Heights, FL 32656
(904) 473-4701

Ichetucknee Springs State Park
Route 2, Box 108
Fort White, FL 32038
(904) 497-2511

Manatee Springs State Park
Route 2, Box 617
Chiefland, FL 32626
(904) 493-6072

O'Leno State Park
Route 2, Box 1010
High Springs, FL 32643
(904) 454-1853

Paynes Prairie State Preserve
Route 2, Box 41
Micanopy, FL 32667
(904) 466-3397

San Felasco Hammock State Preserve
c/o Devil's Millhopper State Geological Site
4232 Millhopper Road
Gainesville, FL 32601
(904) 336-2008

Silver River State Park
c/o Lake Griffin State Recreation Area
103 Highway 441/27
Fruitland Park, FL 34731
(904) 787-7402

Suwannee River State Park
Route 8, Box 297
Live Oak, FL 32060
(904) 362-2746

Waccasassa Bay State Reserve/Cedar Key
Scrub State Reserve
Box 187
Cedar Key, FL 32625
(904) 543-5567

Northeast Florida

Amelia Island State Recreation Area
c/o The Talbot Islands GEOpark
11435 Fort George Road East
Fort George, FL 32226
(904) 251-2320
Seahorse Stables:
(904) 261-4878

Anastasia State Recreation Area
1340-A A1A South
St. Augustine, FL 32084
(904) 461-2033 or (904) 461-2000

Big Talbot Island State Park
c/o The Talbot Islands GEOpark
11435 Fort George Road East
Fort George, FL 32226
(904) 251-2320

Bulow Plantation Ruins State Historic Site
P.O. Box 655
Bunnell, FL 32010
(904) 439-2219

Faver-Dykes State Park
1000 Faver-Dykes Road
St. Augustine, FL 32086
(904) 794-0997

Fort Clinch State Park
2601 Atlantic Avenue
Fernandina Beach, FL 32034
(904) 277-7274

Guana River State Park/
Wildlife Management Area
2690 South Ponte Vedra Boulevard
Ponte Vedra Beach, FL 32082
(904) 825-5071

Little Talbot Island State Park
c/o The Talbot Islands GEOpark
11435 Fort George Road East
Fort George, FL 32226
(904) 251-2320

Ravine State Gardens
Box 1096
Palatka, FL 32178
(904) 329-3721

Tomoka State Park
2099 North Beach Street
Ormond Beach, FL 32174
(904) 676-4050

Washington Oaks State Gardens
6400 North Ocean Boulevard
Palm Coast, FL 32137
(904) 445-3161

West Florida and the Gulf Coast

Anclote Key State Preserve
c/o Gulf Islands GEOpark
#1 Causeway Boulevard
Dunedin, FL 34698
(813) 469-5918

Caladesi Island State Park
#1 Causeway Boulevard
Dunedin, FL 34698
(813) 469-5918

Crystal River State Archaeological Site
3400 North Museum Point
Crystal River, FL 34428
(904) 795-3817

General James A. Van Fleet State
Rail-to-Trail
Region 3 Administration
12549 State Park Drive
Clermont, FL 34771
(904) 394-2280

Hillsborough River State Park
15402 U.S. 301 North
Thonotosassa, FL 33592
(813) 987-6771

Homosassa Springs State Wildlife Park
9225 West Fish Bowl Drive
Homosassa, FL 34448
(904) 628-2311

Honeymoon Island State Recreation Area
#1 Causeway Boulevard
Dunedin, FL 34698
(813) 469-5942

Lake Griffin State Recreation Area
103 Highway 441/27
Fruitland Park, FL 34731
(904) 787-7402

Little Manatee River State Recreation Area
215 Lightfoot Road
Wimauma, FL 33598
(813) 671-5005

Rainbow Springs State Park
19158 SW 81st Place Road
Dunnellon, FL 34432
(904) 489-8503
For camping information, call
(904) 489-5201

Withlacoochee State Rail-to-Trail
Region 3 Administration
12549 State Park Drive
Clermont, FL 34711
(904) 394-2280

Central Florida

Blue Cypress Water Management Area
c/o St. Johns Water Management District
Box 1429
Palatka, FL 32178
(904) 329-4377

Blue Spring State Park
2100 West French Avenue
Orange City, FL 32763
(904) 775-3663

Bull Creek Wildlife Management Area
1239 SW 10th Street
Ocala, FL 34474
(352) 732-1225

DuPuis Reserve State Forest
23500 SW Tanner Highway
Canal Point, FL 33438
(561) 924-5310

Highlands Hammock State Park
5931 Hammock Road
Sebring, FL 33872
(813) 385-0011

Hontoon Island State Park
2309 River Ridge Road
DeLand, FL 32720
(904) 736-5309

Lake Kissimmee State Park
14248 Camp Mack Road
Wales, FL 33853
(813) 696-1112

Lower Wekiva River State Preserve
c/o Wekiwa Springs State Park
1800 Wekiwa Circle
Apopka, FL 32712
(407) 884-2009

Rock Springs Run State Reserve
c/o Wekiwa Springs State Park
1800 Wekiwa Circle
Apopka, FL 32712
(407) 884-2009

Three Lakes Wildlife Management Area
Prairie Lakes Unit
1239 SW 10th Street
Ocala, FL 34474
(352) 732-1225; (407) 436-1818

Tosohatchee State Reserve
3365 Taylor Creek Road
Christmas, FL 32708
(407) 568-5893

Wekiwa Springs State Park
1800 Wekiwa Circle
Apopka, FL 32712
(407) 884-2009

Withlacoochee State Forest
Forest Supervisor's Office
15023 Brad Street
Brooksville, FL 33512
(904) 796-5650

Southeast Florida

Hugh Taylor Birch State Recreation Area
3109 East Sunrise Boulevard
Fort Lauderdale, FL 33304
(305) 564-4521

J. W. Corbett Wildlife Management Area
551 N. Military Trail
West Palm Beach, FL 33415
(407) 640-6100

MacArthur Beach State Park
10900 SR 703 (A1A)
North Palm Beach, FL 33408
(407) 624-6950

John U. Lloyd Beach State Recreation Area
6503 North Ocean Drive
Dania, FL 33004
(305) 923-2833

Sebastian Inlet State Recreation Area
9700 South A1A
Melbourne Beach, FL 32951
(407) 984-4852

St. Lucie Inlet State Preserve
c/o Jonathan Dickinson State Park
16450 SE Federal Highway
Hobe Sound, FL 33455
(407) 744-7603

Jonathan Dickinson State Park
16450 SE Federal Highway
Hobe Sound, FL 33455
(407) 546-2771

Southwest Florida

Cayo Costa State Park
c/o Barrier Islands GEOpark
P.O. Box 1150
Boca Grande, FL 33921
(941) 964-0375

Cecil M. Webb Wildlife Management Area
29200 Tucker Grade
Punta Gorda, FL 33958
(941) 639-1531

Collier-Seminole State Park,
20,200 E. Tamiami Trail
Naples, FL 33961
(813) 394-3397

Don Pedro Island State Recreation Area
c/o Barrier Islands GEOpark
P.O. Box 1150
Boca Grande, FL 33921
(813) 964-0375

Fakahatchee Strand State Preserve
P.O. Box 548
Copeland, FL 33926
(813) 695-4593

Lake Manatee State Recreation Area
20007 SR 64
Bradenton, FL 34202
(813) 741-3028

Lover's Key State Recreation Area
c/o Delnor-Wiggins Pass State
Recreation Area
11100 Gulf Shore Drive North
Naples, FL 33963
(813) 597-6196

Myakka River State Park
13207 SR 72
Sarasota, FL 34241-9542
(813) 361-6511

Oscar Scherer State Park
1843 South Tamiami Trail
Osprey, FL 34229
(813) 483-5956

South Florida and the Keys

Bahia Honda State Park
Route 1, Box 782
Big Pine Key, FL 33043
(305) 872-2353

Indian Key State Historic Site
c/o Lignumvitae Key State Botanical Site
P.O. Box 1052
Islamorada, FL 33036
(305) 664-4815

Key Largo Hammocks State Botanical Site
P.O. Box 487
Key Largo, FL 33037
(305) 451-7008 or 451-1202

Long Key State Recreation Area
P.O. Box 776
Long Key, FL 33001
(305) 664- 4815

John Pennekamp Coral Reef State Park
P.O. Box 487
Key Largo, FL 33037
(305) 451-1202

San Pedro Underwater Archaeological
Preserve
P.O. Box 776
Long Key, FL 33001
(305) 664-4815

Alabama

Gulf State Park
20115 State Highway 135
Gulf Shores, AL 36542
(334) 948-7275

Appendix D

National Forests, Monuments, Parks and Seashores

Big Cypress National Preserve
Star Route Box 110
Ochopee, FL 33943
(813) 695-2000

Biscayne National Park
Box 1369
Homestead, FL 33090-1369
(305) 230-7275

Canaveral National Seashore
308 Julia Street
Titusville, FL 32796
(407) 267-1110

Cumberland Island National Seashore
Box 806
St. Marys, GA 31558
(912) 882-4336

Everglades National Park
P.O. Box 279
Homestead, FL 33030
(305) 247-6211
Shark Valley Office:
(305) 221-8776
Tram Ride: (305) 221-8455

Fort Matanzas National Monument
8635 A1A South
St. Augustine, FL 32086
(904) 471-0116

Gulf Islands National Seashore, Florida
District
P.O. Box 100
Gulf Breeze, FL 32561
(904) 932-5302

National Forests in Florida

Forest Supervisor
Woodcrest Office Park
325 John Knox Road, Suite F-100
Tallahassee, FL 32303
(904) 942-9300

Ocala National Forest
Visitor Information Center
10863 East Highway 40
Silver Springs, FL 34488
(904) 625-7470

Ocala National Forest Pittman
Visitor Information Center
45621 State Road 19
Altoona, FL 32702
(904) 669-7495

Osceola National Forest
District Ranger
P.O. Box 70
Olustee, FL 32072
(904) 752-2577

Appendix E

County and Municipal Nature Preserves

Bivens Arms Nature Park
(904) 334-2056
A small urban park near Paynes Prairie State Preserve. Boardwalk, alligators, wading birds. From I-75, south of Gainesville, take Exit 74 and go east on SR 331 to Main Street. Take Main Street north for a quarter-mile to the park entrance.

Morningside Nature Center
(904) 334-2170
Boardwalk, hiking trails in upland sandhills and pine flatwoods. Good fall wildflowers. In Gainesville, take U.S. 441 to East University Boulevard and go east for 3.5 miles.

Theodore Roosevelt Area, Timucuan Ecological and Historical Preserve
(904) 641- 7155
Salt marsh and maritime hammock and 35 acres of shell mounds left by the Timucuans. Located east of the Fort Caroline National Memorial Visitor Center near Jacksonville.

Smyrna Dunes Park
(904) 423-3373
Many shorebirds year-round; black skimmers and least terns nest here in late spring and early summer. In New Smyrna Beach, go north on Peninsula Avenue. The park is located near the Ponce Inlet Coast Guard Station.

Barley Barber Swamp
(800) 257-9267
An outstanding South Florida swamp walk located near Indian Town that requires one-week-advance reservations from Florida Power and Light.

Avon Park Air Force Base
(813) 452-4119
An active military base with limited access. Birding, particularly around Lake Arbuckle, is excellent. Open to visitors weekends only.

Osceola Schools Environmental Study Center
(407) 846-4312
Boardwalk through an ancient cypress swamp; many nesting birds, gators. Open weekends only. From Kissimmee, go west on U.S. 17/ 92 to Poinciana Boulevard. Turn south onto Poinciana and go 6 miles.

Orlando Wetlands Park
(407) 246-2800
Man-made wetlands with numerous birds, gators, armadillos. Scheduled weekend nature walks. Take SR 50 from Orlando to the town of Christmas. Turn north onto CR 420, then east onto Wheeler Road.

Jay B. Starkey Wilderness Park
(813) 834-3247
Hiking, interpretive trails and a main drive through diverse habitat with many bird species. Deer, turkeys and gopher tortoises are common. From U.S. 19 in New Port Richey, go east of SR 54 to CR 1 (also called Little Road) and turn north. Take CR 1 to River Crossing Boulevard and turn east. Proceed almost 2 miles to park entrance.

Upper Tampa Bay County Park
(813) 855-1765
Coastal wetlands with nature trails and boardwalks. Look for ospreys, ibis, egrets and brown pelicans. From Oldsmar, take SR 580 southwest to Double Branch Road; turn south. Go 0.5-mile to park entrance.

Boyd Hill Nature Park
(813) 893-7326
Boardwalk and hiking trails through an unusually diverse habitat in the middle of the city. Many birds, indigo snakes, gopher tortoises. From I-275 at St. Petersburg, take Exit 4 onto 54th Avenue South. Go east to 9th Street and turn left. Go north to Country Club Way South, also the park entrance.

Fort DeSoto County Park
(813) 866-2484
Well known as a superb birding site for migratory species in spring. Early March to mid-May is best. From St. Petersburg, go west on 54th Avenue South and turn south on SR 679. Follow the signs.

Charlotte Harbor Environmental Center
(813) 575-4800
Nesting bald eagles, spring migrants, gators, turtles and woodpeckers on the west side of Charlotte Harbor. From U.S. 41 south of Punta Gorda, take SR 765 (Burnt Store Road) and go south 1 mile to the park entrance.

Six Mile Wilderness Slough Preserve
(813) 432-2004
A boardwalk and a photo blind are just two of the features of this outstanding wetlands system with many wading birds and bald eagles. Scheduled nature walks available. Take Exit 22 from I-75 south of Fort Myers and go west 0.5-mile to Six Mile Parkway. Turn south and proceed 3 miles, then turn east on Penzance Crossing. Entrance is in 0.1-mile.

Sanibel-Captiva Conservation Association
(813) 472-2329
Wetlands and ridges on an offshore barrier island feature alligators, many wading birds

and ospreys. Good walking trails. Located on the main Sanibel road to Captiva on Sanibel Island, a barrier island off Fort Myers.

Carl Johnson Regional Park
(813) 432-2000
A barrier island and mangroves feature egrets, roseate spoonbills and other wading birds. Located south of Fort Myers Beach on SR 865.

Corkscrew Swamp Sanctuary
(813) 657-3771
Owned by the National Audubon Society, this 2-mile boardwalk features the world's largest old-growth bald cypress forest and the nation's largest concentration of nesting wood storks. North of Naples, take SR 846 for 21 miles; look for the small sanctuary sign.

Briggs Nature Center
(813) 775-8569
Many wading birds, songbirds, woodpeckers and butterflies, which all can be viewed from a boardwalk. Scheduled boat tours available. Located on SR 951 on the road to Marco Island.

Marinelife Center of Juno Beach
(407) 627-8280
A good place to arrange nighttime turtle walks in early summer. Shorebirds present year-round.

Gumbo Limbo Environmental Complex
(407) 338-1473
Educational facility with both hardwood hammock and mangrove communities. Most wildlife except for the free-roaming birds is captive due to the urban locale. Located on A1A just north of the intersection with Palmetto Road Park.

Selected Bibliography

Addison, David. *Boardwalk Guide to Briggs Nature Center.* Naples, Fla.: The Conservancy, n.d.

Akerman, Joe A. Jr. *Florida Cowman: A History of Florida Cattle Raising.* Kissimmee, Fla.: Florida Cattleman's Association, 1976.

Andrews, Jean. *A Field Guide to Shells of Florida.* Houston: Gulf Publishing, 1994.

Ashton, Ray E. Jr., and Patricia Sawyer Ashton. *The Snakes: Handbook of Reptiles and Amphibians of Florida.* Miami: Windward Publishing, 1981.

Bartram, William. *Travels.* Reprint, New York: Dover Publications, 1955.

Belden, Robert C. *The Florida Panther.* New York: National Audubon Society, 1989.

Bell, C. Ritchie, and Bryan J. Taylor. *Florida Wild Flowers and Roadside Plants.* Chapel Hill: Laurel Hill Press, 1982.

Bloodworth, Bertha E., and Alton C. Morris. *The Place in the Sun: The History and Romance of Florida Place Names.* Gainesville: University Presses of Florida, 1978.

Carr, Archie F., and C. J. Goin. *Guide to the Reptiles, Amphibians and Fresh Water Fishes in Florida.* Gainesville: University of Florida Press, 1990.

————. *The Sea Turtle.* Austin: University of Texas Press, 1984.

Carter, Elizabeth F., and John L. Pearce. *A Canoeing and Kayaking Guide to the Streams of Florida (North Central Peninsula and Panhandle).* Birmingham: Menasha Ridge Press, 1985.

Cline, Howard F. *Florida Indians.* Vol. 2. New York: Garland Publishing, 1974.

Connor, Jack. *The Complete Birder: A Guide to Better Birding.* Boston: Houghton Mifflin, 1988.

Douglas, Marjory Stoneman. *The Everglades: River of Grass.* Rev. ed. Saint Petersburg, Fla.: Pineapple Press, 1988.

————. *Florida: The Long Frontier.* New York: Harper & Row, 1967.

————. *Voice of the River.* St. Petersburg, Fla.: Pineapple Press, 1987. An autobiography.

Fairbanks, Charles. *Florida Indians.* Vol. 3. New York: Garland Publishing, 1974.

Florida Audubon Society. *Where to Find Birds in Florida.* Maitland, Fla.: Florida Audubon Society, 1977.

Florida Campground Association. *Florida Camping Directory.* Tallahassee: Florida Campground Association, published annually.

Georgia Ornithological Society. *Annotated Checklist of Georgia Birds.* n.p., 1986.

Gibson, Dot Rees. *The Okefenokee Swamp.* Waycross, Ga.: Gibson Publications, 1991.

Glaros, Lou, and Doug Sphar. *A Canoeing and Kayaking Guide to the Streams of Florida. Central and South Florida, Vol. 2.* Birmingham, Ala.: Menasha Ridge Press, 1987.

Greenberg, Jerry and Idaz. *The Living Reef.* Miami: Seahawk Press, 1985.

Greenberg, Margaret H. *The Sanibel Shell Guide.* Sanibel Island, Fla.: Anna Publishing, 1982.

Griffin, Martha W. *Geologic Guide to Cumberland Island National Seashore.* Atlanta: U.S. Dept. of the Interior, 1991.

Grow, Gerald. *Florida Parks: A Guide to Camping in Nature.* Tallahassee, Fla.: Longleaf Publications, 1987.

Hall, F. W. *Birds of Florida.* St. Petersburg, Fla.: Great Outdoors Publishing Company, 1979.

Hanna, Alfred J., and Kathryn A. Hanna. *Lake Okeechobee: Wellspring of the Everglades.* Indianapolis: Bobbs-Merrill, 1948.

Harrison, Colin. *A Field Guide to Nests, Eggs and Nestlings of North American Birds.* New York: Collins, 1978.

Hiendlmayr, Jackalene Crow. *The Florida Bicycle Book.* Sarasota, Fla.: Pineapple Press, 1990.

Hiller, Herbert. *Guide to the Small and Historic Lodgings of Florida.* Sarasota, Fla.: Pineapple Press, 1988.

Kale, Herbert W., and David S. Maehr. *Florida's Birds.* Sarasota, Fla.: Pineapple Press, 1989.

Lane, James A. *A Birder's Guide to Florida.* Revised by Harold D. Holt. Denver: L & P Press, 1989.

Lanier, Sidney. *Florida: Its Scenery, Climate and History.* Reprint, Gainesville: University Presses of Florida, 1973.

Larson, Ron. *Swamp Song.* Gainesville: University Press of Florida, 1995.

Lockey, Richard F., and Lewis Maxwell. *Florida's Poisonous Plants, Snakes, Insects.* Tampa, Fla.: Maxwell Publishers, 1986.

Marth, Del, and Marty Marth, eds. *The Rivers of Florida.* Sarasota, Fla.: Pineapple Press, 1990.

Martin, Alexander C., Herbert S. Zim, and Arnold L. Nelson. *American Wildlife and Planters: A Guide to Wildlife Food Habitats.* New York: Dover Publications, 1961.

Mayo, Lois B. *Settlers of the Okefenokee.* Folkston, Ga.: Okefenokee Press, 1975.

Milanich, Jerald T., and Charles Fairbanks. *Florida Archeology.* New York: Academic Press, 1980.

Muir, John. *A Thousand Mile Walk to the Gulf.* Boston: Houghton Mifflin, 1981.

Myers, Ronald L. *Plants of Archbold Biological Station.* Lake Placid, Fla.: Archbold Biological Station, 1984.

Myers, Ronald L., and John J. Ewel. *Ecosystems of Florida.* Orlando: University of Central Florida Press, 1991.

National Audubon Society. *Corkscrew Swamp Sanctuary.* New York: National Audubon Society, 1981.

National Geographic Society. *A Field Guide to North American Birds.* 2nd ed. Washington: National Geographic Society, 1987.

National Oceanic and Atmospheric Administration. *Fishes of Gray's Reef National Marine Sanctuary.* Washington, D.C.: NOAA, 1989.

Neill, Wilfred T. *Florida's Seminole Indians.* St. Petersburg, Fla.: Great Outdoors Publishing, 1956.

Nelson, Gil. *The Trees of Florida.* Sarasota, Fla.: Pineapple Press, 1994.

O'Keefe, M. Timothy. *Diving to Adventure.* Lakeland, Fla.: Larsen's Outdoor Publishing, 1992.

————. *Great Adventures in Florida.* Birmingham, Ala.: Menasha Ridge Press, 1996.

————. *Hiker's Guide to Florida.* Helena, Mont.: Falcon Press, 1994.

————. *Manatees: Our Vanishing Mermaids.* Lakeland, Fla.: Larsen's Outdoor Publishing, 1993.

————. *Sea Turtles: The Watchers' Guide.* Lakeland, Fla.: Larsen's Outdoor Publishing, 1995.

O'Keefe, M. Timothy, and Larry Larsen. *Fish and Dive Florida and the Keys.* Lakeland, Fla.: Larsen's Outdoor Publishing, 1993.

Olsen, Chris M. *Wildlife Drive Guide, Darling NWR.* Sanibel, Fla.: Press Printing, n.d.

Orr, Katherine. *The Wondrous World of the Mangrove Swamps of the Everglades and Florida Keys.* Miami: Florida Flair Books, 1989.

Ownby, Miriam Lee. *Explore the Everglades.* Kissimmee, Fla.: TeakWood Press, 1992.

Perry, I. Mac. *Indian Mounds You Can Visit.* St. Petersburg, Fla.: Great Outdoors Publishing, 1993.

Pope, Patricia E. *Seashore and Wading Birds of Florida.* St. Petersburg, Fla.: Great Outdoors Publishing, 1974.

Pranty, Bill. *A Birder's Guide to Florida.* Colorado Springs: American Birding Association, 1996.

Purdum, Elizabeth D., and James R. Anderson Jr., eds. *Florida County Atlas and Municipal State Fact Book.* Tallahassee: Florida State University Press, 1988.

Riley, Laura, and William Riley. *Guide to the National Wildlife Refuges.* New York: Collier Books, 1992.

Russel, Francis. *The Okefenokee Swamp.* New York: Time-Life Books, 1973.

Schoettle, H. E. Taylor. *A Field Guide to Jekyll Island.* Athens: University of Georgia, Marine Extension Service, 1983.

Smith, Harriet. *The Naturalist's Guide of Cedar Key, Florida.* Levy County, Fla.: Rife's Printing, 1987.

————. *Watching Birds in the Cedar Keys.* Levy County, Fla.: The Print Shop, 1993.

Smith, Larry L., and Robin W. Doughty. *The Amazing Armadillo.* Austin: University of Texas Press, 1984.

Sprunt, Alexander. *Florida Bird Life.* New York: Coward-McCann and the National Audubon Society, 1963.

Stevenson, George B. *Trees of the Everglades National Park and the Florida Keys.* Miami: Banyan Books, 1986.

Swinburne, Stephen R. *Guide to Cumberland Island National Seashore.* N.p.: Eastern Acorn Press, 1984.

Taylor, Walter. *The Guide to Florida Wildflowers.* Dallas: Taylor Publishing, 1992.

Tebeau, Charlton W. *A History of Florida*. Coral Gables, Fla.: University of Miami Press, 1987.

————. *Man in the Everglades*. Coral Gables, Fla.: University of Miami Press, 1968.

Toops, Connie. *The Alligator, Monarch of the Marsh*. Homestead, Fla.: National Parks and Monuments Association, 1988.

Toops, Connie, and Willard E. Dilley. *Birds of South Florida: An Interpretive Guide*. Conway, Ark.: River Road Press, 1986.

Truesdell, William G. *A Guide of the Wilderness Waterway of the Everglades National Park*. Coral Gables, Fla.: University of Miami Press, 1985.

Tucker, James A. *Florida Birds*. Tampa, Fla.: Maxwell Publishers, 1986.

U.S. Department of the Interior. *National Wildlife Refuges of the Georgia Coastal Complex*. Washington, D.C.: Dept. of the Interior, Fish and Wildlife, 1983.

————. *Okefenokee National Wildlife Refuge*. Washington, D.C.: Dept. of the Interior, Fish and Wildlife, 1987.

Van Meter, Victoria Brook. *The Florida Panther*. Miami: Florida Power and Light Company, 1988.

————. *Florida's Sea Turtles*. Miami: Florida Power and Light Company, 1992.

————. *Florida's Wood Storks*. Miami: Florida Power and Light Company, 1985.

————. *The West Indian Manatee in Florida*. Miami: Florida Power and Light Company, 1985.

Vanstory, Burnette. *Georgia's Land of the Golden Isles*. Athens: University of Georgia, 1981.

Weber, Jeff. *A Visitor's Guide to the Everglades*. Miami: Florida Flair Books, 1986.

Index

About the Author

M. Timothy O'Keefe, who specializes in natural history and travel writing and photography, has lived in Florida for almost three decades. He holds a Ph.D. from University of North Carolina at Chapel Hill, was an editor at large for the *Florida Sportsman* magazine for 23 years and currently is a professor in the School of Communication at University of Central Florida in Orlando. Tim is the author of 10 published books and an accomplished photographer who continuously searches for new subjects and adventures. Winner of more than 40 regional and national awards, Tim lives in Longwood, Florida, when not out in the field.